NEVER LOST A GAME
(TIME JUST RAN OUT)

by
Bob Fulton

with
Chuck Klausing

Closson Press
Apollo, Pennsylvania

Closson Press
1935 Sampson Drive, Apollo, PA 15613-9209
Library of Congress No. 96-072651
ISBN No. 1-55856-255-9
copyright @ January 1997
Bob Fulton
All rights reserved

To order books, write to:
Closson Press
1935 Sampson Drive
Apollo, PA 15613-9209

To reach Chuck Klausing for speaking engagements, write to:
Chuck Klausing
123 Reston Drive
Indiana, PA 15701-4232

Never Lost a Game
(Time Just Ran Out)

The title, *Never Lost a Game*...what does it mean? It is an attitude that I believe I have had all my life. As a boy growing up in the "tuff two-fisted" town of Wilmerding, I was involved in fights with many bullies. At times they got the best of me, but I always felt I would get a second chance.

As a player, when time ran out and I looked up at the scoreboard and we were behind, I always felt we would get a second chance. If we played that team later that same year I would do everything I could to never lose again. I would practice and prepare to never let it happen again.

In my second year of coaching, I like to say we played eight games and won all but seven. This really happened. I wasn't a coach who would go into a depression after a loss, but I worked on corrections and never let it happen again. Friends of mine who were coaches marveled at how I could solve problems and turn teams around.

This is an attitude that I hope I instilled in my team. I never suffered from "coaches burnout" because I looked forward to making the corrections and solving the problems. I never lost a game, time just ran out. There will be tomorrow.

----Chuck Klausing

About the Author

Bob Fulton is a graduate of Indiana University of Pennsylvania, where Chuck Klausing first worked as a collegiate head coach (1964-69). He is the author of *The Summer Olympics: A Treasury of Legend and Lore*, published in 1996 by Diamond Communications of South Bend, Ind. He has also written on a wide range of topics for a variety of national magazines, including *American Heritage, Sports History, Football Digest, The National Pastime, NFL Exclusive, Delta Sky, Basketball Weekly, Touchdown Illustrated, Sports Heritage* and *International Gymnast*. He lives in Indiana, Pa., where Klausing now resides.

Dedications

To my wife Linda, who provides a limitless supply of encouragement, patience and understanding.

----Bob Fulton

To my wife Joann, who raised our five children while I was busy on and off the field. She is my number one cheerleader and is always there when I need her. My players have always felt that she was a surrogate "Mom" to them. I could not have been successful in life without her.

----Chuck Klausing

Foreward

Glance at the names and Chuck Klausing comes into focus like some football Forrest Gump, his life constantly intersecting with a veritable Who's Who list of luminaries.

Vince Lombardi. Joe Montana. Robert Frost. Harry Stuhldreher, one of the famed Four Horsemen. Art Rooney. Bobby Bowden. Chuck Noll. Billy Eckstine. Harry Truman. And Michael Fay, who achieved notoriety because of something that occurred *off* the field, half a world away.

Klausing crossed paths with them all during an illustrious playing and coaching career that spanned more than 50 years. When he stepped down as a coach in 1993, his teams had forged a composite record of 310-112-10.

The anecdotes in *Never Lost a Game*--many humorous, some ironic, a few downright incredible--range from Klausing's youth in the "tough, two-fisted drinking town" of Wilmerding, Pa., to his current coaching experiences in Europe. Included are his years as a legendary western Pennsylvania high school coach and his 27 successful seasons at the collegiate level.

Klausing discusses a death threat that took an amusing turn; ringers in the Rose Bowl; a prep school game that featured three teams; his experiences as a 155-pound lineman at Penn State; and the Iraqi soldier captured during Desert Storm . . . while wearing a T-shirt touting Klausing's football camp.

His recollections and observations touch on Jim Thorpe, Lee Iacocca, Gen. William Westmoreland, Rocky Marciano, Erwin Rommel, Bob Hope and Frank Sinatra--both the singer and the football manager. William Tell, too.

Never Lost a Game spans more than half a century and 10 countries, provides personal glimpses of national figures, snippets from the game's history and a wealth of offbeat tales, such as "The Phantom Coaches," "Goldilocks Loses Out" and "The Moonshine Recruit."

Acknowledgements

The author would like to thank the following for their contributions to this project: Chuck Klausing, for his willingness to spend long hours recounting stories from 46 years in coaching and answer hundreds of follow-up questions; John Smonski, for providing a wealth of material on the history of Braddock High School football; the many college sports information directors who answered requests for assistance, especially Carnegie Mellon sports information director E.J. Borghetti; Steve Klipa, for providing details of Klausing's career at Pitcairn High School; Kiski School football coach Marcus Muster, for providing information on Klausing's tenure at Kiski; and *The Kiski Bulletin* and *The Indiana Gazette* for their kind permission to reprint excerpts of stories written by the author that appeared in their publications.

----Bob Fulton

I wish I could find words to thank the many people who helped me through my coaching career. I was told to remember the people you meet on the way up, as they will be there to help you on the way down.

- To my wife Joann, I dedicate this book. Thank you for raising our children. You were always there when I needed your support.
- To my five children: Patti, Marylou, Tom, Nancy, and Kathy, I thank each of you. You gave of your precious time with me, so I could be someone else's father.
- To my mother and father, who taught me family values. These are the values I have tried to instill in my teams.
- To my many assistants over the years. Without your loyalty, I could not have been as successful.

I am not going to try to thank everybody, because I know I would leave someone out. You know who you are. I value your help, support and friendship.

----Chuck Klausing

Table of Contents

Introduction
A Man of Definition..Page ix
    A legend by any measure

Chapter 1
Miracle in Milltown..Page 1
    Unbeaten at Braddock High School

Chapter 2
The Early Years..Page 23
    Childhood, college star, a coaching debut

Chapter 3
Back to College...Page 43
    Coaching at Rutgers and Army

Chapter 4
Return of the Native...Page 55
    Winning and 'bowling' at IUP

Chapter 5
Odds and Ends..Page 69
    A collection of unusual tales

Chapter 6
Almost Heaven..Page 87
    Joining Bobby Bowden at West Virginia

Chapter 7
The Pride of Pittsburgh...Page 101
    A renaissance at Carnegie Mellon

Chapter 8
On the Road Again..Page 119
   The search for recruits

Chapter 9
Foreign Affairs..Page 137
   Coaching in Europe and Canada

Chapter 10
Finding Utopia..Page 149
   Idealism and a fond farewell at Kiski

Chapter 11
The Sunday Heroes...Page 163
   Experiences and stories of the pros

Chapter 12
That's Incredible...Page 179
   A collection of unbelievable tales

Appendix...Page 195
  Chuck Klausing--By the numbers
  Chuck Klausing--A man of letters

INTRODUCTION
A Man of Definition

leg•end (lej′-end) *n.* a notable person whose deeds or exploits are much talked about in his own time

Keep the *Webster's* on the bookshelf.

In this instance, the best definition of the word is found not in a dictionary but in a grandfatherly football coach who, his down-home humility aside, ranks among the game's greats.

Chuck Klausing wrapped up his illustrious career in 1993 by leading Kiski School of Saltsburg, Pa., to an Interstate Prep School League championship, the final chapter in a saga of success stretching back 46 years. No matter where Klausing coached, his teams won games and titles with regularity.

"I'll tell you this in all sincerity: He doesn't have to take a back seat to anyone in this country as far as football goes," says Steve Klipa, who played under Klausing at Pitcairn High School in the late 1940s and coached for 36 years. "He's a legend over the whole United States."

Small wonder. Klausing took part in 310 victories, directed teams to 10 unbeaten regular seasons and dozens of conference and regional championships and twice earned national coach of the year honors.

A legend? In an age when the word is so overused its meaning has been devalued like a Russian ruble, Klausing truly fits the definition. And not just because of the extraordinary achievements listed above.

Fact is, they represent merely the tip of an iceberg, but a small portion of the whole picture. For example, cold numbers can't convey the man's warmth, at least not as effectively as a scene from November 1993, only days after Klausing announced his impending retirement.

The Kiski players were practicing for their season finale against Shady Side Academy when a car pulled up alongside the field. Out stepped Klipa, a fullback and linebacker at Pitcairn when a relative greenhorn, fresh out of Slippery Rock State Teachers College, arrived to coach the team. Chuck Klausing by name.

Practice came to an abrupt halt. Preparing for his last game wasn't nearly as important to Klausing as greeting his very first captain.

"He stopped practice and acknowledged me in front of the team," says Klipa, a retired teacher who resides in Monroeville. "I was really touched that he took time out to talk with me."

No surprise there. Klausing always could find time for his players, the ones reared on Milton Berle as well as the ones reared on MTV. To him they were all special--from Klipa at his first coaching stop to Lou Saban at his last.

"I had a cold and Coach came to my room and brought his own humidifier for me," recalls Saban, a running back at Kiski in 1987 and 1988. "I'm in bed and he's bustling around my room making sure everything is set up right. Then Mrs. [Joann] Klausing came over and told me if I needed anything, anything at all, to just call."

With Klausing, the bond between player and coach remains unbreakable, despite a distance of years or miles or both. Many former players paid homage to him in his final week as a coach by either making a pilgrimage of sorts to Kiski, as Klipa did, or by calling. Klausing's telephone was tied up for days.

"There's a special kind of relationship there," says Marcus Muster, who played under Klausing at Carnegie Mellon University, served on his Kiski staff for seven seasons and then succeeded him as head coach. "I don't know of one person that I've run across that ever had an ill word to say about the guy, because he always went out of his way for you. He's touched all his players somehow, some way, and they appreciate it."

They realize that when Klausing prepared them for football, he actually prepared them for life. Instilling discipline and the ideals of sportsmanship in his players and teaching the value of hard work was more important to Klausing than the numbers appearing on a scoreboard at game's end.

That explains why Kiski headmaster John Pidgeon coaxed Klausing out of retirement in 1987. He looked beyond the wins and losses and saw a man of character whose presence would be of benefit to all Kiski students, not just the football players.

"His won-lost record was probably the least important factor," says Pidgeon. "We're not the kind of school that places a lot of emphasis on winning. We like to win, but we were interested in him more for the kind of person he is. He fulfilled a role here beyond that of a football coach. Just having Chuck walk around campus talking to the kids was worth having him because he was such a tremendous influence."

Klausing has been influencing kids since 1948, when he began his coaching career at Pitcairn. He wasn't much older than his players, a veritable youngster still able to strap on the headgear when circumstances required it. Klipa recalled one such instance for the Cougars during his visit to Kiski.

"He told a story about how one day they were padding up for a scrimmage," says Jeff Simmons, who quarterbacked his grandfather's last team. "They had only 21 players. They needed one more for 22."

So Klausing, an all-state lineman at Wilmerding High School who later distinguished himself at Penn State and Slippery Rock, suited up. The scrimmage proceeded as planned.

It was at another suburban Pittsburgh high school--Braddock--that Chuck Klausing the coach evolved into Chuck Klausing the legend. A 53-0-1 record and six WPIAL (Western Pennsylvania Interscholastic Athletic League) championships in as many seasons gained the Tigers national recognition. *Sports Illustrated* devoted four pages to Braddock and its unprecedented unbeaten streak in a 1959 feature.

Klausing continued his winning ways after moving up to the collegiate level. Four successful seasons as an assistant at Rutgers and Army were followed by a 47-10 record in six years as head coach at Indiana University of Pennsylvania, including the school's first perfect regular season in 34 years and first bowl berth. Only a last-second touchdown by mighty Delaware deprived IUP of an upset victory in the 1968 Boardwalk Bowl at Atlantic City.

Klausing made two more bowl trips at West Virginia University, where he served as an assistant under Bobby Bowden for six seasons. He returned to head coaching in 1976 and led Carnegie Mellon University to a 77-15-2 record and six Presidents Athletic Conference championships. The Tartans advanced to the national playoffs on four occasions and twice reached the semifinals. Klausing was named the NCAA Division III Coach of the Year in 1979 and 1983.

He left CMU following the 1985 season, spent a year at nearby Pitt and then decided to hang up his whistle for good. But he postponed retirement at Pidgeon's request.

Why would a man who could have headed for the nearest easy chair instead tackle a new challenge? Because Klausing's enthusiasm for football never waned, even after his birthday cakes began sprouting in excess of 60 candles.

Even in "retirement" he rivals the Energizer bunny, constantly on the go. Klausing travels several times a year to Europe, where he conducts football clinics, teaches courses in American football and acts as an advisory coach to national teams. Klausing also directs as many summer football camps as he can squeeze into his schedule.

This is a man with an unquenchable passion for the game. "It's just unbelievable that someone could love something as much as he loves football," says Muster. "I remember one time he was in the hospital with phlebitis. The doctors told him he had to relax and stay in the hospital, so I went in on Monday, Tuesday and Wednesday and we put a game plan together. Well, I walked into the field house on Saturday and he was here, watching film. The will and desire and the love he has for the game is just phenomenal."

As is Klausing's love for his players. There's never been any doubt he cared for them as if they were family members, offering counsel and guidance and encouragement.

"He became like a relative to me," says Klipa. "I think all our successes in life are a tribute to him. He helped mold us into successes."

And that, after all, is the best measure of Chuck Klausing, not the gaudy numbers in a record book. Ask him what he's proudest of in his coaching career and he mentally fast-forwards past the Braddock years, the Boardwalk Bowl team, the playoff appearances at Carnegie Mellon.

"I'm very proud that so many guys I've coached have graduated from college. The rate has to be up in the higher 90th percentile," says Klausing. "I've had guys that played for me who are CEOs of large corporations, who are public school administrators, who are doctors, who are preachers. They're people that, I hope, I influenced to try and do things the right way."

Their achievements off the field thrill Klausing more than their achievements on the field ever did. Games and championships won have never been the focus of his work. Why, even Klausing's farewell season--despite a 7-1 record and a league title--wasn't necessarily the highlight of his seven years at Kiski.

"I think you judge a season by the effort your kids have made, not the won-lost record," he says. "That's what was most satisfying about that last team. We didn't have great physical talent--I had bigger teams at Kiski, maybe more gifted players--but that was an overachieving-type team."

The Cougars provided a storybook finish to the Chuck Klausing era by whipping Shady Side Academy 33-8 in the season finale. And when the 432nd game of his career was over, after the teams exchanged handshakes at midfield, Klausing addressed his players.

"Usually it's a good time for me to find out if anybody's been hurt--if they need to see a doctor," he explained that day. "It's also when I make any announcements I need to make. Today I just thanked them for letting me be their coach."

The Cougars will likely remember that noble gesture long after the game's final score slips from memory. They'll never forget the coach who shared a special bond with all his players, be they teen-agers of the '90s or teen-agers of the '40s.

Yes, Chuck Klausing has long been a man of definition. The one listed beside legend in *Webster's*.

CHAPTER 1
Miracle in Milltown

Chuck Klausing first came to prominence at Braddock High School in suburban Pittsburgh, where he coached for six seasons (1954-59)--and never lost.

Klausing's teams posted a 53-0-1 record, won or shared six WPIAL Class A championships and surpassed the national scholastic record for the longest unbeaten streak, set by Massillon (Ohio) High School when the legendary Paul Brown was coach. The Tigers gained national exposure during their record run, even garnering a feature article in the Nov. 2, 1959, edition of *Sports Illustrated.*

Those feats were remarkable, especially in light of Braddock's history. The Tigers suffered through a 21-54-4 record in the nine years prior to Klausing's arrival, including one abysmal season when they scored only 25 points.

"I ran into the guy that had been coaching at Braddock [Henry Furrie] at graduate school at Pitt," Klausing recalls. "He heard that I was looking into the Braddock job and might be getting it. He talked to me as a friend: 'Chuck, don't take the job. It's the worst job in America. I could've stayed there but I just saw it was an impossibility. You'll have pretty good material, but the kids are very undisciplined: They don't come to practice and they come late for the games. It's a bad situation.' "

But Furrie's counsel fell on deaf ears. Klausing accepted the position . . . and the daunting challenge. Working under appalling conditions--cinders were actually scattered over the Tigers' practice field--he restored discipline and pride, launched a golden age in Braddock High School football and rejuvenated the spirit of an entire town.

"We had a lot of great players at Braddock," Klausing says. "I just happened to be the right coach at the right time."

Fact is, he was the *only* coach. The position was so utterly devoid of appeal that no one else had even bothered to apply. No matter, for Klausing *was* the right coach at the right time. He turned the downtrodden Tigers into conquerors and launched an era of dominance unparalleled in the 91-year history of the WPIAL.

Klausing wore a Notre Dame hat throughout his reign at Braddock--not because he was a fan of the Fighting Irish, but because the initials emblazoned on the cap served as a battle cry for his Tigers. To them, ND stood for No Defeat.

And for six seasons there wasn't one.

Boarding a Sinking Ship

More than a few of his fellow coaches thought Klausing daft for even considering the Braddock job. He had turned the Pitcairn program around, leading the Railroaders to a 7-2 record in 1953.

Why board a new ship--especially one that was barely afloat?

"The reason I wanted to take the Braddock job, I was scouting East Pittsburgh High School when I was coaching at Pitcairn. We were to play East Pittsburgh the next week. Braddock had two running backs, Joe Reaves and Jim Gilliam. Boy, they were great runners. One was a sophomore and one was a junior. I catalogued that in my mind, that those were two guys I'd like to coach."

So Klausing, paying little mind to Furrie's advice, accepted the position. The situation was anything but ideal. Braddock prepared for games on "a grimy, stony practice field that looks like a flattened coal heap," according to the *Sports Illustrated* feature. There was no game field--the Tigers played home games at North Braddock Scott High School, their chief rival. The shower room at Braddock consisted of one working shower. Klausing's office could be likened to a dungeon: It was located in a congested equipment room in the basement of a brownstone schoolhouse constructed in 1890. He barely had room for visitors.

But instead of wallowing in despair, Klausing worked diligently to overhaul the program, with the assistance of the administration. The victims became the victors in short order.

"Mike Sullivan was the president of the school board in Braddock. When he and the school board hired me, they made a commitment. They wanted to win. They told me whatever you feel you need to win, ask for it and we'll try to get it for you. They just solved all the problems that people told me were problems. They did a pretty good job."

So did Klausing. The foundering ship was swiftly transformed into a juggernaut, inspiring dread in foes that had once feasted on the Tigers. In six seasons at Braddock, his teams outscored the opposition 1,431-289.

All Fired Up

Before firing up his first Braddock team, Klausing fired up some uniforms.

"After I was hired I went and looked at the uniforms. There were, I think, 30 uniforms from the year before. They had played their last game on a rainy night and they never were cleaned. They still had mud on them. I looked at them and just shook my head.

"So I went to Mike Sullivan and showed him the uniforms that we had. And he says, 'Chuck, get a wheelbarrow.' "

A puzzled Klausing did as he was told, wondering all the while what Sullivan wanted with a wheelbarrow. He soon had his answer. Sullivan piled the uniforms on the wheelbarrow, carted them to the school furnace room and tossed them into the flames. The Tigers wore brand new duds for their 1954 opener against Wilkinsburg.

A Dandy Debut

The Klausing era officially began at Braddock on Sept. 10, 1954, when the Tigers squeezed past Wilkinsburg 7-6 on a rainy night at Graham Field. Substitute halfback Bill Macko scored on a first-quarter 6-yard run and Chuck Myers kicked the extra point to provide the margin of victory.

"At the time Wilkinsburg was a dominating power in the largest division, which was Double A at the time. It was the equivalent to what is Quad A now. We had a close, nip-and-tuck game and won against a Wilkinsburg team that went on and challenged for the WPIAL championship in their division. For us to be able to stay with Wilkinsburg surprised everybody because they were a dominant team in that era."

No one could have imagined it at the time, but the Tigers had taken the first step toward the school's first unbeaten season since 1924. That squad was later forced to forfeit all nine of its victories because of an ineligible player.

The only blemish in 1954 was a 7-7 tie with Midland in the WPIAL championship game. In fact, that was to be the *only* blemish in Klausing's 54 games as head coach of the Tigers.

A Championship Shared

Klausing's team came within three minutes of a perfect season in 1954 before some perfectly awful bad luck surfaced on--fittingly enough--Friday the 13th at Ambridge Stadium. Braddock forced a Midland fumble yet somehow surrendered a touchdown on the play.

There were no black cats in sight on that most ominous of dates--just a gang of Leopards. Midland forged a 7-7 tie and earned a share of the title despite gaining only 144 yards to the Tigers' 309. One fluky play made all the difference.

"We were actually dominating, if you can dominate someone in a 7-0 game. We have them backed up on their own 20 with three minutes to play. Ivan Toncic was their quarterback. He drops back and throws a 10-yard hook pass to an end, Gene Lake."

The father of Pittsburgh Steelers defensive back Carnell Lake, incidentally.

"Their coach, John Petchel, explained to me later that it was supposed to be a hook and lateral. Lake was gonna pitch the ball to a back. But one of our guys hit him so hard that he didn't lateral the ball, he fumbled it. The ball bounces out to the side and everybody's trying to get it. The back who was supposed to get the lateral--Jack Flara--scoops up the ball and goes 70 yards for a touchdown."

Henry Suffaletta, who like Toncic and Flara would later play at Pitt, kicked the extra point (there were no two-point conversions back then) that clinched a share of the championship for the Leopards--and denied Braddock a perfect season.

Hitting 'Pay'-dirt

During the Klausing era, Braddock's fiercest rival was neighboring North Braddock Scott, whose fans were as frenzied over football as the Tiger partisans. Emotions ran high during the annual showdown between the schools.

The action in the stands was nearly as compelling as the action on the field when the Raiders and Tigers clashed. Bets were made on the outcome, often with thousands of dollars changing hands.

"You have to understand, Braddock and North Braddock are divided by the Pennsylvania Railroad tracks. Braddock is below the tracks and North Braddock is above the tracks. The big employer was the Edgar Thompson steel mill, where people from both communities worked.

"Both communities were very proud of their football teams. North Braddock had a 45-game winning streak at one time [1932-36] and sent a lot of great players to major colleges, just like Braddock.

"There was a lot of betting when the teams played. In that time, when you heard of $500 or $1,000 bet on a game, it wasn't uncommon."

While he was at Braddock, Klausing learned that wagering was rampant even when other teams were involved. He was told a story about North Braddock standout Fran Rogel, later a fullback with the Pittsburgh Steelers (1950-57).

"North Braddock had a great game against Turtle Creek Union and the star player on the Turtle Creek Union team was Leon Hart [who went on to earn the 1949 Heisman trophy as a Notre Dame end]. Rogel has a great game and North Braddock wins.

"As he was walking off the field going toward the locker room, Rogel was carrying his helmet. And the story is told that the fans that had won betting on the game were putting $5 and $10 bills in Franny's helmet. They said he received over $200."

An afterthought on the heated Braddock-North Braddock rivalry that produced so many memorable games: The long-time adversaries became allies in 1971 when the school districts merged with Rankin High School to form General Braddock High School. Larry Reaves, the last Braddock High coach, played offensive and defensive tackle under Klausing from 1955 through 1957.

'Recruiting' at Braddock

After graduation losses devastated the Tigers in both 1954 and 1955, Klausing was desperate to replenish his roster. So he started recruiting. Legally, of course.

"Some people might look down on this. I don't--you have to understand the time and the situation. I'd lost just about everybody who had played on my first two teams and I was looking for some replacements. There were some decent replacements within our school system, but not enough to keep our streak going."

The Tigers were by then unbeaten in 19 consecutive games, including a 15-7 win over Rankin in Furrie's final game in 1953. But prospects for future success were dim--at least until Klausing began looking beyond Braddock for players.

"In that time there were school districts that did not have high schools. Their kids, after ninth grade, had their choice of going to whatever high school they wanted to. There was a school district near us called North Versailles, which had no high school. They had a running back by the name of Ben Powell who broke the junior high school's 100-yard dash record. So I recruited Ben Powell to go to Braddock.

"He could've gone to two or three other high schools, whose coaches were doing the same thing I was. But he decided on Braddock, even though there were other schools closer to where he lived that he could've walked to. I used to pick him up on the way to school because he was on my route.

"To my good fortune, several other great players lived in North Versailles Township. One was Curtis Vick, who was a great fullback for us and later played at Purdue. Another boy was John Jacobs, our quarterback. Jake went on to become a great player at Arizona State. I had several other players come from North Versailles, but probably none with great backgrounds like those three."

Real Operators

Klausing's players would sometimes go to extraordinary lengths to satisfy his wishes. Even if it meant "borrowing" something that wasn't theirs.

"We had a very good quarterback coach, John Zuger, who wanted to sit up in the press box and call the plays to me down on the field.

This was in 1954, before people professionally were selling telephone systems.

"I was visiting with our electrical shop teacher one day and I explained to him what we wanted was a portable telephone that would have a two-way connection with a wire a couple hundred feet long. He said that would be no problem, that he could rig it up for us and that he had the wire. The only thing that he needed was a hand-held telephone.

"A couple of our football players were in his electrical shop class and they said they knew where they could get a set of telephones. Next day I went to make a call at the pay station in our high school and, sure enough, there was no hand-held telephone there. I assumed where we got our telephone system."

His Name is Mudd

The Tigers once won a crucial game on a field goal--with their regular placekicker on the bench.

Klausing rolled the dice in 1958 when he tabbed Roland Mudd, a 220-pound tackle, to attempt a 37-yard kick. Mudd's field goal provided the margin of victory as Braddock edged North Braddock 9-6 in a titanic battle of 8-0 teams. More than 9,000 fans, including members of a Notre Dame squad that would battle Pitt the next day, attended the showdown.

Mudd, who later played for the University of Minnesota's 1960 national championship team, barely made the kick to give Braddock a 9-0 halftime lead. Ironically, he wasn't even the Tigers' regular kicker.

"It was a long field goal for a high school kid. Normally we wouldn't have even let Mudd kick it, because he wasn't our placekicker. We had a real good extra point-type kicker [Jim "Rosey"

Graham], but he could never have kicked one that long. Mudd was a big, strong kid so I let him try it. The ball actually hit the crossbar and wavered a little before it rolled over."

Deciding the outcome in the process. In another bit of irony, Mudd's game-winning field goal was the only one made by a Braddock player during Klausing's six-year tenure as head coach.

Disgusted Dough Boy

The Tigers celebrated a stirring come-from-behind 9-7 victory over Midland in 1958--everyone, that is, but running back John Gay.

Gay, nicknamed "Dough Boy" for his less-than-sleek physique, slammed his helmet to the turf moments after teammate Ben Powell capped a long drive with a 1-yard run, erasing a 7-2 deficit.

"We had a great game against Midland. We both had undefeated teams. Anyway, Midland's beating us with about six minutes to play and we've got the ball on our own 20.

"We started a drive and every play was John Gay going off tackle. He'd go off tackle eight yards to the right, 10 yards to the left, six yards to the right, 11 to the left. We just marched steadily down the field. We get the ball to the 2-yard line, first and goal, with enough time for four plays."

Whereupon the Midland defense suddenly stiffened.

"Gay goes off right tackle for about a foot. He goes off left tackle for a foot and then goes off right tackle for about a foot. I call timeout and talk to our quarterback [Mark Rutkowski]. I said, 'Look, don't call that same play again because everybody's gonna close in to stop Gay.' "

So Rutkowski handed the ball to Powell, who slashed through the defense for the winning touchdown--much to Gay's disgust.

"Ten players were celebrating. Gay took his helmet off and threw it down. He was mad. He was saying, 'Coach doesn't have any confidence in me.' "

Mental Lapse

Athletes are advised by their coaches, ad nauseam, to maintain their focus. But at the high school level, the players' concentration tends to wander, as Klausing learned in 1958.

"We were going to New Brighton, so we took the bus early and stopped about 5 o'clock at a dairy store. I gave each of my players a couple dollars and they went in this store and got two or three hot dogs and a couple milkshakes each. The kids really enjoyed it. They said it was the greatest pre-game meal they ever had.

"We get back on the bus and make the hour drive down to New Brighton and start getting dressed. I always try to give a pep talk before the game and I wrote on the chalkboard, 'mental lapse.' And I talked about avoiding mental lapses.

"I went through every player on my team. After I went through the offense, I told the defensive linemen, 'You have to key the man in front of you.' I told the linebackers to read the guards in front of them. And I told the safety man, 'Above all, no one ever gets behind you. You've got to stay deeper than any of their pass receivers.'

"My safety man was a very good athlete, a boy by the name of Melvin Coburn. Almost the first play of the game the New Brighton quarterback drops back and throws a long pass for a touchdown.

"I take Melvin out of the game and I say, 'Melvin, what happened to you? The receiver got behind you.' 'Coach, I had one of those.' 'What are you talking about?' 'The thing you wrote on the board.' 'Oh, mental lapse.' 'Ya, Coach, that's what I had, a mental lapse.'

"And I said, 'Well, what in the world were you thinking about?' And he said, 'Coach, I was wondering, are we gonna stop at that same dairy store on the way home?' "

The Death Threat

What could have been the most frightening moment of Klausing's coaching career turned into one of the most humorous, thanks to a case of mistaken identity.

One of Braddock's victories during the 1959 season--a 15-12 decision over rival North Braddock--was achieved under trying conditions for a man considered a legend by some. And an enemy by others.

"I get a letter saying that if I show up for the game against North Braddock I'm gonna get shot. They wrote, 'To prove we mean business, we're gonna smash your car this week.'

"Well, I always parked my car right next to the high school, a reasonably safe area. The Wednesday night before this game, our team was honored by the Variety Club in Pittsburgh. We came back on the bus. We get off the bus and the kids say, 'Coach, look at your car.' Every window is broken, every fender is smashed, the hood is smashed. Someone had taken a sledgehammer and just ripped it up.

"So I started to think these people were serious. My dad was the mayor of my hometown [Wilmerding], which was close by. I showed the letter to him and he said, 'It's probably a prank. He just wants to upset you. He's probably a fan of North Braddock and he wants to have you worried about this rather than the game. But I'll put two of my policemen in plain clothes to protect you at the game, just in case.'

"So we go to the game and these two plainclothesmen, they're in the locker room and they have pistols in their holsters and everything else. The kids on the team are wondering what the heck is going on. We go up and we play the first half and we don't play very well at all. So I'm running off the field at halftime and a guy steps up to me with something in his hand and he points it at me."

Klausing's bodyguards immediately wrestled him to the ground. Turns out the poor man was armed with nothing more deadly than a tape recorder microphone.

"The guy was a radio man wanting to get a comment from me to put on the air at halftime. He didn't know what hit him."

Job Insecurity

Mark Rutkowski, who quarterbacked Braddock to WPIAL Class A championships in 1956, 1957 and 1958, was in uniform the last two years only because of some skullduggery involving Mike Sullivan, the president of the Braddock School Board. Sullivan ensured Rutkowski wouldn't defect to rival North Braddock.

"The final game of Mark's sophomore year, we beat Carmichaels for the championship [38-0]. That night after the game he told me in tears that his family was moving to North Braddock.

"I said, 'Why? What's happening, Mark?' He said, 'North Braddock is hiring my dad to be a custodian at the school.' So I mentioned it to Mike Sullivan. He said, 'I don't care for Bud Rutkowski, but he has a job paying more as a custodian at Braddock starting Monday.' So that little tragedy was solved.

"Mark led us to undefeated seasons his junior and senior year. We were having a party after the last game when the Braddock School Board walks into the party. They see Mark's dad and say, 'Bud, you're fired.' "

No Excuse

When Klausing arrived at Braddock in 1954, he heard a multitude of stories about one of his predecessors as Tiger football coach, Dan Rice. Rice, a Braddock grad who coached his alma mater's football team for four seasons (1942-45) and was employed as a phys ed instructor, was a real character.

"Dan had an 11 o'clock gym class. He'd take the kids up to the playground to play softball, then he'd leave them there. The kids were taking off, not staying, and causing trouble around town.

"The principal was getting phone calls on it, so he says to Dan, 'You've got to watch your class and make sure they're not leaving.' So he takes them up to the field the next time. He gives them the ball and the bat and picks up sides. They're ready to play softball.

"He says to them, 'Look, it's 11:05, I'm going over to North Braddock High School. I've got to make arrangements for this week's football game. I don't want anyone to leave till I come back to excuse you. No one is permitted to leave until I come back.'

"So the kids start playing, Dan goes over to North Braddock and he gets to talking about the game. Someone from North Braddock says, 'Dan, let's go down to the Elks for lunch.' So Dan takes off with him.

"At 1 o'clock he's coming into the school building and the principal's there waiting. He says, 'Dan, what happened to your class?' Dan says, 'I told them they weren't permitted to leave. Don't worry, they weren't running all over town today.'

"The principal says, 'Dan, I'm not worried about them running around town--they didn't come back for lunch!' They were still up at the ballfield, waiting for Dan to excuse them."

A Betting Man

Rice led Braddock to a 19-7 victory over Farrell in 1944--even though he missed the opening kickoff. Klausing heard the following tale from Stan Zajdel, the Tigers' captain that season.

"During World War II, travel was restricted. They didn't have gasoline, so you couldn't go by bus. Braddock was scheduled to play a road game at Farrell and the only way to get there was to take a streetcar into Pittsburgh and get on a Pennsylvania Railroad train up to Farrell.

"The only train before the game was like 11 o'clock in the morning. So the Braddock team gets into Farrell and Dan goes over to the high school and picks up the $600 guarantee check. He goes to the bank, cashes it and gives each of his players a dollar or two to get something to eat.

"Well, Dan must have started to brag about what a great team he had and how they were gonna beat Farrell. The people from Farrell ran up and down the street and got $500 and challenged him to bet $500 on the game. And Dan accepted. They gave the money to the chief of police to hold.

"Anyway, 6 o'clock comes and the team goes out to warm up. At five minutes to seven the official comes to Zajdel and says it's time for the coin toss. He says, 'But our coach isn't here.' The official says they've got to toss the coin. So they toss it, Farrell wins, they choose to receive and the Farrell back returns the kickoff 90 yards for a touchdown.

"Just about that time Dan Rice comes onto the field. He runs out and grabs the official and says, 'It doesn't count, it doesn't count.' The official says, 'What do you mean, it doesn't count?' 'Well, the coach wasn't here.' 'The coach doesn't have to be here.' "

The touchdown stood, of course. And Rice, to use a term not yet in vogue in the '40s, went ballistic.

"His team had to sit him on the bench--had to actually sit *on* him--because they were afraid he was gonna lose his cool."

Rice was afraid he'd lose something else--his $500 bet. But Bob Sandidge scored two touchdowns to rescue the Tigers. And his coach.

Joe and Oscar

Halfback Joe Reaves scored 21 touchdowns as a senior for Klausing's 1955 team and, predictably, was courted by a swarm of recruiters. But he never developed into a collegiate standout. Fact is, Reaves never even survived his freshman year.

"In the fall of 1956 he's at the University of Cincinnati--they played freshman football at the time--and he's the star of the team. He did OK his first semester, but then he started getting into trouble along with one of the basketball players.

"I hear the story that the president of Cincinnati called the football and the basketball coaches in and told them they had to get rid of one of the two--either Joe Reaves or the basketball star. 'You two go into a room and fight it out.'

"Well, the basketball coach won out. What they did, all of a sudden, instead of PE [phys ed] 101 and PE 102, Joe was taking anatomy and physiology. He couldn't pass those courses and wound up going home. The star basketball player stayed."

From that day forward, Oscar Robertson caused trouble only for Cincinnati opponents. The Big O won three consecutive NCAA scoring titles (1958-60), averaged 33.8 points per game for his career and twice led the Bearcats to a third-place finish in the NCAA tournament. He was also a member of the 1960 United States Olympic squad that earned a gold medal in Rome.

Robertson later earned NBA Rookie of the Year honors, a prelude to a marvelous 14-year career with the Cincinnati Royals and Milwaukee Bucks during which he scored 26,710 points and dished out 9,887 assists. Robertson is a member of the Basketball Hall of Fame.

Glove Story

Wide receiver Jimmy Hux enjoyed a big night in Braddock's 1958 championship-game win over Waynesburg--while wearing a pair of gloves. Not gloves of the sort worn by modern-day players, mind you. *Dress* gloves.

They weren't even his. They were Klausing's.

The coach had forgotten the gloves at home, but his wife, Joann, delivered them just before game time. Klausing didn't don them for long, though.

"Jimmy Hux, one of my best wide receivers, was having trouble before the game because his hands were cold. So I gave Jimmy the gloves. They were a good pair of gloves--fur-lined black leather."

It must have been a strange sight, Hux lining up while wearing dress gloves. But if the Waynesburg players were snickering at first, they weren't snickering for long.

Hux, his hands warmed on a numbing night, caught a 37-yard touchdown pass from Mark Rutkowski on the third play from scrimmage. That was all the scoring the Tigers would need en route to a 21-0 victory--and their fifth consecutive WPIAL Class A title.

The Arrival of Big Bertha

Klausing's fourth WPIAL title the year before was achieved at the expense of Glassport High--and a respected colleague. The Gladiators were coached by George Hays, a former Steeler end (1950-52) who had served as Klausing's line coach for two seasons.

Hays provided the inspiration for a piece of equipment that contributed to Braddock's success. And, indirectly, to Glassport's 14-0 loss to the Tigers in a 1957 showdown for the Class A championship.

"George was a guy that really believed in developing his linemen by hitting a seven-man sled. He told me about a sled that the Pittsburgh Steelers had built by a steel company in Pittsburgh.

"He got the plans for this sled and I took it to one of our boosters who worked in the Edgar Thompson steel mill in Braddock. Their mechanics visited with me and two weeks later a big truck came to our practice field. It had a crane to lift this heavy, all-steel sled off the truck."

The players dubbed the sled Big Bertha.

"Several executives of the steel company, one of them [former Notre Dame All-American] Harry Stuhldreher, were there to give it to us. They claimed that no one would ever be able to move this sled, it was so heavy. The first time our line hit it, they maybe budged it about six inches. But by midseason they were driving it up and down the field. It was a valuable piece of equipment in developing our line."

Camp Corbley

Every year, the Braddock football team would leave the city and spend two weeks of the preseason at rustic Camp Corbley, located about 80 miles northeast of Pittsburgh in Curwensville. The players got so chilled there they donned long underwear at bedtime. In *August.*

"The little cabins we stayed in had no insulation. It got very cold at night, so the kids were told to take long winter underwear to sleep in."

Two of them, William Branch and Charles "Spider" Webb, made the mistake of wearing their long johns even after they climbed out of bed.

"When we started practice at 8 o'clock in the morning it was still cold. But then it got pretty hot. By mid-morning those kids were sweating like anything. It was terrible for them.."

Camp Corbley is also where Melvin Coburn slept in his uniform. Coburn reasoned that by eliminating that daily morning chore, he could grab some extra winks.

"I don't know whether it was me or one of his teammates, but we'd just get him up and push him out the door. He would start jogging around the practice field. About halfway around he'd finally start waking up."

The Befuddling Muddle Huddle

Klausing was never above resorting to trickery to defeat an opponent. One of his favorite weapons was what he calls the muddle huddle, which is designed to leave a defense utterly confused--and therefore vulnerable.

Klausing utilized the formation to great effect during his career, especially at Braddock.

"The big question is, What is a muddle huddle? It's a lineup where a man goes over the ball and the other six linemen line up quickly to his side, forming an unbalanced line. The man over the ball snaps it sideways to one of the backs and you attempt to run the opponents' end, where you have an unbalanced advantage.

"It's a lineup that our teams used before every extra point or field goal try. The man over the ball studies the situation to see if we have an advantage to the unbalanced side and, if we do, he quickly snaps it to that side. If opponents overmatched our unbalanced line, he could snap the ball to the holder, who was also a quarterback. And since the snapper was on the end of the line, he was eligible to receive a pass."

Klausing conjured up a magical muddle huddle play one time, using a staged dispute to score a touchdown.

"As we lined up to kick a field goal, our left halfback and right halfback came to the right side and argued about who was supposed to be in the game. One of them finally started to run towards our bench, but he was actually running in motion. When no one covered him we snapped the ball and threw a pass to him running down the sideline."

He caught the ball without a defender in sight.

Going Batty

Opposing teams likely dreaded Tiger field goal attempts. When they weren't dealing with the muddle huddle, they were dealing with other Klausing tricks.

"I officiated high school games while I was coaching at Pitcairn and Braddock. I discovered a rule that if you batted a ball forward, you could pick up the ball and run with it.

"So we developed a play where, on a field goal try, the holder would take the snap and just flip the ball up in the air. Our kicker would then bat the ball forward like a volleyball. The defensive linemen who were trying to rush the kicker would never realize that this was a batted ball. They would think it was a muffed kick.

"Very few players even knew the rule. The rule was you could not advance a kicked ball, but you could advance a batted ball. So this batted ball would go into the secondary and one of our players would just pick it up and run with it.

"Early on when we used the play it was very successful. It was something we could do maybe once or twice a season. We scored some touchdowns off of it. Unfortunately, the rules committee felt it was something that we were taking advantage of and they eventually changed the rule."

Double Dare

Klausing used an offer from another school to double his paycheck--and that of his assistants--in a most unusual negotiating session with Mike Sullivan, president of the Braddock School Board.

Officials from Canon-McMillan approached Klausing and offered him a position as assistant superintendent and football coach. He was given assurances that he could bring along his entire coaching staff.

"Gee, it seemed like a great opportunity. So I went to Mike Sullivan, with my coaches, and I told him what was happening. He said, 'Are they paying you more?' 'Considerably more.' He handed me a sheet of paper and told us to go in another room. 'Talk it over and write down what you would need to stay here.'

"We went in the other room and started to discuss coaching salaries. The assistants all said, 'Let's double our salaries.' I said, 'Aw, they'll never go for that.' One of them said, 'Let's try. What have we got to lose?'

"So I wrote on the paper 'double what we're being paid' and we walked back into the room with Mike Sullivan. He took the sheet of paper, folded it up and put it in his pocket. He said, 'You have it.' He never even looked at the paper."

Just Holding On

One of those assistant coaches once earned a letter at Indiana University as a sophomore--even though he never actually played a minute of football that season.

"We had a quarterback coach at Braddock by the name of John

Zuger. John had been a great football player at Indiana University in Bloomington. The rules there were you had to play half the total number of quarters to earn a letter. They played 10 games so you had to play in 20 quarters.

"John never played a minute of football his sophomore year, but he lettered because he played in almost every quarter. He was the holder on extra points."

And since the clock does not run on extra points, Zuger's official playing time that year amounted to zero.

The Disjointed Tiger

Melvin Coburn scored four touchdowns in a 26-0 rout of North Braddock in 1956--as a substitute halfback.

But he's perhaps best remembered for his miracle cures. Coburn dislocated his ankle and shoulder in separate incidents that season, but he didn't miss any playing time. He healed himself.

"We have a preseason scrimmage with Monroeville Gateway and he completely dislocates his ankle. I took him to Braddock Hospital and the doctor said he'd have to relocate it the next day. I said, 'What kind of anesthetic are you gonna use?' He said, 'We'll just inject him with a little Novocaine, freeze it up that way and then jerk it back into place.'

"So I go down the next morning. The operation's supposed to be at 9 o'clock. I go into the hospital and run into the doctor. I asked him if he'd done the operation yet. He said, 'Chuck, it's amazing. We took an X-ray of the ankle this morning and it's in perfect position. We sent the boy home.' "

Turns out Coburn feared the pain of a needle piercing his skin more than the pain of a relocation procedure. During the night he jerked the ankle back into place himself.

"We go through the season and this kid, he scores 10 touchdowns and every week there's a long run--he's having a great year. We're practicing for the championship game against Carmichaels when he tries to make a tackle after an interception. He reaches out and grabs the kid's jersey--the back goes one way and Melvin's body goes the other. He completely dislocates his shoulder."

Coburn was in such obvious pain that the other Tigers dropped to their knees and began praying for God to help their teammate. Coburn, still in dire dread of needles, quickly grabbed his elbow, gave it a jerk and pronounced himself healed.

"When the players heard that they all looked up to heaven and one of them said, 'The good Lord, He done answered our prayers for Melvin.' "

Klausing later discovered, while interrogating Coburn about his miracle cures, that his running back was double-jointed. He could dislocate--and relocate--his joint on a whim.

Delayed Reaction

A week after defeating Midland in 1959 to equal the national record for the longest unbeaten streak, Braddock thumped Derry, 32-7. But the Tigers and their fans weren't especially exuberant afterwards.

It seems Braddock hadn't surpassed the record after all.

"See, we thought a team in Abilene, Texas, had the record at 49 games. But then the week of the Derry game someone found out Paul Brown's Massillon team had a 52-game streak."

The Tigers ripped Swissvale 34-7 to push their streak to 51, mauled Monaca 28-8 to tie the mark and then eclipsed Massillon's milestone with a 45-27 victory over Canon-McMillan. The score was somewhat misleading since Braddock led 38-0 at halftime.

Lopsided scores were commonplace during the Tigers' 56-game run, during which they outscored the opposition 1,471-302. Klausing's team never played as if all the attention focused on the streak was any kind of burden.

"The surprising part is that after the first few games, there seemed to be more pressure on our opponents. They tried so hard to beat us that they didn't play their normal game. Fear seemed to take over."

An interesting point about the Derry game: The Trojans' only touchdown was scored by sophomore tailback Mickey Watson, who later quarterbacked Klausing's IUP squad to Pennsylvania Conference Western Division championships in 1964 and 1965. Watson finished third in the nation as a senior with 2,080 yards' total offense.

He later coached under Klausing and his successors, Bill Neal and Owen Dougherty, at IUP.

Tale of the Tape

The Braddock streak survived its biggest scare on Nov. 6, 1959, when the Tigers entered the final minute of their annual showdown with North Braddock facing a 12-9 deficit.

But Ray Henderson--with an assist from NFL All-Pro Ray Berry--saved the day. He snagged a 26-yard touchdown pass from John Jacobs with 37 seconds left to spoil North Braddock's perfect season and catapult the unbeaten Tigers into another WPIAL championship game.

The winning drive officially covered 83 yards, although a sack of Jacobs had actually pushed Braddock back to its own 9-yard line at one point. Jacobs completed five passes on the march, the last transforming Henderson--known as Butch--into the most unlikely of heroes.

For, as Klausing recalls, Henderson was not an ideal target.

"Butch did not have great hands. In fact, he had boards for hands. He was always dropping the ball. But he could block. He played end because he was a great blocker. Anyway, the day of the game I'm reading a *Sports Illustrated* and there's a story about Raymond Berry."

Berry was then a record-setting receiver for the reigning NFL champion Baltimore Colts.

"In this story Raymond is talking about his great success as a pass receiver. One of the things that he said he did, he wrapped his wrists very tight with tape every game. And during the game he would make sure the tape was still tight because it relaxed his fingers. If you almost shut off the circulation, your fingertips are gonna relax.

"Well, I showed this article to Butch and he read it. That night he asked for a roll of tape and wrapped his wrists. All during the game he's checking his wrists--we haven't even thrown a pass to him--to see if the tape is still tight."

Henderson's efforts were not in vain. In the closing minutes the Tigers finally turned to their usually stone-handed receiver, whose impersonation of the incomparable Berry suddenly went beyond mere wrist wraps. Henderson caught three passes for 61 yards during Braddock's crucial, last-gasp drive, the last an acrobatic, over-the-shoulder grab in the end zone for the decisive score.

Klausing later called that game the "toughest I've ever been involved in." It would've been tougher to take without Henderson's heroics.

"The wrapping of the wrists helped him psychologically, I think. On that last play he made a great catch to win the game."

The End of the Line

The Tigers' streak, just like Joe DiMaggio's, reached 56 games before it was snapped in 1960 by Hopewell--a team directed by a former Braddock assistant coach.

Bill McDonald had worked to extend the Tigers' streak in 1956 and 1957 before taking over the Hopewell program the following season. Klausing was coaching at Rutgers when the Vikings pulled off a shocking 7-6 upset at Aliquippa High Stadium, ending a monumental stretch of success dating back to 1953.

"When George Hays left Braddock to coach in his hometown of Glassport, we hired Bill McDonald, who was from my hometown of Wilmerding. Bill coached for me later on at IUP (1966-68) and then became the head coach at Edinboro University."

McDonald led the Fighting Scots to a 54-34-7 record in 10 seasons, highlighted by a Pennsylvania Conference championship in 1970.

In another ironic touch, one of McDonald's assistants was Rey Dempsey, a former quarterback at Pitcairn--under Klausing.

CHAPTER 2
The Early Years

Chuck Klausing is most identified with Braddock High School, where his teams put together a 54-game unbeaten streak, won six WPIAL Class A championships in as many years and attracted national attention. But Klausing had achieved success long before winning his first game at Braddock.

He earned all-state honors as a center at Westinghouse Memorial High School (popularly known as Wilmerding High School), beating out future Pro Football Hall of Famer Chuck Bednarik, who was relegated to the second team. Klausing started as a freshman at Penn State and later transferred to Slippery Rock, where he was selected to the school's all-time team. He also played basketball, ran track and boxed during his collegiate career.

Not long after graduation from Slippery Rock, Klausing accepted his first coaching positions: head football coach and assistant basketball coach at Pitcairn High School, located not far from his hometown of Wilmerding. Pitcairn provided a steppingstone to Braddock and national fame.

Klausing seemed destined for a career in athletics as far back as the eighth grade, when he penned a paper for civics class. The title? "My Career in Coaching."

"I had to write about my career," he recalls. "I wrote that I wanted to be a phys ed teacher and coach, why I wanted to be a coach and what I had to do to prepare to be one. I still have a copy of it."

Though yellowed and crumbling, he keeps the paper as a reminder of the youngster who realized his dreams--exceeded them, in fact. Not only did Klausing become a coach--he became one of the best.

In 1995 Klausing was inducted into the Pennsylvania Sports Hall of Fame for his achievements in the coaching profession.

This chapter focuses on the years preceding his breakthrough at Braddock, when the foundation for later successes was laid.

Success for Mr. Fails

Klausing's first football team at Pitcairn in 1948 finished with a 3-6 record. He doesn't recall all that much about the first two victories, but memories of the third are branded indelibly in his memory. All due to the presence of a special fan.

"The game that I remember at Pitcairn more than any other was the last game of the year against Trafford, our rival. We had sort of a psychological edge.

"George Fails had been the principal at Pitcairn for 40 years. In his 39th year or so he developed cataracts. They operated, but he went blind. He was really well-liked. The kids just idolized him. He had taught most of their parents.

"We're getting on the bus to go to the last game of the season and he walks up to me with his white cane. He says, 'Coach, can I ride with you?' Boy, the bus got silent. He said, 'I can't see the game, but I'd like to sit on the bench and hear the blocking and the tackling.' So he goes with us and sits on the bench.

"Well, our kids blocked and tackled over their heads. I honestly think that psychological edge he gave me meant so much."

The Railroaders, long a doormat in battles with their rivals, rose up and conquered Trafford, 20-0.

Beware of Sleepers

When Klausing coached at Pitcairn and Braddock, so-called sleeper plays were all the rage. Many a coach would rack his brain like some demented Dr. Frankenstein to create a different kind of monster: variations of a play that featured more deception than the typical afternoon soap. (Alas, sleepers have since been outlawed.)

Players dressed as officials, fans, even cheerleaders--male ones, of course--would creep stealthily onto the field and wind up in the middle of a play that, if it succeeded, would have the spectators rolling in hysterics and the opposing coach tearing out so much hair he could double for Michael Jordan.

Klausing occasionally sprang such plays on unsuspecting foes and was, in turn, victimized by them.

"People would stay awake nights trying to think up new ones. You'd get hit maybe once a year. There were some coaches that every game they would be trying some kind of sleeper play. I guess where it got its name, a player laid on the field and he pretended he was sleeping.

"One of the best sleeper plays I ever saw--I can't claim I invented this one--this team dressed a player up as an official. Most of the games back then had three officials, but every once in a while there was a four-official game. This team rolled a guy off the field somehow on the opening kickoff and had only 10 players on the field.

"The first play after the kickoff this official comes on the field with the other three and lines up as a side judge near the bench. And real fast, he rips his shirt off and throws it down. And they throw a helmet out and he puts it on. And then they throw a pass to him.

"That helped me think of another way of doing a sleeper play. When I was coaching at Pitcairn--we were a Class B school--we played Wilmerding [Klausing's alma mater], which was a Class A school and had a great team. Well, our field only had bleachers and benches on one side. On the other side of the field there was a steel cable and a lot of our fans would stand two, three deep behind it to watch the game.

"So we got the opening kickoff, ran it back towards our bench and the guy got tackled out of bounds. We ended up with 10 players in the huddle. Over behind the steel cable we had a young freshman player, standing in among our fans. He was wearing a faded out red jersey and blue jeans and he was carrying a children's helmet.

"We lined up with 10 players on the right hash mark and he steps inbounds on the left sideline and we throw a pass to him and it goes all the way for a touchdown. Well, the coach from the other team immediately comes out on the field with a rule book. He says to the officials, 'Illegal play,' and he read the rule.

"The one official comes over to me then and says, 'Coach, we think we have an illegal play here because your player isn't in uniform.' So I say, 'What does the rule book say as far as a uniform?' He starts reading: 'Must have a jersey with numbers front and back.' He had a jersey with numbers front and back. 'Must have a helmet.' He was wearing a helmet. 'Uh-oh. Must have knee pads.' And the official rolls up his blue jeans and he had a pair of basketball knee pads on.

"That made him eligible."

Suiting up at Pitcairn

There were times when visitors to Pitcairn's practice field probably blinked in disbelief. For there among the scrimmaging players was a slightly older man, wearing a helmet. Chuck Klausing.

Klausing, who had concluded his collegiate career at Slippery Rock not long before, thought nothing of lining up across from his players when the Railroaders didn't have enough bodies for a workout. He would don a helmet and join in.

"Coaching was different in the late '40s and '50s. Even the coaching uniform--in that era we all wore football pants which had knee pads in them. Sometimes we made sure the thigh guards were in, too, because we demonstrated so much full tilt.

"We didn't have very many tackling dummies, if we even had such a thing, so we would line up across from one of our players and say, 'Block me.' The kids would come at you pretty good.

"At times we'd only have 21 players, so the only way we could have a scrimmage was for me to join in. The kids loved trying to hit me, I'll tell you that."

Barroom Brawlers

To spice up Pitcairn scrimmages, Klausing occasionally requested the participation of outsiders--denizens of neighborhood watering holes. Assistant coach Pete Antimarino would recruit several rough-and-ready types to give the Railroaders a challenge.

"I remember getting ready for one big game. We wanted to give our first string a real workout, so I sent Pete, who was from Pitcairn, across the street. The main drag was right next to the football field.

"So he went in and out of a couple bars and came out with about five pretty decent football players. We gave our kids a real good scrimmage that day.

Fortified by their workout--much as the "recruits" had been fortified by liquor--the Railroaders easily disposed of their opponents the following Saturday.

The Armchair Quarterback

Coaches invariably receive unsolicited advice from fans. Sometimes they're even moved to follow that advice--with beneficial results.

Railroad workers who toiled at the yards adjacent to Pitcairn's field were always on hand to offer suggestions when the team was struggling.

"We played Saturday afternoon football at Pitcairn. The railroaders who worked the second trick [shift] at 4 o'clock would come to our games, which started at 2:30. The railroaders would stand right behind my bench. I could always hear them yelling advice.

"This one railroader was always yelling, 'Throw the ball out in the left flat.' I'm ignoring him, so at halftime, as I'm walking off the field, I bump into him and he says, 'Coach, look out in the left flat, it's wide open.'

"I go in the locker room at halftime and he must have gone across the street, where there was a bar, and had a few drinks. He comes back just as I'm coming out of the locker room and again he says, 'Coach, look out in the left flat, it's wide open.'

"We start the second half and we're not doing very good. I finally look out in the left flat and, sure enough, there's no one covering. So I call a pass play and we throw it out in the left flat. We march down the field with passes out in the left flat and score a touchdown. We're ahead now.

"At about five minutes to 4 I get a tap on the shoulder. I turn around and this railroader says, 'Coach, I work the second trick. I have to leave to be at work at 4 o'clock. You're on your own the rest of the game.' "

Crisis of Confidence

In 1952 and 1953, Klausing coached a quarterback at Pitcairn who initially had no faith in his ability. Rey Dempsey probably never figured he'd amount to much in football.

Hard to believe, given the fact that he wound up in the NFL.

Dempsey displayed no shortage of confidence when he took a coaching position with the Detroit Lions in 1975, or eight years later when he led Southern Illinois to the NCAA Division I-AA championship. Dempsey obviously overcame the doubts that beset him as an untested quarterback at Pitcairn.

"Rey Dempsey in his first football game threw a couple interceptions. It got to where he was afraid to throw the football. Well, we had a great wide receiver by the name of Kenny Mignogna. He was the first guy that I ever saw who could dunk a basketball.

"We had a pass play where we opened up the middle and Kenny went down the middle. If you threw the ball down there he would outjump anybody and catch it. So I called Rey to the sideline and told him, 'Just shut your eyes and throw the ball up like a punt, because Kenny is gonna get it.' I kept calling that play down the middle.

"He finally started throwing down the middle and Kenny would outjump everybody for the ball. Rey eventually became a pretty good high school quarterback. He went on to Geneva, then became a high school coach.

Dempsey later graduated to the collegiate ranks, working as an assistant at Bowling Green (1971-72) and a head coach at Youngstown State (1973-74), Southern Illinois (1976-83) and Division I Memphis State (1984-85). He spent the 1975 season as the Lions' special teams coach.

Today Klausing takes pride in his role in transforming Dempsey from tentative high school quarterback to self-assured coach to, lastly, a nondenominational minister.

"It was just a case that he had to get confidence in himself. And he certainly has shown since that he has confidence."

Up in Smoke

Klausing once doused a fire that could have burned down Pitcairn High School. Of course, he'll confess that he was the indirect cause of the near-catastrophe.

"I was in charge of general discipline because the principal, Mr. Fails, had a cataract operation and went blind. There was one section in the school where the kids would smoke. I would come past there after lunch. When they saw me coming they would 'choke' their cigarettes and put them in their pockets."

To avert a run-in with Klausing's ever-present--and much-feared--wooden paddle, understand. But one student's burning desire for tobacco nearly brought disastrous consequences--he or she hadn't completely snuffed out their cigarette.

"In the classrooms there were cloakrooms, that had sort of folding doors, where the students would hang up their coats. It was late fall or winter. I'm in my class and the typing teacher came running through the door, very excited, and said, 'My room is on fire.' "

Smoke had begun billowing out of the cloakroom. By the time Klausing arrived on the scene, flames were crackling menacingly.

"I grabbed a fire extinguisher and ran in and, boy, when I opened up the cloakroom door, the fire started to shoot out at me. I doused it good with the fire extinguisher and put it out. I might have caused the school to burn, but at least I helped prevent it from burning *down*."

Encore Performance

Klausing's reputation as a strict disciplinarian dates back to his first year of teaching at East Pittsburgh High School. Students in those days knew that using the wrong words would get them more than words in return.

"A kid said a four-letter word to me once and I threw him up against a chalkboard. He ran to the principal, so the principal comes back with the boy and asks me, 'Why did you do this?' I told him the kid swore in front of the girls in his class."

The principal listened intently to Klausing's explanation.

"Then he goes, 'You mean you grabbed him by the shirt and threw him against the wall--like this?' And he threw the kid harder than I did."

The English Lesson

Klausing always wanted to teach, either through coaching or in a classroom. But an impromptu lesson in English vocabulary landed him in hot water during his childhood in Wilmerding.

"Mike Theodore was a great basketball player, a high school teammate of mine. He was our center. He went to Carnegie Mellon--Carnegie Tech at the time--and this was when Carnegie Tech played Pitt, Duquesne, West Virginia, all the big teams. He was the leading scorer in the tri-state area one year.

"He came from Bulgaria. When he was five years old he moved to our block during the summer. He couldn't speak any English. The first week of school the teacher asked him, 'Michael, you've been in this country for a month or two--do you know *any* English words?' And he goes, 'Ya, ya.' She says, 'What do you know?' And he goes, 'Son . . . of . . . a . . . beetch.' "

The teacher scowled. "She says, 'Who taught you that?' And he points to me and says, 'Charles.' "

Beaten by a Heisman Winner

Klausing turned black and blue after using some blue language later in his youth, courtesy of a future Heisman trophy recipient.

"I grew up in a time and in an area where half our vocabulary was swear words. Well, I had a good thing happen to me--I think it was between my junior and senior year in high school.

"I had a chance to be a counselor at Camp Fitch, which was a YMCA camp in Youngstown. I go to this camp and I'm out in the lake swimming and helping to be a lifeguard. I had a few kids who were going out too far and I let out a few curse words--'Get yourself back in the shallow end.' "

Except that Klausing interposed some more colorful words among the ones listed above.

"The head lifeguard was a guy by the name of Frankie Sinkwich, the Heisman award winner [as a Georgia tailback in 1942]. And he shouts at me, 'You come in here. You're not gonna use that kind of language again.'

"Well, I was a pretty smart 16-, 17-year-old guy. I said, 'You want me, you come in and get me. I'm not coming in.' He said, 'I'll outlast you.' So I just stayed out there in the water for about a half hour.

"I got tired finally and I came in. Well, he put me on the dock there and he whacks me about 10 times with a canoe oar. He really blistered me. I'll tell you what, I can count on the fingers of my hand the times I've sworn since then. That was one of the best lessons I ever had."

Uncle Mike and 'Chook'

Mike LaGorga lived in Wilmerding when Klausing was growing up there. Whether they were a relative or not, everyone addressed him as Uncle Mike.

"He was born in Italy and came here when he was 20 years of age. And at 80 he was still speaking very broken English. When I was a young boxer, I was having a fight in my hometown, so Uncle Mike went to the fights with my dad.

"He didn't have real good eyesight, but I can remember him yelling all through the first round: 'Hit him, Chook, hit him Chook, hit him in the breadbasket, Chook.' You could hear his voice over everybody else's.

"The second round, he'd go, 'Hit him Chook, rabbit punch him, Chook, hit him again, Chook.' Third round, the same thing. Well, they tell me he nudged my dad at one point and he said, 'Pardon me, *compa*, but which-a one is-a Chook?' "

Recruited by a Priest

In his youth, Klausing was recruited by Father John Flaherty. Not to join the priesthood--to join a Catholic League football team. And Klausing wasn't even Catholic.

"His parish and his school was St. Aloysius. I'm an eighth-grader going to public school--I'm Lutheran--but all my buddies were going to St. Al's grade school. They had a football team, but because I wasn't in their school, I couldn't play for them."

Until Father Flaherty intervened, that is.

"St. Aloysius' big rival was St. Colman's of Turtle Creek. They're playing at Turtle Creek against St. Colman's and I go down to watch the game. Father Flaherty and a priest from the other school had a bet on the game.

"St. Al's is losing at halftime and he asks the kids, 'How come you're losing?' They say, 'Aw, Father, they have three or four ninth-graders playing for them.' He says, 'Well, what can we do to get competitive with them?' They said, 'If you let Chuck play, we'll beat them.' "

And so Father Flaherty bolstered the St. Al's roster, mid-game.

"They got one of the kids who was a substitute to take his uniform off. Some of the players rode to the game in a hearse, so I dressed in the back of a hearse and went out and led them to a win over St. Colman's."

Long after playing for the Catholic school team, Klausing converted to Catholicism. On May 9, 1948, he and Joann Wit were married by an old acquaintance--Father John Flaherty.

Time-Tested Official

Under normal circumstances, when an official spots a fan rushing toward him on a football field, he braces for the worst. Klausing did. But instead of delivering epithets or uppercuts, this particular fan delivered compliments.

"When I was a young high school coach I got my officiating license and I officiated on Friday nights, because Pitcairn played on Saturday afternoons. I was just starting out so I didn't have many games to officiate.

"Well, I get a call saying that an official was needed for a Wheeling vs. Wheeling Catholic game at Wheeling, W.Va. I met the other officials part way down the route and we drove down to Wheeling. We got there, got dressed and went out on the field. The two coaches had been arguing about officials, which is why they got a crew from Pittsburgh to come down--they felt that they needed neutral officials.

"There were four of us and we were all rookies. It was decided that I was to be the field judge, which I was happy to do. I said to the other three guys, 'Who has the watch?' Well, no one has a stopwatch. This was an era when there was no scoreboard clock, so I had to use my wristwatch to keep time.

"Generally speaking, a high school football game lasts about two hours. There's about a 20-minute break at halftime, so I figured each quarter would be 25 minutes. I looked at my watch and when it came to 25 minutes, I blew the whistle to end the first quarter. I even pretended I was stopping a stopwatch.

"So we go into the second quarter and when 25 minutes is up, I blow the whistle. We have a 20-minute half, go out for the third quarter, play for 25 minutes and go into the fourth quarter. The Catholic team is behind, but late in the fourth quarter they're driving for a touchdown. Players from both teams are coming up to me--'How much time? How much time?' 'Five minutes.' 'How much time?' 'Three minutes.' They're even trying to look over my shoulder, so I sort of shield my watch from them, because they could see it's just an ordinary wristwatch.

"The Catholic team's inside the 10-yard line and, boy, the second hand passes 12 and the 25 minutes are up. I had to be fair, so I go in and pick up the football--the game's over. I'm running off the field and a guy comes running up to me and he has a stopwatch--it's a Catholic priest.

"For a brief moment Klausing wondered if the priest, perhaps irate over his timekeeping and the Catholic team's aborted scoring opportunity, was about to rebuke him.

"He says, 'Mr. Official. I want you to know that it's my hobby to keep time at football games.' "

Klausing felt his knees weaken, fearing that he'd been exposed as a fraud.

"He says, 'I want you to know that in the first quarter you and I were about 45 seconds off, the second quarter we were about 30 seconds off and the third we were about 15 seconds off. But that fourth quarter . . . we were right on the button.' So how lucky can you be?"

The Mettle (and Metal) to Play at Penn State

In 1943 and 1944, Penn State football fans were understandably incredulous when Klausing lined up at center for the Nittany Lions. After all, few major-college teams, despite the manpower shortages of the war years, featured a 155-pound lineman.

But then, Bob Higgins didn't know that's all Klausing weighed. The youngster fooled his head coach through an inventive bit of chicanery.

"When I went to Penn State I wasn't very big. I know I boxed at 155 pounds, so that was probably my playing weight. They must have had some kind of rule that if you were gonna go out for the team you had to weigh a certain amount. I think they were saying 175 pounds.

"So I got my dad to get two 10-pound pieces of metal. I strapped one to each thigh and went up and got weighed. Instead of weighing 155 pounds, I weighed 175. That was the only way I got a uniform."

Today, when 300-pound centers are commonplace, the story seems utterly preposterous. What makes it even more incredible is that Klausing not only played, but wound up starting at center and linebacker by midseason of his freshman year.

Higgins recalled his lightweight sensation in 1961, when Klausing returned to Beaver Stadium as an Army assistant coach.

"I don't think he ever weighed much more than 150 pounds, but I can still remember him mixing with the big fellows," Higgins said. "He was a hard-nosed kid who had more grit than any boy on the squad."

That grit--along with 20 pounds of hidden metal--helped Klausing earn a spot on the Penn State roster.

The Unlucky 13th

Klausing fancied himself a "pretty good basketball player," having started at guard for a Wilmerding High School team that won a section championship in 1942 and participated in the WPIAL playoffs.

But he was in for a rude awakening at Penn State.

"I went there and I thought I was gonna play at least two seasons--football season and basketball season. I got to start as a freshman in football, so I thought I had a good chance of making the basketball team.

"I go out for the team and the coach--his name was John Lawther--had a heckuva good way of picking his team. I thought it was very fair. He liked to play at lunchtime, so he'd play with us at noontime.

"I think he sort of liked to play with me--he picked me real early when we chose sides. At practice there were 25 guys, then it was down to 20, then down to 15--I think he was gonna keep 12. Well, I must have been the 13th.

"He says to me, 'Chuck, I really like playing with you because you set me up so well. Will you keep playing at noontime?' He was the kind of guy who liked to shoot all the time. I'd set good screens for him so he could shoot."

While Lawther cut Klausing from the varsity squad, he did make a suggestion that landed the freshman on another varsity team.

"I wasn't real tall, but I was a pretty good athlete. He suggested I try boxing."

Klausing, who had fought some as a youngster, approached coach Leo Houck and requested a tryout. He made the team and earned a varsity letter during his freshman season (1943-44), but that was the extent of his ring work at Penn State. Klausing left school on Nov. 1, 1944, to begin active military duty.

Meeting the Mauler

Perhaps Klausing's biggest thrill as a Penn State boxer took place outside the ring. He had the honor of meeting Jack Dempsey, who enjoyed an extended reign (1919-26) as world heavyweight champion.

Dempsey, an icon during the Roaring '20s, when America embraced its sports heroes as never before, finished his career with a 62-6-1 record. Two of those losses occurred in memorable bouts with Gene Tunney, who succeeded Dempsey--the so-called Manassa Mauler--as world champion.

Houck, Klausing's coach at Penn State, had fought both Dempsey and Tunney.

"We went on the train to New York, because we were to box West Point the next day. We stayed overnight in New York City, so

Leo took us to Dempsey's restaurant. Dempsey was there and Leo introduced us."

Klausing recalls the occasion for another reason, too.

"I remember that's where I had my first beer. They served it in a cocktail glass--for a dollar."

Jack Be Nimble

Besides Dempsey, perhaps the most memorable boxer Klausing ever encountered was Jack Chabek. Chabek and Dempsey shared the same first name; there the similarities ended.

"We have preseason boxing at Penn State and every weight division had two or three guys, but Chabek was the only heavyweight. He had no one to spar with to show whether he was any good. The closest guy would've been a 175-pounder and this guy was afraid to go against Chabek, who weighed about 225.

"So no one knew how good Chabek was. But, boy, did he look good. He was the most beautiful shadow boxer I've ever seen. He would snort around that ring, he'd hit the light bag, he'd hit the heavy bag--he was a big, strong guy.

"We go up to West Point to open the season against Army and they're having weigh-ins. Chabek weighs in at 225. Army had a heavyweight by the name of Dewitt Coulter, who was an All-America football player. He was 6-foot-6 and about 245 pounds.

"So they measure Coulter and announce 6-6 and Chabek goes, 'I never thought that they could pile crap that high.' Coulter gets on the scale and they announce his weight and Chabek goes, 'I never thought crap was that heavy.

This match had eight divisions and we go into the final fight of the evening tied 3½-3½. Whoever wins the heavyweight bout will win the match. We're all saying, 'We're sure winners. Not only does Chabek look good, he's not afraid of Coulter.' You could tell that.

"The bell rings and Chabek rushes across the ring and he just pelts Coulter something terrible. Coulter covered up rope-a-dope, like Muhammad Ali used to do. I don't think Chabek gets one punch in on him, but he dominates the round.

"We're all so happy, we're sure we're gonna win this match. The bell rings and Coulter goes and sits down on his stool. Our guy doesn't even sit down--he tosses the stool out of the ring, as if to say, I'm not even tired.

"The bell rings for the second round and he rushes across the ring again and that dang Coulter, he's ready this time. He hits Chabek and down he goes. Chabek crawls to the corner of the ring and he starts climbing up the post. One punch and he's knocked down. After the referee counts him out, he starts screaming that he got robbed, that it was a lucky punch, that the referee had a fast count--he complained about everything."

The referee, incidentally, was Arthur J. Donovan, whose son, Art, gained fame as a Baltimore Colts lineman (1950-61), commercial pitchman and comical talk show guest.

"We go down to Maryland the next week and Maryland's coach had scouted our match at West Point. So when Chabek rushes across the ring at the bell, their heavyweight [Dan Marowitz] throws one punch and down he goes--the same act. Our coach is so disgusted he just takes a towel and throws it in the ring. And that was the last of Chabek."

The Boxer Rebellion

Brotherly love was strained to the limit in the Tomosky family in 1928. Especially after Rags cost his sibling some riches. Or at least a shot at some riches.

"I had two guys from my hometown that were boxers. One was a guy by the name of Andy Tomosky, who fought under the name Bobby Murphy. His brother, Rags Tomosky--I don't remember his real name--was a great hitter. Rags became an alcoholic. I heard what caused him to turn to alcohol was that he killed a man in the ring.

"The Tomoskys were both little guys--I'm gonna say flyweights. Andy wasn't a knockout hitter, where Rags was just the opposite.

"Anyway, Andy had won about 40 straight bouts, so he got the chance to fight for the world championship. But he needed somebody to train with. So he went to Rags. 'My manager will pay you $5 a round to spar with me. Can you give me six good rounds tomorrow?'

Rags said, 'You know I can always give *you* six good rounds. I'm better than you.'

"So the next day they step into the ring. Andy was a great defensive boxer, a great jab guy, and he's peppering Rags all over the ring--bing, bing, bing--hooking him, and one-twoing him and hitting him low and coming up, using all kind of combinations.

"Rags is taking a beating. The whole time he's thinking, A lousy $5 a round. And he starts getting mad. Finally he hauls off and hits his brother and breaks his jaw. Andy never got the chance to fight for the world championship because of Rags getting mad at him."

Joining the Marine Corps

Klausing was a senior at Wilmerding in February of 1943 when he and four friends--all teammates on the school's basketball squad--ventured into Pittsburgh.

It was a trip that would change Klausing's life.

"The moral of this story is, don't do things because your friends are going to do it. World War II was on and we were all feeling patriotic. We decided to join the Marine Corps.

"So we take a streetcar into Pittsburgh and go to the Marine recruiting station. We walk in and the first thing they give you is two or three pages of forms to fill out. For some reason I took a little longer than the other four guys.

"There were about five or six different rooms of doctors, giving eye tests, checking our blood pressure and our heart and so forth. My four friends were always ahead of me. Sometimes I would see the last one just as I was entering the room.

"So I come into the final room and there was a Marine colonel there, sitting behind a desk. And he said, 'Are you ready to take the Oath of Allegiance to the Marine Corps?' I said, 'Oh, yes, sir, I'm all ready.' 'Raise your hand, repeat after me.' And I take the oath.

"He told me I'd be getting a letter in a couple weeks to report to Parris Island. I was looking forward to that. So I go out and my four buddies are waiting on the corner. We get on the streetcar and we're going back home and I say, 'Boy, are we gonna have fun--five of us going to Parris Island together. We'll have a ball down there.'

"And the other four guys look at me and say, 'You didn't join up, did you?' "

They hadn't. And they never did.

A Visit from the President

Klausing attended Penn State as a V-12 trainee before he was called to active duty in the fall of 1944 and assigned to the Norfolk (Va.) Naval Station. It was there that he found himself practically standing next to Harry Truman, the 33rd president of the United States.

"I was a Marine Corps officer at the Naval Operations Base in Norfolk. This was right after World War II ended. The *Missouri*, the battleship where they signed the treaty with the Japanese, had just come back from the Pacific.

"I have officer of the day duty on a weekend. I'm in my office when two FBI men come in and tell me they were going to have to go over security because President Truman was coming down from Washington and wanted to go aboard the *Missouri* and congratulate the crew.

"So I first of all took them to the ship and we went over the procedures and so forth. And the sergeant major said to me, 'Lieutenant, we're gonna have to have a parade. Any time the commander in chief comes aboard, you have to have a parade.'

"We have about 250 Marines there at the time. Here I am a young lieutenant, I don't know what to do. The sergeant major says, 'I've been through a hundred of these. I'll stand right next to you and give you every command you have to give.'

"Well, I was as close to Truman as I was to the sergeant major. He inspected my troops. He must have been an old serviceman himself. He asked for the rifle of one of the guys and opened it up and looked in to see if it was clean. It was an interesting experience."

Water Hazard

Klausing had another interesting experience at Norfolk, this one--fortunately--not involving the president.

As a driver, he was still wet behind the ears back then.

Consequently, a young Marine nearly got wet--period.

"My family had never had an automobile while I was growing up, so I didn't know how to drive a car. I had guard duty one night, which meant I had to check all the guard stations between 2 a.m. and 6 a.m.

"Part of my tour was about 10 piers at Norfolk Naval Station. I had a car I could use, so at 2 o'clock in the morning I drove a car for the first time in my life. It wasn't an automatic--it was clutch and gearshift.

"I had watched some people start a car and I watched how they got in reverse and so forth, but I wasn't real sure how to do it. I took this car out on one pier and at the end was a young Marine. He snapped to attention when I stopped the car.

"I asked him what his fifth general order was and he gave the fifth general order and I saluted him and got back in the car. I thought I had the car in reverse, but I must have put it in second instead. I almost knocked the poor kid off the pier."

'Landing' at Slippery Rock

After playing football for two seasons at Penn State and spending 29 months on active duty in the military, Klausing chose to continue his education at Slippery Rock. The end of World War II brought an influx of gridders--many far brawnier than Klausing--to Penn State. His days as a starter, he presumed, were numbered.

Preferring to play at a small school rather than sit at a large one, Klausing transferred to Slippery Rock. But getting a uniform there was not a foregone conclusion, even for a player who had distinguished himself at Penn State.

"Right after the war Slippery Rock was physical education school. It jumped from about 500 enrollment to 900. Four hundred GIs came in and about a hundred guys wanted to go out for football. They only had about 30 uniforms left over from before the war, so the coach [Bill Storer], who didn't have much help as far as assistants or anything, used sort of a physical education method to pick his team.

"He had us run the cross country course, do jumps over hurdles and do forward rolls in a sawdust pit. I didn't exactly understand how that could determine whether you were a good football player or not. Anyway, it came down to 35 players left and there were 30 uniforms.

"He couldn't think of anything else to determine whether a guy was good enough to get one of those uniforms. Here I am, I went through OCS [Officers Candidate School] and the Marine Corps and I'm in pretty good shape and I still might not get a uniform.

"Well, I remembered something they did in the Marine Corps at boot camp--I think it might have been some kind of punishment. On a concrete drill field the drill instructor made us stand at attention, put our hands behind our backs and fall on our chests. I could do it. I almost rolled down into it.

"So I said to the coach, 'I can show you how to find out if any of these players have enough guts to play.' He says, 'What?' I said, 'Have them repeat after me,' and I fell on my chest.

"He said, 'OK, you get a suit.' None of the other 34 wanted to do it."

Rocket Red, the Pioneer

Like Eric the Red, Rocket Red ventured into uncharted waters, a discoverer in his own right. Paul Uram, known to his buddies as Rocket Red, was Klausing's roommate at Slippery Rock and the player to whom he snapped the ball.

Apart from his quarterback duties, Uram was also an exceptional gymnast. But it was his study of athletes--not his own athletic feats--that commanded attention. And ultimately earned him a position in the NFL.

"He was the originator of what we call stretching exercises. He wrote a term paper about how bouncing calisthenics--one, two, three, four--were no good for you. He told us one time that he pulled a hamstring because a coach was making him do one-two-three-four exercises to stretch his leg.

"He said that's wrong, that the muscles were like a rubber band--you stretched it too much, it's gonna break. You should stretch it slowly--that was his philosophy. He took that thesis and made it into a book [*Refining Human Movement*].

"I think Michigan State was the first school that had him speak at a clinic. A number of NFL coaches were there and they liked what he said. So NFL teams started asking him to come in for a week and show their coaches how to stretch their guys. And the Pirates baseball team had him go to spring training in Bradenton [Fla.]. He was sort of free-lancing."

Until the Steelers, despite initial resistance from head coach Chuck Noll, hired him full-time.

"Noll was always slow to take on anything new like that. I think it was [assistant coach] George Perles who finally sold Noll on what Paul was doing."

Uram served as the team's strength and flexibility coach from 1972 through 1981. Which means that his pioneering efforts in the field of stretching helped stretch his bank account--he cashed four Super Bowl championship checks in his 10 years with the team.

CHAPTER 3
Back to College

Klausing had no idea a speech he delivered at a football convention on Long Island in 1958 would take him in a new direction--away from his western Pennsylvania roots and away from the high school game his Braddock teams had dominated.

John Bateman, the line coach at the University of Pennsylvania, was in the audience that evening when Klausing spoke on football fundamentals. Duly impressed, he approached Klausing afterward and introduced himself. If I ever become a head coach, he told Klausing, I'll hire you. Bateman kept his word in 1960.

"I'd always wanted to coach college ball," Klausing recalls, "so when John became the head coach at Rutgers, I didn't hesitate when he offered me a job."

Klausing worked as head recruiter and tutored the defensive backs. He stayed one year before moving 75 miles north to West Point, where he served as an Army assistant for three seasons.

During that four-year span in New Jersey and New York, Klausing laid the groundwork for his later successes as a collegiate head coach at IUP and Carnegie Mellon, where his teams were a combined 125-24-2 (.828). Through the 1995 season, the latest for which information was available from the NCAA as this book went to press, only 14 coaches (minimum 10 years' experience), regardless of division, rank ahead of Klausing on the all-time list.

A Loss at Last

On Nov. 5, 1960, the Rutgers freshman team suffered its first loss of the season. Ordinarily, freshman games draw scant attention from anyone besides the players and coaches and their families, but this game was different.

This one caught the eye of fans as far away as western Pennsylvania for one simple reason: A Klausing-coached team had finally lost. His monumental streak, covering in excess of seven years, was over.

Incredibly, Klausing's last defeat had come 2,590 days before, on Oct. 3, 1953, when East McKeesport squeaked past his Pitcairn team, 6-0. He had been unbeaten since.

Klausing's 1953 Pitcairn squad finished the season with five consecutive victories and his teams at Braddock fashioned a phenomenal 53-0-1 record from 1954 through 1959. The Rutgers freshmen then won their first four games in 1960, extending his personal unbeaten streak to 63.

The Rutgers frosh had bumped off Princeton, Penn, Lehigh and Lafayette before Delaware--a school that would hand Klausing's IUP team a heart-wrenching setback eight years later--marched into New Brunswick and posted a 12-6 victory.

"It was a nip-and-tuck game that could've gone either way. They had a great running back. We would 5-yard them to death. They would go one foot, one foot, then 80 yards."

That was sufficient to beat Rutgers and end Klausing's seven-year streak. Undaunted, he began a new one the following week.

Special Delivery

Klausing fondly recalls his year with Bateman, whom he regarded as a first-class coach--and a first-rate deliveryman.

"John resembled Jackie Gleason physically. He had his doctorate, was a very articulate, bright guy and did a great job in turning the Rutgers program around. In his second year he had an undefeated season [9-0, with a team dominated by Klausing recruits].

"There's one thing that I remember about John that I really appreciated. I was away recruiting and they had a major snowstorm in New Jersey--my wife was snowed in. She tells the story that a guy pulled up in an automobile, got out with a snow shovel, shoveled the walk, went back to the car and came back to the door with two brown bags full of milk, eggs, bread--the staples that you need."

It was Bateman.

"He just knew that she was snowed in and needed some help. You really respect a guy you're working for who's thinking of your family."

The Timid Knight

During his time at West Point, Klausing kept in shape by occasionally playing in pickup basketball games that pitted Army's football and basketball coaching staffs. Included was a brash, young assistant basketball coach, Bobby Knight.

Knight had played for Ohio State's NCAA championship squad in 1960, but he was no match for the behemoths that joined forces with Klausing.

The most notable of Klausing's teammates was Don Holleder, who had earned All-America honors as a junior end in 1954. A year later, Army's head coach, Col. Earl "Red" Blaik, asked Holleder to move to quarterback.

The outcry was instantaneous. Shift a returning All-American to a new position? Vitriol flowed like the nearby Hudson River. Critics called for Blaik's scalp and even the Army brass wore anxious expressions as the debate raged.

Holleder defused a potential crisis by agreeing to the move, even though it meant sacrificing his opportunity for personal honors. By subordinating his own ambitions for the sake of the team--a concept glorified at the service academies--he ensured his place among the athletic legends at West Point.

Army excelled under Holleder's command in 1955, finishing 6-3. The highlight was a 14-6 victory over archrival Navy.

Klausing learned of the Furor of '55 from Holleder himself. They met in 1961 when Klausing arrived at West Point from Rutgers to join Dale Hall's staff. Holleder was an assistant plebe coach.

"Col. Blaik was the kind of guy who believed in putting his best leader at quarterback. He asked Holleder to be the quarterback even though Holleder's coming up to his senior year and he's a sure-fire All-American again at end. And Holleder accepted the assignment to be the quarterback.

"He led his team pretty well, but he couldn't throw worth a lick. The story goes that someone found an opposing team's scouting report. And on the scouting report it told the defensive backs to stand still, because Holleder's liable to throw the ball to you as well as to his own teammates. But Holleder was a great leader and led his team to a big win over Navy, which was the important thing.

"Holly came back to West Point while I was there. He and I used to play basketball together against Bobby Knight. The other players on our team were Bob Novogratz, who was about 6-4 and 240, and Bill Rowe and Chuck Lytle, who were about that size. And Holleder was 6-4, 210.

"Believe me, Bobby Knight wasn't as tough a basketball player as he is a coach, because he wouldn't come near that basket when those guys were standing under it."

Novogratz, Rowe and Lytle had all played on the 1958 Army football team--along with halfback Pete Dawkins, the Heisman trophy recipient--that finished 8-0-1 and trounced Navy, 22-6.

Holleder went from the football field--and the basketball court--to Vietnam, where he lost his life in 1967.

General Orders

General William Westmoreland, who played a prominent role in the Vietnam War, was the superintendent at West Point when Klausing arrived. Westmoreland was an imposing figure who could unnerve even the most unflappable officers.

He nearly unnerved Klausing once.

"Dale Hall gets fired and they're looking for a new head coach. I was asked to stay on and take care of the interim business. Naturally, recruiting was a big part of the interim business.

"But maybe the most important thing was to keep the players eligible in school. So I would call the professors at West Point, asking how key players were doing. One night I get a phone call, which goes something like this: 'Klausing. This is Westmoreland. I understand you've been badgering my professors about the players' grades.'

Klausing composed himself and then answered.

"I said, 'General, I don't know whether you'd call it badgering, but

I'm trying to save some potential officers for the academy.' He liked that. He said, 'I want you to know that if any of the professors [who were all Army officers] are giving any of your players a rough time, let me know. There's a war going on in Vietnam and they could be over there rather than being a professor here.'

"I had no trouble after that. He was very supportive."

Showdown with Westmoreland

Westmoreland usually got his way at West Point, at least until Paul Dietzel interviewed for the vacant head coaching position following Hall's dismissal. Dietzel called Westmoreland's bluff and walked off with a jackpot.

"Gen. Westmoreland had a hot list of three coaches that he wanted to interview. All three had been ex-assistants at West Point. One was Paul Dietzel from LSU, who had won the national championship in 1958. Another was Murray Warmath of Minnesota, whose team had just won the Rose Bowl. The third was Vince Lombardi, who had just won the NFL championship with the Green Bay Packers. They were all hot candidates and Westmoreland felt he could get any of the three.

"Well, when the Army does things they do them in a special way. They called it Operation Pelican: They were gonna go into New Orleans and interview Dietzel. Operation Gopher, they were gonna go into Minneapolis and interview Warmath. And Operation Packer, they were gonna go into Green Bay and interview Lombardi.

"The first interview was with Dietzel. Anyone who knows Dietzel, he had great communication skills. He did a great job on his interview. When the officers who were interviewing him finished, they asked him if he had any questions. His question was, 'What's going to be your procedure from now on?' Westmoreland told him they were gonna interview Warmath and Lombardi.

"Well, Dietzel had passed out these beautiful playbooks to every officer interviewing him. He gets up and goes around picking up all the playbooks that he had put in front of them. He tells Westmoreland, 'You can withdraw my name from the list.' And he walks out in a huff.

"Westmoreland was so impressed with Dietzel that he goes running after him. He says, 'What did we do wrong, Mr. Dietzel?' And Dietzel says, 'If I am not the only candidate for this job, I don't want to be considered.'

"Westmoreland talks him into going back in the room. There must have been 10 officers there and they were all for Dietzel. They didn't even bother to talk to Warmath or Lombardi. Dietzel got the job."

The Chinese Bandits

Under Dietzel, it was often difficult to discern the difference between East and West: the Far East and West Point, that is. The Army band played Chinese music during football games and the cadets in the stands wore coolie hats.

What's more, Chinese Bandits ran amok on the field.

The Bandits formed part of a three-platoon system that caught the fancy of fans across the land. It was billed as innovative and novel, but Klausing knew better.

"When you're a coach, you copy from other coaches' ideas. Knute Rockne at Notre Dame used what he called Shock Troops. He would start his second team, see how the opposition was playing, and then put the first team in.

"In the late '30s, Duquesne [then a national power] used a two-team system. They had a team made up of mostly seniors and another team of good, young sophomores. They were sort of interchangeable.

"Then when I went to Army I was fortunate to be involved in a three-team system. The rules at that time were if you played in a quarter and were substituted for, you could not come back in that quarter. So to beat the rule we had a three-team system.

"We had our regulars, who would play offense and defense. Then we had a team called our Go team that would just play offense. And then we had the Chinese Bandits, who would just play defense."

With wreckless abandon, it might be noted.

And who christened the Bandits? None other than the head coach.

"There was a comic strip in the paper called Terry and the Pirates. And in that strip the meanest people in the world were Chinese bandits. So that's what Dietzel called them."

Foot Fault

With the Chinese Bandits leading the way, Army played sensational defense in the early '60s, especially against Penn State.

But then, the Cadet defenders had a distinct advantage--Chuck Klausing. He knew what plays the opposition was running. The tip-off was the quarterback. His feet, actually.

"When their quarterback had his right foot back it was gonna be a sprintout pass to the right. If he had his left foot back, it was gonna be a sprintout pass to the left. When his feet were even, it was gonna be a running play.

"All of their running plays came off a reverse pivot of the quarterback, so as soon as we saw the shoulder starting to turn we angled to that side and we were able to shut them down."

In Klausing's three seasons at Army--1961 through 1963--the Cadets won all three meetings with Penn State, surrendering only 20 points in the process.

Sound Barrier

To partisans of Army football, nothing is quite as unpalatable as a loss to Navy. Few defeats in the storied, century-old series were more revolting--or more riveting--than a 21-15 setback in 1963.

The game ended with the Cadets poised on the Navy 2-yard line, unable to run a play because of the deafening din. Quarterback Carl "Rollie" Stichweh, who engineered a dramatic fourth-quarter comeback, stood helplessly at the line of scrimmage as time expired.

The second-ranked Midshipmen (8-1), led by Heisman trophy recipient Roger Staubach, were favored over Army (7-2) in the showdown at Philadelphia Stadium (later renamed JFK Stadium). The game went according to form until Stichweh scored on a 1-yard run and then tacked on the two-point conversion with six minutes left, slicing the deficit to six points.

The Navy fans in the crowd of 100,000 stirred nervously in their seats, especially after Stichweh--a seemingly omnipresent force--recovered Dick Heydt's ensuing onside kick. Klausing, like most of the Army players and coaches, sensed an upset.

"We started a drive and it was like three yards and four yards every play--a very consistent drive, no big plays. We get the ball down inside the 10-yard line with a minute and a half to play."

Fullback Ray Paske gained two yards to the 5 on first down, tailback Ken Waldrop picked up a yard on second down and Waldrop plowed ahead for two more. The Cadets faced a fourth-down play from the 2. That's when the nightmare began.

"We go up to the line of scrimmage, the clock is live and there's no timeouts available--we'd already used them. We're on Navy's end of the field and their fans are making so much noise that Rollie Stichweh turns around and appeals to the official.

"The official stops the clock with about 30 seconds to play and our team goes back in the huddle. They're waiting for the referee to tell them to go ahead and try again. And the official--I remember his name was [Barney] Finn--he winds the clock. The clock ticks off at least 10 seconds and our kids don't even know it. They're still in the huddle.

"We coaches run towards that end of the field screaming to our kids to run a play. They go to the line of scrimmage--there's about 10 seconds on the clock--and the noise now really gets loud. You can see Stichweh yelling 'set, hike'--you see his head bobbing--but the ball doesn't get snapped because no one can hear him.

"He looks around at the referee, again appealing for help, and the referee does nothing. The time finally clicks off and one of the other officials runs in, picks up the ball and runs off the field."

The Cadets stood motionless, unable--or unwilling--to comprehend what transpired. Klausing's view was shared by those in the tomblike silence of the Army locker room.

"We really felt we got robbed of a chance that we should've had."

Afterwards, Navy accepted a bid to play top-ranked Texas in the Cotton Bowl on New Year's Day. Army's season was over.

"The irony was, in 1946 the opposite situation happened. Army was ahead 21-18 and Navy did not get the opportunity to win because of noise."

That game ended with the Midshipmen on the Army 5-yard line.

The Lonely End

There were probably times when Army end Bill Carpenter felt like a carrier of bubonic plague, shunned by teammates who kept their distance. While they would huddle, he would stand far removed, seemingly isolated.

Actually, it wasn't a contagion that separated Carpenter from his teammates. It was an innovation that coach Red Blaik termed the Lonely End.

"Prior to 1960, everyone got into very tight formations. The single-wing was tight--even the T formation was tight. There were no flankers or anything of that type.

"Col. Blaik and Dale Hall, his successor, developed what they called a Lonely End. The reason they called him that, he would stand out wide to the side. He never came into the huddle.

"A lot of people wondered how he even got the signals. All he'd have to do was look in at the ball; when the ball was snapped, that's when he would leave the line of scrimmage. And the quarterback would have signals--he'd hitch his trousers up on certain plays or he'd touch his chinstrap. He would have his right foot forward in the huddle if the play was going to the right and his left foot forward if it was going to the left."

Carpenter, who earned All-America honors in 1959 after catching a school-record 43 passes, was the first--and certainly most acclaimed--of the Lonely Ends. The second was Bob Fuellhart, whose nephew, Sean, later played for Klausing at Kiski School.

The Daring Captain

Carpenter had graduated by the time Klausing arrived at West Point in 1961, but he nearly had the opportunity to coach alongside the original Lonely End.

"Part of my work at West Point was getting graduate assistants. The head coach told me, 'We ought to get an officer to be a grad assistant. Would you call Bill Carpenter and see if he would want to come back here and be a coach?' Carpenter had been out on duty.

"I called him and he said, 'Chuck, I'd love to be a coach. But I've been trained to fight wars and there's a war going on.' The Vietnam thing was just starting. So he winds up going over to Vietnam."

And becoming a hero.

"Later on the story comes out that his company was pinned down by enemy fire--they were completely surrounded by Vietnamese. There was no way they could get out. So he called in his coordinates--exactly right where he was--and asked for napalm to be dropped. He lost some of his own men--a few--but the majority of the people that got killed were Vietnamese. And because of that his company was able to fight their way out of that position.

The New York Times chronicled Carpenter's heroism under the headline "A Daring Captain Saves a Company." For his actions, Carpenter received the Silver Star, the second-highest medal awarded by the Army.

Going AWOL

Klausing once did something that his superiors at West Point would most definitely have frowned on, had they only known about it.

He told a soldier to go AWOL.

"One of my duties was to find enlisted men with a football background to come to West Point to be graduate assistants. So I would look for college football players who had joined the Army. They would have to put two years in, but once they finished with boot camp, then they could come to West Point to be grad assistants for the last 21 months of their service.

"Some of the people who did this were Bill Parcells, the coach of the Patriots, and Tom Modrak, who played for me at IUP and is now with the Steelers [as their college personnel coordinator].

"Well, we had a guy by the name of Steve Medwed, who was from McKees Rocks and had played at Slippery Rock. He was interested in coaching. The way I explained it to him, when he was finished with boot training, he would get an assignment to come to West Point, to be attached to the football team.

"I get a call from Steve about two, three months later and I said, 'Steve, you got your orders?' He says, 'Coach, I got my orders, but they're bad orders. I'm calling from Norfolk, Va., and my outfit is going to Europe. There's a Berlin incident going on and everybody's being called up to go there.

"Here's a kid I had given my word to that I was gonna get him to West Point. Somehow the orders were mixed up. So I called the second or third in command at West Point, who handled all these things, and he says, 'Tell the kid to find a way to West Point and I'll have his orders straightened out by then.'

"Steve's waiting by a telephone in Norfolk. I call back and I said, 'Steve, you have to have nerve. You walk away from there.' He says, 'I'm gonna have real difficulty walking away. I have a big pack and a rifle and everything else.' I said, 'Just leave it. Get away from there and work your way up to West Point.' "

Medwed did as he was told and wound up spending 21 months as a grad assistant at Army. He never did make it to Berlin.

CHAPTER 4
Return of the Native

When the head coaching position at IUP opened up in 1964, Chuck Klausing had just finished his third season at West Point. He applied, in part because he longed to return to his western Pennsylvania roots.

Klausing landed the job, although perks were practically nonexistent. In the early years, he operated with a skeleton coaching staff, had no trainer or equipment manager and often laundered the team's uniforms himself.

"The best way to describe the IUP situation, we were lacking a coaching staff, a practice field, equipment, trainers . . . just about everything that you would like to have in a first-class operation," he says. "Maybe I was spoiled, having been at places like Rutgers and Army. But I wanted my program to resemble them in every way possible."

Fortunately, Klausing found an ally in President Willis Pratt, whose steadfast commitment to the program helped turn IUP into a consistent winner.

"When I was hired," he recalls, "Dr. Pratt said to me, 'I know nothing about football. You are my expert in football. Whatever you need, ask for it. But if I get it for you, you better win.'"

Klausing adhered to that mandate and led the Indians to a 47-10 record in his six seasons (1964-69) as head coach. Ironically, IUP's crowning achievement in that period was actually a rare defeat. Klausing's 9-0 team put up a gallant fight against heavily favored Delaware in the 1968 Boardwalk Bowl, played before a crowd of 9,849 at Atlantic City's Convention Hall and a regional television audience.

Oddsmakers, declaring the game a mismatch, installed the vaunted Blue Hens as three-touchdown favorites. Even Klausing conceded his team's role as the longest of long-shots. Of Delaware he said, "They're about as close to major-college football as you can get.

But the anticipated rout never materialized. In fact, IUP stunned the experts--and most assuredly the opposition--by battling the Blue Hens on even terms. And when Bob Tate kicked a 32-yard field goal with one minute remaining to send the Indians in front, 24-23, underdogs everywhere rejoiced.

The rejoicing came too soon for IUP, however. The Indians' dream of a perfect season was shattered in excruciating fashion moments later. Quarterback Tom DiMuzio quickly marched Delaware down the field and drilled a 9-yard touchdown pass to Ron Withelder with 15 seconds remaining for the deciding score.

The Cakewalk Bowl

Al Cartwright, sports editor of the Wilmington (Del.) *Evening Journal*, refused to call the 1968 Boardwalk Bowl by its official name. After appraising the two participants, he sharpened his barb and, in print, offered what he maintained was a more fitting name: The Cakewalk Bowl.

"To prolong the season by two weeks to play Indiana University of Pennsylvania is more embarrassing than prestigious," he wrote.

Sam Bechtel, sports editor of *The Indiana Gazette*, reprinted Cartwright's column in its entirety. The inflammatory words contained within became a weapon that Klausing wielded with telling effect.

"His story was very motivating to us. We put a copy of the article in everyone's locker and it made the kids want to go down there and show the people from Delaware that we had a football team. So I had no trouble getting them to focus on the game.

"A couple years later I go to Delaware State to visit. Delaware State is a black university with a very good football program. I walked in and introduced myself and they said, 'Aw, coach, we know you.' I said, 'How do you know me?' It turns out some of the coaches there had played and been assistants at Delaware when we played them.

"This one guy, Joe Purzycki, said, 'I was the guy who returned the opening kickoff in the Boardwalk Bowl. Your kids really hit me. I never was hit like that before--I got knocked out. They're taking me off the field after I come to and I say to the rest of the Delaware team, 'Cakewalk Bowl my ass.' "

Al Cartwright had been wrong. To his credit, he admitted as much in print.

"The Big Indians, they call the team from Indiana," he wrote. "Not really big, physically. Just inside. They seldom lose, and now everybody around here knows why."

The Gas Man

Klausing describes Ernie Vida as a man who could accomplish just about anything. Why, he even talked the *Sports Illustrated* editors into covering a Braddock High School football game.

Vida was Braddock's unofficial public relations man during the Klausing era (1954-59), when the Tigers posted a 53-0-1 record and broke Massillon (Ohio) High School's national record for the longest unbeaten streak.

He convinced *Sports Illustrated* to cover the milestone victory in 1959 after intimating to the editors that *Life* and *Look* were interested in featuring the team and might just beat them to the punch.

That was a bluff, of course. Vida hadn't talked to anyone from *Life* or *Look*. But his attempt at subterfuge succeeded. A four-page spread on Braddock, titled "A Town and its Team," appeared in the Nov. 2 issue of *Sports Illustrated*.

Nine years later Vida was still lending Klausing a hand whenever and however he could.

"We get invited to the Boardwalk Bowl and, sure enough, Ernie shows up two days before the game. Anything that we needed done, it would be taken care of. Ernie was gonna get it done. If we needed a change in dining procedure, he changed it. If we were going to a movie, Ernie would go and talk to the people that owned the theater and not only get a reduced price, but get us in free. He was the kind of guy who could accomplish anything.

"Well, at that time you hardly ever heard of oxygen on the bench. One of the coaches said maybe we ought to get some oxygen for the game. I said, 'Gee, we never had a canister of oxygen before. Why do we need it now?'

"My son, Tom, was a pretty good student. He says, 'Dad, there's sod on that floor at Convention Hall and the sod will seek oxygen and take it out of the air. It might be difficult to breathe in there.'

"So I purchased a canister of oxygen, never thinking it would be used. We start the game and, gee, every time there was a timeout or every time the offense or the defense came off the field, the players were going to the oxygen canister.

"We go in at halftime and my team's laying on the floor of the locker room--every player is just exhausted. And they're all yelling, 'Get me the oxygen,' and they're passing it around. One of the players finally says, 'Coach, there's no more oxygen left. What are we gonna do in the second half?'

"So Ernie, who was in the locker room, comes up to me and says, 'Coach, do you need oxygen?' I said, 'Ya, but how are we gonna get it?' He says, 'Don't worry, I'll get it.'

"He goes to a pay phone right outside the locker room door and they tell me he called Atlantic City Hospital and said there was an emergency in the IUP locker room. One of the players was having a heart problem and they needed oxygen, quickly. Two minutes later we hear a siren blowing. They came right down the boardwalk and through a back door into our locker room. In come two attendants with two big canisters of oxygen. 'Where's the guy that needs it?'

"Well, everybody was raising their hands. The ambulance people realized they'd been had, but they were happy to give us the oxygen. That kept us going."

A Dented Ferrari

Defensive tackle Tony Ferrari, who was selected to IUP's 1960s All-Star Team at the close of the decade, was a pillar of strength for the Boardwalk Bowl squad. His only weakness was vanity.

That discovery made an indelible impression on Klausing in the wake of the loss to Delaware.

"I go up to the locker room after the game and I'm soaking wet. I dressed in a blazer and everything, but I was soaking wet and I had to get a shower.

"I go in the shower room and Tony, who was a big kid--he was 5-11 and 245 pounds, maybe 250--was in there. And I'll tell you what, I never saw a guy whose hips were so black and blue. I thought he must have taken a couple terrible hits.

"I said, 'Tony, what the heck happened to you?' He says, 'Aw, coach, I knew we were gonna be on TV and I didn't want to look fat, so I didn't wear any hip pads today.' "

California, Here We Come

From the most crushing defeats can come the most sublime victories. Case in point, what Klausing considers IUP's most critical win during the Boardwalk Bowl season of 1968.

California visited Miller Stadium on Nov. 2 for a showdown with the 7-0 Indians. IUP had also sported a 7-0 record entering the 1967 California game, but a perfect season was spoiled with 4:14 remaining when the Vulcans scored on a fourth-down 23-yard hook-and-lateral play. Jim Trombetta caught a pass from quarterback Jeff Petrucci and then pitched the ball to Jim Boggio, who crossed the goal line unmolested while the IUP defenders buried Trombetta.

A year later, Klausing realized that the Vulcans were again a formidable threat to the Indians' spotless record.

"In that '68 season the best team on our schedule, I think, was California. The year before we had a real hard-luck loss to them--and that was our only loss. So we knew we'd have to be ready.

Were they ever. Spurred on by the bitter memories of 1967, the Indians rolled to a 41-0 victory. They held Cal to minus-17 yards rushing and even put the clamps on Petrucci, who had ranked third nationally in total offense coming in. He threw for only 121 yards, was intercepted three times and spent much of the afternoon on his backside.

The Indians and Klausing had their revenge.

"It was supposed to be a very even game, but we were up for it mentally. Because of what had happened the year before, it was sort of satisfying to beat them so bad. Everything just went perfect."

Which kept IUP's record perfect.

A Game of Inches

Many long-time IUP fans contend that Klausing's best team at the university was not the one that played in the Boardwalk Bowl, but the one that followed. Klausing is inclined to agree. "I thought we were as good or better in 1969."

That team might have finished with a 9-0 regular-season record, just like its immediate predecessor, were it not for a critical decision that Klausing still regrets. The situation bore eerie similarities to the previous year's Boardwalk Bowl, but this time his strategy backfired. IUP trailed 23-21 in both instances.

During the waning moments of the game in Atlantic City, tight end George Stark made a spectacular catch to set up a fourth-and-inches play from the Delaware 15-yard line. Klausing elected to kick and senior Bob Tate booted a 32-yard field goal to give IUP a short-lived 24-23 lead with one minute remaining.

He wonders now if he should've followed the same script when Slippery Rock visited Miller Stadium the following season. The Indians were 5-0 at the time.

"We had a drive going late in the game and we were on about the 20-yard line. We had fourth and a foot. We could have kicked a field goal to go ahead, but we were gaining three, four yards every play. So we go for it on fourth and a foot and they stopped us. It was my decision--plus the fact we didn't execute--that caused us to lose."

Slippery Rock prevailed, 23-21. That was the only defeat suffered by the Indians in Klausing's last 19 regular-season games at IUP.

Part-time Partners

By the time that 1969 season rolled around, Klausing was blessed with a coaching staff that could devote ample time to football. It was a far cry from 1964, when he first arrived on campus.

Back then Klausing was operating the program on a shoe-string budget that allowed for only one assistant coach. But he found a way to bolster his staff, thanks in part to the IUP music department.

"I had studied the college catalogue and in the music department I noticed there were a number of one-fifth time instructors: piano instructor, one-fifth time, voice instructor, one-fifth time, brass instructor, one-fifth time, and so on.

"I asked Dr. Pratt what that meant. He explained that he took one instructor's salary and divided it five ways with part-time people. So that's how I got five assistant coaches."

For the price of one.

Tough Sledding

In Klausing's first year at IUP, the team had only two weeks to prepare for the season opener against Frederick (Va.) College. And what a strange opener it was.

Fans at Miller Stadium were treated to the bizarre sight of the Indians squeezing in some extra practice time on an adjacent field only moments before kickoff.

"I was big on hitting a seven-man blocking sled. I told our kids that we were gonna have to hit that sled a thousand times before the first game if we were gonna win. We only had two weeks of practice and we had two practices a day. So let's say we had a potential of 20 practices, because we had some scrimmages on the weekends. So we were gonna have to hit that sled 50 times each practice.

"Those kids would count 'em. We pushed that thing up and down the practice field. Then the day before our first game it rained and we didn't practice. I was kind of glad because we needed to get our legs back.

"Anyway, I'm giving a pep talk before the game the next day and John Tate, who was one of my linemen, said, 'Coach, we've only hit that sled 950 times. If we're gonna win this game, we have to go out and hit that sled 50 times.'

"Sure enough, that's what they did. They went out on the back field right before the game and we ran that sled up and down the field."

The Indians then ran Frederick *off* the field, posting the first victory of the Chuck Klausing era at IUP.

The Phantom Coaches

When Klausing first came to IUP in 1964, his coaching staff could've fit comfortably in a VW. For one memorable game during the 1965 season, Klausing *was* the coaching staff.

The Indians opened that year at Ball State, located in Muncie, Ind. IUP should have been outclassed against such a big-time opponent--especially since the Cardinals were en route to a 9-0-1 season--but the Indians battled their hosts right down to the wire. Due in no small measure to their "phantom coaches.

"We arranged for a bus and buses weren't as big then as they are now. There might have been 35 seats at the most on this bus. I started to figure out the travel squad, and because I had to take 33 players, myself and the team doctor, Dr. [C.E.] D'Zmura, I couldn't take any assistant coaches.

"We get there Friday night and I get a call from a coaching friend at Western Michigan University in Kalamazoo, Bill Doolittle, who had coached with me at Army. He says, 'Chuck, what defense are you expecting tomorrow?' I said, 'They've used what I call a 50 monster defense.' And he says, 'Uh-oh. Better get prepared for something different. I have a young assistant who came from Ball State and he told me they've been practicing a Notre Dame 4-4 defense.' "

In the little time available before kickoff, Klausing worked feverishly to alter his game plan in order to counteract the Cardinals' 4-4. Those adjustments nearly paid enormous dividends. Behind the passing of quarterback Mickey Watson, the Indians gave heavily favored Ball State fits before finally succumbing by a 26-14 score.

"When we went out for the game, everything was laid out for us. They had about three sets of telephones laying on the sidelines. I said, 'What am I gonna do with these?' One of the kids said, 'Coach, please put the earphones on. At least pretend you have a coach up above.' So I put them on.

"Well, we went up and down the field that day, but they were just physically too much for us and they ended up winning. So I walk out to the middle of the field after the game and shake hands with their coaching staff. They were the most complimentary people I've ever been around.

"They said, 'Coach, we want to congratulate you and the guy that was upstairs on the phones. Every time we made a change, you adjusted. You had the best information that you could ever get about what we were doing defensively from that guy upstairs.'

"Well, my guy upstairs was in Kalamazoo, Mich."

You Deserve a Break Today

That journey to Muncie is also memorable for the trip back--and a late-night stop at a McDonald's outside Columbus, Ohio, where 33 famished football players laid waste to the fast-food restaurant's supplies.

"I announce we're gonna stop at this McDonald's and I tell the kids, 'Get all you want to eat.' The kids haven't eaten in a while, so they get two or three Big Macs and two or three milkshakes, every one of them."

Then I realized I didn't have any money. I ask Dr. D'Zmura, 'Do you have any money?' He says, 'I have $100.' The girl at the cash register rings everything up and I ask, 'How much is it?' She says, '$99.90.' "

Whereupon a relieved Klausing handed D'Zmura his change: one thin dime.

The Unpolished Gem

Guard Bob Prokay starred on Klausing's Boardwalk Bowl squad and was later selected to IUP's All-'60s team. What's remarkable is that Prokay hadn't even played football in high school.

He was "discovered" by Klausing . . . on a handball court.

"I used to play a lot of handball when I was coaching at IUP. One day I got to the handball courts and there were three students playing a game. I put my head in the door and said, 'Do you mind having a fourth? Let's play two against two,' which they were happy to do.

"Boy, one of these three students, a youngster about 6-4, 235, had good agility. He was quick as a cat and would throw himself on the floor to try and get a low shot. I was just so impressed with how competitive he was playing a game he wasn't necessarily gifted at.

"After playing I asked him if he was a student. He said yes, he had just entered mid-term as a freshman. I asked him if he played football. He said, 'I've never played football, but I'd like to.' He told me he'd always wanted to play, but he traveled with an older group of guys in high school and they weren't football people. 'When they graduated, I was coming up to my senior year. I went to the coach and asked to go out for the team, but he wouldn't let me because I was a senior.'

"So he came out for spring football practice, very raw, but anxious to learn. He was something that we as coaches really enjoy. We're taking a raw talent and teaching good techniques and fundamentals. Because he hadn't played before he had no bad habits.

"He was without a doubt the best offensive lineman I've ever coached. There were others more gifted physically, but as far as techniques and fundamentals, he was the best. He became a great team leader."

Prokay is today a leader in business. He works as the vice president of finance and treasurer at National Gypsum Company in Charlotte, N.C.

Wheeling Past Ferris

Ferris State arrived in Indiana for the 1966 homecoming game much as those unfortunates sacrificed to the lions at the Roman Colosseum, their doom virtually assured. After all, IUP had crushed the Bulldogs 57-0 the year before.

But at halftime, the Indians were clinging to a 10-6 lead as the 12,000 fans crammed into Miller Stadium fidgeted in their seats, wondering if their team would ever shift into gear. They needn't have worried. IUP struck for two touchdowns in a span of eight seconds in the third quarter, the two quickest scores by a Klausing-coached team in his 46-year career.

Fullback Dave Cessna scored on a 5-yard run to open the second half and Bob Tate added the extra point, increasing the Indians' lead to 17-6. Ferris State then resorted to some sleight-of-hand on the ensuing kickoff that backfired miserably. Walter Haskins fielded Tate's kickoff, headed up the right side, stopped in his tracks and fired a cross-field lateral pass to a teammate.

"That's one of those plays people have in their bag of tricks. That was a play Bobby Bowden has had success with. I saw his Florida State team take an opening kickoff against Miami eight or nine years ago and the return man ran to the right and then threw to a guy running up the left sideline. He went for a touchdown."

The Bulldogs' attempt at razzle-dazzle also wound up in the end zone. Their own. Ed Unruh deflected the pass and Moe Smith fell on the ball for a gift score.

"We defended it pretty well and turned it into a touchdown. That was probably a turning point in the game."

Barely a bark was heard from the Bulldogs after that. Final score: 44-6.

Sinatra Comes to IUP

Klausing's reign at IUP was highlighted by the presence of Frank Sinatra, who carried water to the players during timeouts. *This* Frank Sinatra never broke into song; he was a team manager.

Sinatra wasn't related to "Ol' Blue Eyes," though that didn't stop him from making claims to that effect. Repeatedly. Klausing will never forget his first meeting with the other Frank Sinatra.

"I asked if he was a relative. No, he wasn't a relative. I told him, 'Well, it's a catchy name. I'm sure I'll always remember you.'"

And he has. Many coaches can't recall the name of their manager from five years ago. But there's little chance Klausing will ever forget his manager from three decades ago.

"I still see Frank. He's a very loyal guy to IUP. He comes out for those spring alumni golf outings and so forth."

In a postscript, Klausing coached another Sinatra in his final season at Kiski School. Frank's nephew, Tony.

Sunday Night at the Movies

Think Siskel and Ebert are unforgiving movie critics? Klausing was an even more exacting judge during his Sunday night film sessions at IUP, where players cringed in the darkness and fervently prayed they wouldn't be singled out by the perfectionist at the projector.

As halfback Norman "Munk" Amorose wrote in a 1964 story for *The Indiana Gazette*, "There is no place to hide when the all-too-perceiving eyes of Chuck Klausing or one of his assistants find a flaw on the 4x8 screen and demand restitution." Offensive tackle Gene Epley found a parallel to *1984*, the foreboding novel by George Orwell: "You know that 'Big Brother' is watching."

Klausing chuckles today as he recalls what was surely a harrowing experience for his players.

"They were scared of me. I must have been a real tyrant. We met on Sunday evenings from 7 o'clock to whatever it took. I ran each play 11 times if I saw a big mistake and would yell their name. Boy, everybody's waiting for what I'm gonna say.

"But they must have enjoyed it in a way, too, because they'd go back to their dorms then and jag each other. 'Oh, boy, I only got yelled at 10 times. You got yelled at 20 times,' or something to that effect. They liked to repeat the story I told about how one of my Braddock players, a guard, was supposed to lead a sweep to the right and he went left instead. He got around the end and he sees everybody going right, so he tried to cover up his number with his hands."

To prevent recognition come movie time, you see. But as Klausing's players through the years learned, there was no escaping what Amorose termed restitution.

The unforgiving movie critic would inevitably pass judgment. And 250-pound players shuddered in fear at the prospect.

Snow Job

In the final game of Klausing's tenure at IUP, his team battled two opponents--the Wilkes College Colonials and Mother Nature. The Indians conquered both, with the help of some unusual garments.

Full-length plastic clothing bags.

When Klausing awoke the morning of Nov. 15, 1969, he discovered the Indiana area had been transformed into a winter wonderland. Four inches of snow blanketed the ground and temperatures had plunged into the 20s. A biting wind added to the arctic ambience.

There was some sentiment, at least initially, to postpone the game. But because the Colonials were already in town, the decision was ultimately made to play. Klausing, whose team was 7-1, was anxious to face Wilkes (6-1), which had owned the nation's longest winning streak (32 games) until a recent loss to Ithaca.

An army of maintenance workers, along with members of the freshman football team who had answered Klausing's appeal for assistance, wielded shovels and ran snowplows that morning, clearing the Miller Stadium playing surface and stands.

Once that task was complete, Klausing faced his next challenge: How to protect his players against the dangerous wind chill? Fortunately, Joann Klausing provided a solution.

"We were scrounging for gloves and woolen clothing to wear under our pads. That's when my wife came up with a good suggestion. No woman has seen more football games than she has. She always goes to the games prepared.

"What she had found is if you put a pair of socks on and then a plastic baggy and then put another pair of socks over that, your feet will stay warm. She suggested we try that. She also said, 'Let's go down to the dry-cleaning place on Philadelphia Street and get some big plastic full-length clothing bags.'

"So my team dressed for the game in these plastic full-length clothing bags with plastic bags on their feet. They were a little doubtful that this was gonna help, so I mentioned that I had just gotten off the phone with Vince Lombardi and this is what the Packers did to stay warm. I bent the truth a little bit--I *did* just get off the phone, but not with Vince Lombardi. But my kids believed me."

IUP went out and dominated the first half against the favored Colonials, scoring twice on runs by Dan Cox for a 14-0 lead. That's how the game ended, no small thanks to three interceptions by Barry Ruffner--and the Indians' plastic wraps.

"I remember we came in the locker room at halftime and the kids asked if they could change into drier clothes for the second half because they were sweating so much from those plastic bags. I honestly believe the comfort of the plastic bags helped us win the game."

CHAPTER 5
Odds and Ends

When he's not running summer camps, attending clinics, coaching overseas or scouting at football games, Chuck Klausing can usually be found at a podium, a rapt audience at his feet. His popularity as a banquet speaker is predicated on a bottomless store of sports tales that come spilling out like coins in a Las Vegas slot machine. He regularly leaves listeners convulsed in laughter.

One of Klausing's favorite stories deals with one of his favorite acquaintances: the late Art Rooney, beloved owner of the Pittsburgh Steelers for many years. Rooney founded the team during the Depression, funding the enterprise, legend has it, with racetrack winnings.

Klausing first met Rooney some 50 years ago when the Steelers were still lovable losers.

"I went to their training camps when they were up at Alliance College [in Cambridge Springs, Pa.] and later when they were at St. Bonaventure in New York," he says. "That really goes back to the late '40s and early '50s. I went every year for the longest time. I'd spend three or four days at training camp. That's how I got to know Mr. Rooney."

Some years later Klausing would accept the head coaching position at IUP, where a certain youngster from Pittsburgh's North Side had distinguished himself in a number of sports. Art Rooney.

Art Rooney's Homecoming

Ever since the franchise was born, the Steelers have shared a close relationship with IUP that transcends their geographic proximity. The association is particularly strong where Klausing is concerned: He coached a number of future Steeler employees during his years at the university (1964-69).

Dave Smith, a member of Klausing's famed Boardwalk Bowl squad, suited up as a Steelers wide receiver for three seasons (1970-72). Guard Jack Henry, a captain on that Boardwalk Bowl team, coached the Steelers' offensive line during Chuck Noll's final two seasons in command (1990-91). Another Klausing protege, Tom Modrak, is now the Steelers' college personnel director. And Tom Donahoe, a 1969 IUP grad, serves as the team's director of football operations.

The bond between the university and the Steelers dates all the way back to the man who founded the franchise in 1933, after the repeal of Pennsylvania's Sunday Blue Laws. Art Rooney (1901-88) graduated from Indiana Normal School, the forerunner of IUP.

Rooney ranks as one of the premier athletes in the school's history. He participated in baseball, basketball, track and, most notably, football during his time at INS. A 1921 yearbook entry jokingly noted that, "Notwithstanding the fact that Art was in love throughout the entire football season, he was the individual star of the team." Indeed, with Rooney in the backfield, Indiana won Pennsylvania Normal School championships in 1920 and 1921.

But it was another title--in boxing--that earned Rooney a special homecoming, recalled fondly by Dean of Students Walter Whitmyre nearly half a century later, when the school dedicated the Rooney Hall dormitory. Klausing, then IUP's head coach, was in charge of the ceremonies.

"We had a lot of the Rooney family there and Bill Austin, the head coach of the Steelers, came out, too. We had a party afterwards and one of the people that I invited was Dean Whitmyre. The reason I invited him was that Art Rooney, when he was a student at IUP, used to baby-sit the Whitmyre kids.

"Well, Dean Whitmyre told the story that in 1920 Mr. Rooney won an international boxing championship, I think in Toronto. School was in session at the time, so when he came back to Indiana on the train, the entire student body was out to meet him.

"When he got off the train [the stop was then adjacent to campus], he said he never felt so good. Here were all his classmates out to greet him. And what really shocked him, it was like 8:30 in the evening and all the girls were out. Back then, the girls were locked up in the dormitory at 7:30 every night. None of them ever got out in the evening.

"So as he gets off the train, Dean Whitmyre walks up to greet him. Mr. Rooney had taken a good blow to the nose or the eye and both his eyes were swollen and black. And Dean Whitmyre looks at him and says, 'Arthur, I thought you *won*.' "

The Road Not Taken

Whether recruiting a prospect, motivating his team, speaking at a clinic or simply regaling banquet crowds with humorous stories, Klausing's way with words is legendary. But while visiting western Massachusetts in the late '50s, he met someone whose mastery of the language far exceeded his own.

Exceeded most mortals', for that matter.

"I'm being interviewed at Amherst College for a coaching job around 1958 or 1959. They took me over to the faculty lounge. They had some pool tables there--one was a three-ball billiards table.

"There was an old man practicing his billiards. I had learned to shoot billiards at the Wilmerding YMCA when I was a kid. I asked the man if he needed somebody to play with, because I had to kill a half hour.

"So I shot billiards with him. He was good, but I gave him a pretty good game. He asked me why I was there and I said I was being interviewed for a coaching job. He said, 'I sure hope you get it because I need someone like you to play against.' "

Robert Frost's wish wasn't granted, for neither was Klausing's. He didn't get the job. Frost continued to teach literature at Amherst, when not searching for a worthy foe at billiards.

Frost won four Pulitzer prizes for poetry, the first in 1924. He read one of his works at the inauguration of President John F. Kennedy--a fellow New Englander--in January of 1961.

One of Frost's most famous poems, "The Road Not Taken," begins:

"Two roads diverged in a wood, and I--
I took the one less traveled by,
And that has made all the difference."

Not getting the Amherst job made all the difference for Klausing. He was available when Division I Rutgers came calling in 1960.

Fit to Be Tied

Red Blaik just couldn't comprehend how his football team, unbeaten and top-ranked in the nation, failed to defeat a rather ordinary Pitt squad in a 1958 classic at Pitt Stadium. So he came up with a wacky excuse for the 14-14 tie.

"Col. Blaik claimed the reason that Army didn't beat Pitt that day was that the officials, who were told to put the laces up when they marked the ball, put the laces down. And that caused bad exchanges between the Army center and the Army quarterback."

One can just imagine the gathering of reporters, probing for a reason behind Army's failure, rolling their eyes at that ludicrous explanation. Some did more than just roll their eyes.

"Stanley Woodward was the sports editor of the *Herald Tribune* in New York. He wrote in his article that that was like blaming the Johnstown Flood on a leaky commode in Altoona."

That tie cost the Cadets a national championship. Army finished with an 8-0-1 record, good for third in the final poll. And Pitt? The Panthers checked in at a rather pedestrian 5-4-1.

Klipa Gets Clobbered

Steve Klipa played under Klausing at Pitcairn and John Galagaza coached under him there. Together they figured in one of the worst defeats in Geneva College history.

West Virginia pummeled the visitors--especially Klipa--on Oct. 20, 1951, winning by a score of 89-0. The most lopsided winning score in WVU history, by the way.

"Gal was the Geneva captain and a star of the team. Klipa was a sophomore. He's not on the travel squad to make the trip to play West Virginia down in Morgantown. Gal goes to the coach and says,

'If Klipa doesn't go, I don't go.'

"The coach gave in, but now they had to find a way to put Klipa on the team bus. They found a little bench that they put in the aisle and Klipa sat on this bench and made the trip to Morgantown."

To his everlasting regret.

"Klipa was the No. 3 fullback. The first series of downs the No. 1 fullback gets hurt. The second series of downs, the No. 2 fullback gets hurt. So Klipa has to go in and he plays the rest of the game.

"West Virginia beats them real bad and Klipa just gets smashed up--broken nose, bruised shoulder, bruised knee, hips all bruised up. So he goes up to Gal after the game and he says, 'Please, Gal, don't insist on me making any more trips.' "

Taking a Shine to Cortazzo

Chuck Klausing grew up in Wilmerding, Pa., and Bobby Bowden was reared in Birmingham, Ala. Yet despite the distance in miles between them, these future football coaches idolized the same athlete during their childhood.

A baseball player, strangely enough. John Francis Cortazzo by name. Little John--5-3½, 142 pounds--stood tall in their youthful eyes.

"We all look up to role models, people in our life we think are great. The only man to ever make it to the major leagues from my hometown was a guy by the name of 'Shine' Cortazzo. He was only up for a cup of coffee with the Chicago White Sox [one game, one hitless at bat in 1923], but he was a great minor league baseball player.

"I attended a banquet back many years ago where they were honoring the president of the Middle Atlantic League [Art Rooney played briefly for the league's Wheeling, W.Va., club], a guy from Ebensburg by the name of Elmer Daley. And they asked him, 'Who was the greatest player to ever play in the Middle Atlantic League? Was it Stan Musial? Was it Joe Cronin? Was it Ducky Medwick?' He said it was the guy who batted .400 every year--Shine Cortazzo.

I was with Bobby Bowden once and he found out my hometown was Wilmerding. He knew Shine was from there, too. He said he idolized Shine Cortazzo. Shine played for the Birmingham Barons, his hometown team."

Football's Desert Fox

Coaches sometimes draw inspiration from the most unusual sources. When Klausing found himself in a predicament during games, he would think of Field Marshal Erwin Rommel and act accordingly.

Rommel commanded Germany's Afrika Korps in the Sahara during World War II and earned a distinctive nickname for his cunning maneuvers afield: the Desert Fox.

"I had read Rommel's letters in a very interesting history book. At the time he was having great success in North Africa. He would run trucks up and down the desert, stirring up dust. The British and Americans thought it was his tanks coming. But then he'd send the tanks in from the flank and surprise them.

"Well, I'm an admirer of Rommel's tactics. So I would sometimes use a strategy in coaching similar to Rommel's. I would call the play that my opponent did not think we were going to use.

"For example, there's been times when I've had the ball third-and-one, fourth-and-one, in critical situations. Everybody thinks it's going to be a power off tackle or a quarterback sneak, but I'd throw a pass off it."

Klausing leaned toward the unpredictable throughout his career. But two of his most unconventional calls occurred while he was coaching at Carnegie Mellon.

In his very first game at CMU--the 1976 season opener--the Tartans were clinging to a 16-14 lead, facing a fourth-and-six play deep in their own territory with under a minute remaining. Punter Dick West took the snap, but he didn't kick. On Klausing's orders he ran with the ball. West gained 22 yards on the play, enabling CMU to keep the ball and run out the final 25 seconds.

Klausing also sprang the unexpected during a 1978 game against John Carroll University. Following a personal foul on a CMU extra point attempt, the Tartans kicked off from the John Carroll 45-yard line. He told Mike Kostic to try an onside kick, a common strategy under the circumstances. But what followed was definitely uncommon.

Kostic slipped as he kicked the ball and it went out of bounds, costing CMU a 5-yard penalty. The element of surprise now gone, Klausing--a sly fox inspired by the Desert Fox--told Kostic to try another onside kick anyway. The unsuspecting John Carroll players watched, astounded, as CMU's Pat Olivo recovered the ball.

The Tartans scored a touchdown two plays later and rolled to a 27-0 victory.

Lessons from the Wizard

If Klausing could draw inspiration from a German tank commander, then it should come as no surprise that he could also learn from a basketball coach.

Not just any basketball coach, of course. UCLA's basketball coach, the so-called Wizard of Westwood.

"I've had the good fortune to observe a lot of great coaches and one of them was John Wooden. I spent some time once at Pauley Pavilion watching him coach his basketball team.

"He was the same at practice as he was on the bench during a game. He always had his practice plan rolled up in his hand [substituting for the program he waved during games]. He would stop practice and correct his players, using that rolled up piece of paper as a pointing stick.

"I saw him reach up high to point at Bill Walton's chest. He would correct him and show him how to get in position to rebound, how to screen an opponent and how to turn and pivot properly.

"This was great correction, not criticism. Chuck Noll was very similar. I watched him critique his players. The great coaches correct, not criticize. They show their players how to do the technique properly."

Few could argue with Wooden's methods, given his success at UCLA. The Bruins won 10 NCAA championships in a 12-year span between 1964 and 1975, seven in succession.

No Rest for Red

Klausing learned about deception from Rommel and correction from Wooden. He learned a little about work ethic from Zigmund

"Red" Mihalik, an indefatigable official who abhorred idleness.

"Red Mihalik is probably the most famous basketball official ever to come out of western Pennsylvania. If any man ever made a living just officiating--there's very few who ever did--Red might have been one.

"I remember when I was the athletic director at Pitcairn, Red refereed a junior high school basketball game for us at 4 o'clock on a Friday afternoon for $8. He refereed a JV game at 7 o'clock for $8. Then he refereed a varsity basketball game at 8:15 for $15.

"After the game he asked me for directions to Morgantown, W.Va., because he was gonna drive that night to Morgantown to officiate a college game the next afternoon. Then he was driving to Raleigh, N.C., to officiate a college game on Sunday afternoon."

Mihalik's odometer kept climbing, and so did Red. Before he put away his whistle for the last time, Mihalik had officiated in six NCAA championship games, the 1964 and 1968 Olympic Games and the NBA. He was inducted into the Basketball Hall of Fame in 1986.

Groat and Cousy

Paul Birch, an All-America basketball player at Duquesne University in 1935, once made a decision as coach of the NBA Fort Wayne Pistons that backfired. He drafted the College Player of the Year.

Unfortunately, Dick Groat's professional career consisted of only 26 games. The guard Birch passed up--Bob Cousy of Holy Cross--spent 14 seasons in the NBA with the Boston Celtics and Cincinnati Royals.

Klausing knew of Birch through a good friend, Brute Kramer, the Pistons' general manager.

"Right after playing for Duquesne, as a 22-year-old right out of college, Birch coached the Homestead High School basketball team to the state championship. At 65, right before he retired, he coached the General Braddock High School team to the state championship.

"You might think that Paul Birch coached high school ball from age 22 to 65, but actually at age 23 he was the playing-coach for the New York Celtics, who were one of the first professional basketball teams. Then he went and coached in the NBA with the Fort Wayne Zollner Pistons, who are now the Detroit Pistons."

Birch coached the team for three seasons. One year he agonized over the Pistons' first-round draft selection, which distilled to a choice between Cousy and Groat. Cousy was an extraordinary playmaker at Holy Cross, coveted by a number of teams. But Groat had scored 26.0 points per game as a senior at Duke and earned national Player of the Year honors.

"Birch chose Dick Groat because he felt Dick was a better athlete."

Too good, as it turned out. Groat, who signed with the Pittsburgh Pirates after graduation, decided to forsake basketball after Pirates GM Branch Rickey pressured him to choose between the sports. He spent 14 seasons in the major leagues, won an MVP award and a batting title with Pittsburgh in 1960 and played on two World Series-winning teams: the Pirates in 1960 and the Cardinals in 1964.

Cousy was no stranger to championship celebrations, either. The Boston Celtics won six titles--five in succession--between 1957 and 1963 with him in the lineup.

Hide and Seek

Birch was a no-nonsense coach who ruled his team with an iron hand. Players would avoid him at all costs when the Pistons faltered--even hiding out, as Press Maravich did.

"Press was playing for Birch at Fort Wayne--Birch was a very volatile type--and he had done something wrong. Right before the end of the first half he took Maravich out of the game and he said, 'I'm gonna kill you when I meet you down in the locker room.'

"People that knew Birch told me he was one of the toughest guys to ever come down the pike. Maravich ran down to the locker room and Brute Kramer, the general manager, was there. And he said, 'Brute, please hide me. Birch is gonna kill me.'

"So he locks Maravich in a locker. When Birch came down, he searched the locker room from top to bottom. There was no other door out, no window out. Fortunately, he couldn't find Press, because he was going to really take him on."

Maravich survived his time with Birch and eventually went into coaching. But he never did approach the fame achieved by his son, Pete, who averaged an NCAA-record 44.2 points per game during his collegiate career at LSU--where Press coached. "Pistol Pete" then followed in his father's footsteps, playing in the NBA for 10 seasons.

The $1 Million Man

Klausing accepted a coaching position on the West Virginia University staff after the 1969 season, when Bobby Bowden succeeded Jim Carlen as the Mountaineers' head coach.

He did not follow Bowden to Florida State six years later, though there are probably times Klausing wishes he had. At least for the sake of his bank account.

"When I was coaching at IUP I was running summer camps. Bobby had worked for me at my camps. One day he calls me--this is right after the 1969 football season--and he says, 'Chuck, I just got the head job at West Virginia and I want you to come as my first assistant.'

"I said, 'Bobby, I know what assistant coaches are getting paid. There's no way I can come there for an assistant coach's pay.' So he says, 'We're gonna put two or three salaries together. I'm getting paid $20,000 a year. We can pay you $19,999. One dollar less.'

"I think I was making about $12,000 a year at IUP and that was a big raise, so I went. Then a couple years ago I see where Bobby got a new contract at Florida State for a million dollars a year. I called him up and I said, 'Bobby, I'm ready to come back and work for you--for one dollar less.' "

No Nostradamus

WVU assistant coach Greg Williams was obviously operating with a defective crystal ball in 1976 when he declined a position on Bowden's Florida State staff.

Williams chose to remain in Morgantown rather than follow Bowden to Tallahassee. The Seminoles were ranked last among the three Division I programs in the state and, he presumed, weren't likely to improve their standing any time soon.

Klausing, by then, had accepted the head coaching position at Carnegie Mellon.

"He calls me from Florida State, telling me he's been offered a job by Bobby, but he's gonna turn it down. He said, 'Bobby will never win at Florida State.' And he gave his reasons. He said, 'There's 40 great players every year in the state of Florida. The one or two who live around Miami are going to go to Miami, Florida State might get one and all the rest are going to Florida.'

"What happened, Florida went on probation the next year and kids who might have gone there started going to Florida State instead. That was what put Bobby over the top."

Williams misfired on his prediction. Bowden *has* won--and is still winning--at Florida State. The Seminoles are 197-50-4 since his arrival and capped 11 consecutive seasons (1985-95) with a bowl victory, an NCAA record. That streak was snapped in the 1997 Sugar Bowl--by Florida.

Rhodes to Success

Klausing coached dozens of All-Americans during his college career, but he derives more satisfaction from his players' achievements in the classroom than on the field.

He's especially proud to have coached Danny Williams, Alex Kroll and Terry Bowden, exceptional students who followed widely divergent paths to success.

"I'll tell you, success stories like theirs keep you going. The most important thing, I've found, is not what kids accomplish during their football careers, but seeing them go on and be successful in life."

Williams, a quarterback at West Virginia during Klausing's six-year stint as a Mountaineer assistant coach, earned a Rhodes scholarship to study at Oxford University in England. He later became a radiologist and today teaches at the Wake Forest University Medical School.

Kroll, who gained All-America honors as a Rutgers center in 1960 when Klausing was an assistant at the university, is now CEO of a prosperous Madison Avenue marketing firm. It was at his suggestion that Chrysler-Plymouth head Lee Iacocca stepped before the camera and appeared in the company's television commercials, a masterstroke that helped launch a period of record sales.

Like Williams, his former West Virginia teammate, Bowden studied at Oxford, though not as a Rhodes scholar. The numbers on his coaching resume are nearly as impressive as those on his academic transcript: Since succeeding Pat Dye as Auburn's head coach, Bowden's record is 36-9-1.

Twists of Fate

Few college football coaches are as identified with a school as Joe Paterno is with Penn State. Yet if events had followed a slightly different course, he might never have set foot in State College.

Klausing traces the twists and turns that brought Paterno from Brown University to the resignation of Bob Higgins--his own coach at PSU--following the 1948 season.

"Higgins was about the same age as his first assistant, Joe Bedenk. He had another assistant, Earl Edwards, who was five years younger than Bedenk. Bedenk and Edwards both were very respected, but Higgins felt Edwards was the right guy to be the next head coach at Penn State."

The athletic committee instead selected Bedenk, who doubled as the Nittany Lions' head baseball coach.

"Well, Edwards was very disappointed that he didn't get the job. So he leaves Penn State and goes to Michigan State as an assistant coach. Sort of a step to the side because he doesn't want to work under Bedenk.

"Bedenk coaches one year and decides he doesn't want to continue coaching both football and baseball. He gives up football and goes back to baseball. Well, Edwards is gone and for some reason the athletic committee went out on a national search and hired Rip Engle [then head coach at Brown].

"Rip Engle brings Joe Paterno along as a grad assistant because there were no coaching openings. Everybody was tenured on the football staff at Penn State. Where I got a little bit of this inside story, Rip Engle's No. 1 assistant at Brown was a guy by the name of Bill Doolittle, who coached with me at Army.

"We had played Penn State while I was Army and you could tell that Doolittle was upset at Rip Engle. He told me the story that Rip Engle had promised that he'd be the first assistant he would hire when there was an opening at Penn State. But there weren't any when Rip went to Penn State to coach.

"Well, a year later, after Engle had been at Penn State a year, Earl Edwards, who was at Michigan State, gets the head coaching job at North Carolina State. He hires one of his best friends who was on the Penn State staff, Al Michaels, to be his assistant there. That opens up a position on the Penn State staff.

"So Bill Doolittle calls Rip and says, 'Coach, I'm ready to come. You promised me I'd get the job if there was an opening.' And Rip says, 'Oh, Bill, I'm sorry, but the people here in State College have taken a liking to young Joe Paterno and they want me to hire him in Al Michaels' place.'"

So Engle added Paterno, who had quarterbacked his Brown team, to the Penn State staff. And when he retired following the 1965 season, Paterno assumed the reins. He's been coaching in the shadow of Mount Nittany ever since.

"You sometimes ask yourself, What if Joe Bedenk hadn't taken the Penn State job? Earl Edwards would've been the head coach at Penn State. Or what if Earl had never gotten the North Carolina State job? Al Michaels might not have left Penn State and Paterno might have become the lawyer that he wanted to be. Or what if Engle would've gone along with his commitment to Bill Doolittle and brought Doolittle in instead of Paterno?

"There's a lot of what ifs there.

Bedenk, Edwards, Michaels and Doolittle were all fine coaches, but it's difficult--if not impossible--to imagine any of them achieving the kind of success at Penn State that Paterno has: two national championships (1982, 1986), five undefeated seasons, an 18-8-1 bowl record and 289 victories. Only three Division I coaches in history have won more games: Bear Bryant (323), Pop Warner (319) and Amos Alonzo Stagg (314).

It's a Small World

When Klausing met Northern Arizona head coach Steve Axman at a football clinic several years ago, he knew a little of Axman's background. What Klausing didn't know was his personal role in Axman's development as an expert in handling the blitz.

"We were at a clinic, killing some time in the evening, and I said, 'Steve, you're the greatest coach I've seen as far as teaching your quarterbacks to handle the blitz. Where did you get influenced about being able to handle the blitz?'

"He said, 'I was a quarterback at C.W. Post when we played against your teams at IUP. No one ever blitzed us as much.' He said our team did such a great job of blitzing that he made up his mind if he ever coached quarterbacks, he was gonna have a plan and have them prepared for blitzes like we were doing."

Axman quickly gained a reputation as a first-rate quarterbacks coach. In fact, he tutored both Super Bowl XXX quarterbacks during their college days: the Cowboys' Troy Aikman at UCLA and the Steelers' Neil O'Donnell at Maryland.

Axman's success as a coach has helped erase the memories of his experience as a backup quarterback at C.W. Post. Although the Long Island school produced some outstanding teams in the late '60s, the Pioneers went 0-3 in their series with IUP, losing by scores of 32-24, 35-13 and 35-8.

C.W. Post never did solve the Indians' relentless blitz scheme. Not even quarterback Tim Carr, the eventual ECAC Division II Player of the Year, could rescue the Pioneers in 1968. IUP defenders sacked him seven times.

When a Win Equals a Loss

NCAA regulations prohibit cheering in the press box by media and sports information department representatives. But the rules were disregarded during a game between Pitt and Syracuse--by the man in charge of the Pitt Stadium press box.

Even stranger, Carroll "Beano" Cook was cheering for the other team. Sort of.

Klausing heard the story from Beano himself while he was

coaching at Kiski School. Cook, who later worked as a network football analyst, is a 1949 Kiski graduate.

"When Beano was the sports publicity man for the University of Pittsburgh he would run a pool where you would guess the total number of points scored in the game. He would get like $5 off everybody that came in the press box. There usually was a pot of $200-plus.

"Pitt was playing Syracuse and losing the game, 35-31, with a minute to play. Beano was right on the button--he had guessed 66 points. In the last minute, Pitt throws a long pass and their back is running for a touchdown."

The fans at Pitt Stadium cheered wildly, but Cook reacted in a decidedly different fashion.

"Beano kicks the table in front of him. He was happy because Pitt had won the game, but mad that he had lost the pool."

And a couple hundred dollars.

Stand and Deliver

Bud Wilkinson didn't just rock the world of college football when his Oklahoma University teams reeled off a record 47 consecutive victories from 1953 to 1957. He started a trend.

The Sooners stood on the sidelines during games, which was a departure from the norm, according to Klausing.

"Back in the '30s and '40s, everyone sat on the bench. In fact, the coaches had folding chairs and sat out in front of the bench. No one ever stood up. The only time anyone stood up was when the coach called your name and told you to go in the game.

"Well, Oklahoma won 47 games in a row during the '50s. The interesting thing, Oklahoma's players all stood. And you know how coaches are--they'll copy anything that they think helps them win. That's why everybody started to stand."

A Word to the Wise

One of Klausing's long-time acquaintances, Bill Peterson, was regarded as an outstanding head coach during his career, which featured stops at Florida State and Rice and a stint with the Houston

Oilers.

He was also regarded as the second coming of Casey Stengel. Like the Hall of Fame baseball manager, Peterson sprinkled his speeches with malaprops, mangled the language in endearing fashion and was susceptible to bouts of absent-mindedness, as the following illustrates.

"When he was at Rice he went to the library and got a book on owls, because Rice's mascot is the owl. So he's giving a pep talk to his team. He says, 'You know, our mascot is a bird that sits quietly at night and when anything comes by, it'll attack that prey. And it'll fight to the last minute.'

"He goes on and on like that. He's really getting his team fired up for the game. Finally he says, 'So let's go out and play like a bunch of Rice . . .' And he turns to his assistant and he says, 'What the heck's the name of our mascot?' "

A Gift from Beyond

Ed Hirshberg had a knack for always finding a way to win on the football field. Even more impressive, he found a way to keep treating his friends--*after* his death.

"Eddie was originally from McKeesport and he played at Pitt, coached at Dartmouth, coached at West Point, coached at Carnegie Tech. I got to be good friends with him because of my Carnegie Mellon background.

"I went to Eddie's funeral and afterwards his niece read his last will and testament. He wanted his ashes dropped over the Great Divide, gave a percentage of his estate to his wife and children and so forth."

The typical bequests. With one exception.

"His last wish was, if any of his friends are ever thirsty, there will always be a tab at the Lincoln Hills Country Club bar. And you can go in and have a drink on old Eddie."

A Football Dynamo

Neil Brown, whom Klausing considers one of his mentors, coached a succession of winning teams at long-defunct Har-Brack High School in the Allegheny Valley. Three of his best players came from the same family.

All three ultimately played for Division I programs and two went on to the NFL.

"He coached the Modzelewski brothers, Ed and Dick, who were known as Big Mo and Little Mo. Big Mo [Ed] went to Maryland. Jim Tatum, the head coach at Maryland, was recruiting the second Modzelewski [Dick]. They were sitting outside the Modzelewski home in the backyard and the mother was hanging clothes on the line.

"The boys must have got their build off their mother--she was about 5-8, 250 pounds. That's sort of the way those two guys were. Well, Big Mo and Little Mo had a brother [Gene], who they called Dyna-Mo."

With good reason, it seems.

"He was like an 8- or 9-year-old kid when Dick was being recruited by Tatum. Tatum rubs Dyna-Mo on the head and says, 'Dyna-Mo, are you gonna be a football player?' 'Oh, ya, Mr. Tatum, watch me.' His mother is hanging a sheet on the line. Dyna-Mo runs full speed and tackles his mother.

Mrs. Modzelewski went sprawling and clothes flew in every direction.

Dyna-Mo graduated from tackling his mother to tackling ballcarriers at New Mexico State, but he couldn't quite live up to the standards set by his older brothers: Ed and Dick both earned All-America honors at Maryland, Ed as a running back in 1951 and Dick as a tackle in 1951 and 1952.

Ed Modzelewski, Pittsburgh's first-round draft choice in 1952, spent six seasons in the NFL with the Steelers and Browns. Dick played defensive tackle for the Redskins, Steelers, Giants and Browns during his 14-year career, appeared in eight NFL title games and was a member of championship teams in 1956 (Giants) and 1964 (Browns).

Driving Miss Nicholson

Klausing doesn't claim to possess the prognosticating powers of Punxsutawney Phil, but he does recall one prediction of his that was as accurate as a Dan Marino spiral. It involved a young student named Milene Nicholson, who took a driver training course from him at Braddock High School.

"Two years or so later I'm taking my football team to a Pirate baseball game. We had complimentary tickets, so I stop into the office to pick up the tickets and I get directed to a secretary--Milene. I said to her, 'This is a great job for a girl. You'll probably meet one of the players and get married.' She says, 'Fat chance. All the players on the team are married.' "

A few months later the Pirates recalled a young infielder--a bachelor--from Hollywood of the Pacific Coast League, who took a liking to the secretary and ultimately married her. Bill Mazeroski's wife has never forgotten Klausing's prophetic words.

"I bump into them once in a while. She always says, 'You're the guy who predicted this would happen.' "

CHAPTER 6
Almost Heaven

Following six consecutive winning seasons at IUP--and three postseason appearances--Chuck Klausing returned to Division I in 1970 when he was hired as Bobby Bowden's top assistant at West Virginia.

With Klausing acting as defensive coordinator and head recruiter, the Mountaineers went 42-26 and twice played in the Peach Bowl, splitting a pair of decisions with North Carolina State.

Klausing was coaching at IUP when he first met Bowden in 1966. The two immediately hit it off and became fast friends.

"I was down at Florida State visiting Bill Peterson, the head coach," Klausing recalls. "Bobby had left there a month before to take a job as the offensive coordinator at West Virginia. He was back at Florida State tending to some business and he had stopped in the office. My friends on the Florida State staff introduced us.

"We sort of said, 'Oh, we're only 60, 70 miles apart, we'll spend some time together.' So I started to visit him at spring practice and he started to work my summer camps."

When head coach Jim Carlen left for South Carolina following the 1969 season, Bowden succeeded him. One of his first acts was to appoint his friend from IUP to the West Virginia staff.

The highlight of Klausing's six years in Morgantown was unquestionably a dramatic, last-second 17-14 victory over archrival Pitt at old Mountaineer Field in 1975. The win helped WVU nail down a Peach Bowl invitation and just might have kept Bowden's coaching career alive.

The Suitcase Game

A walk-on kicker named Bill McKenzie drilled a 38-yard field goal on the final play against 20th-ranked Pitt that not only won a game, but might have saved some jobs.

The WVU coaches, under fire because of a mid-season skid, had their suitcases packed--figuratively, at least--so certain were they that their days were numbered. But McKenzie's kick pulled out a critical victory that was instrumental in Bowden's landing the Florida State job he's held ever since.

"We started off that season winning four games, but then we hit a slump. The assistant coaches were talking among themselves, saying, 'Let's all start looking for another job.' In fact, I had the Carnegie Mellon job in my pocket at the time.

"That was Tony Dorsett's junior year and we did a great job of defensing them: It was three downs and punt for Pitt. Our offense was doing a pretty good job, too. Anyway, we came down to the last few minutes of the game tied, 14-14."

Quarterback Dan Kendra--whose son now plays for Bowden at Florida State--brought the sellout crowd to its feet with a 26-yard pass to Randy Swinson, who bobbled the ball just before stepping out of bounds at the Pitt 22 with four seconds remaining. That's when the most unexpected of heroes stepped into the spotlight.

"This kid, Billy McKenzie, was a walk-on. We had had sort of a tryout to find a kicker. When you're trying kids out, you ask, 'Did you kick off in high school?' He says, 'Yes.' 'What was your average kickoff?' He tells me 20 yards. 'Why only 20 yards?' He says, 'Well, my coaches made me put the ball down flat and I squib-kicked it every time.' 'OK, what was your record as a field goal kicker?' 'We never tried a field goal.' 'How were you at extra points?' He said three out of six."

McKenzie's credentials were as weak as Popeye without his spinach. But Klausing decided to withhold judgment, a wise move in light of later events.

"The kid had a strong leg. It was my responsibility to work with the placekickers, so we worked with him and he got pretty good. Then he makes a great pressure kick on national TV, last play of the game. Everybody goes on one big pile where the kicking tee was.

"Bobby said that was the greatest win of his career. Someone asked him about the [1994] Orange Bowl game, when Florida State beat Nebraska to win the national championship. Wasn't that the greatest game of his career? He said without a doubt he would not be coaching today if his team hadn't beaten Pitt that day in Morgantown."

The Mountaineers turned their season around and wound up defeating Lou Holtz's North Carolina State squad 13-10 in the Peach Bowl. Klausing tendered his resignation the next day and moved on to CMU. Three weeks later, Bowden accepted the Florida State job.

His successor was Frank Cignetti, who once played and now coaches at IUP--where Klausing held forth before joining Bowden in Morgantown.

It Takes a Thief

Chuck Klausing was caught stealing during that 1975 showdown between West Virginia and Pitt. He freely admits his guilt.

Fact is, he was a thief throughout his coaching career. He stole signals.

"If you used signals in games Chuck Klausing coached, he might have stolen them off you. That might have been the most sensational thing I've ever done. I saved a career."

Namely Bowden's. Klausing, long a master at deciphering the signals opponents sent from the sidelines, was an even bigger factor in WVU's upset that day than Bill McKenzie. His expertise enabled the Mountaineers to know what play Pitt was running--before the snap.

"In scouting Pitt we noticed they were signaling every one of their plays. We used stick figure drawings of the coach giving the signals and then matched those stick figures with plays from the films that were sent to us.

"When the coach gave a certain signal, it was a dive play. We had like 11 rats going to a rat hole to stop that dive. Another signal, it was an option play. A certain signal, it was a pass. We matched up our defenses that day with their signals and we held a great Pitt team of [tailback] Tony Dorsett, [quarterback] Matt Cavanaugh and [wide receiver] Gordon Jones to 14 points."

The explosive Panthers were limited to 11 first downs and 281 total yards. The WVU defense was especially hard on Cavanaugh, who passed for only 93 yards and threw two interceptions.

Nightmare in Pittsburgh

Pitt and West Virginia staged another classic in 1970, only this time the Panthers were celebrating wildly at the finish, having mounted a comeback that defied belief.

The Mountaineers bolted into a 35-8 halftime lead, which sparked a mass exodus of Panther fans from Pitt Stadium. Those who hung around witnessed a stirring rally spearheaded by quarterback Dave Havern, who later served as a graduate assistant coach under Bill Neal--Klausing's successor--at IUP.

Havern, a mere wisp of a player at 5-9, 160 pounds, engineered a 70-yard drive that culminated in his 5-yard TD pass to Bill Pilconis with 55 seconds left. The catch by Pilconis, who "was enjoying monastic solitude in the end zone," according to a *Pittsburgh Post-Gazette* account, gave Pitt a 36-35 victory in a game that had seemed all but lost 30 minutes before.

The defeat was one of the most wrenching in Klausing's six seasons at West Virginia. The WVU players and coaches milled around the locker room like zombies, stunned by such a remarkable reversal of fortune. Some were sobbing.

"The kids had started to celebrate at halftime in the locker room. They were all charged up because West Virginia just hates Pitt. You could lose to Penn State a hundred straight times, but, boy, if they lost to Pitt once, that was something they didn't care for.

"We go out in the second half and played very conservative. We had scored easily because we combined a great option game with the forward pass. But in the second half we'd dive right, dive left, run a draw and then punt. Pitt kept drives going, controlled the ball [62 plays to 18] and just kept scoring. It was a hard-to-believe situation."

And a hard-to-swallow defeat.

'Going' in the Air

As head recruiter at WVU, Klausing had access to a private plane piloted by Raymond Dellagatti. The two made some memorable flights on what Klausing jokingly called Air Italia.

One trip included Bowden, whose fear of flying is legendary.

"We go over to play golf at the Saucon Valley Country Club, a private course owned by Bethlehem Steel. The secretary of Bethlehem Steel is a West Virginia alumnus.

"We play the game and have dinner and go back to the airport and our pilot, Raymond, is waiting for us. He says, 'I have bad news. The winds are dangerous, so we're gonna have to stay here tonight. I've already booked us rooms.'

"The next day we start flying from Bethlehem back to Morgantown. The winds have died down some, but it's still pretty bad. We're flying at 120 mph, but we're bucking a 70 mph head wind--we're only gaining 50 miles an hour. So we're up there about four hours.

"Bobby and I are in the back seat and we're bouncing all over the place. Raymond and his co-pilot, Wayne, finally decide to land in Altoona. Four hours in an airplane and we're only to Altoona.

"We come down and Wayne jumps out of the front seat and runs into the hangar. Bobby says to Raymond, 'Why did Wayne run into the hangar so fast?' Bobby's afraid that there's something wrong with the airplane. He's a real white-knuckler. Raymond says, 'Aw, he just had to go to the bathroom.'

"Bobby says, 'I wish you'd have told me about an hour ago we were gonna stop. I already went.' "

The Bowden Clan

Klausing has the utmost respect for his former boss at WVU, Bobby Bowden. He also holds Terry Bowden--Bobby's son, now the head coach at Auburn University--in high esteem.

Klausing regards the younger Bowden as one of the most remarkable players he's ever coached. Not so much because of what Terry achieved on the field, but because of his single-minded desire, against odds longer than Rapunzel's hair, to play football at the

Division I level.

"Terry was a unique guy. He wasn't gifted physically as a player, but he was a gutty kid. He played on the high school team [Morgantown High] with his brother, Tommy, and my son, Tom. The three of them were the defensive secondary when the team went to the finals of the West Virginia Quad-A playoffs.

"Terry was a good little high school player, but he was a 'B' squader, a practice player, at West Virginia. He was there for the year or two after I left, when Frank was the head coach. I get the impression he was a little mad at Frank because Frank wouldn't play him."

While Cignetti admired Bowden's grit and determination, he couldn't overlook the fact that Terry lacked the size (5-9, 180 pounds), speed and quickness to excel--or even survive--as a Division I running back. Bowden, a demon on special teams, did play enough to earn letters in 1977 and 1978. Brother Tommy also lettered twice at WVU as a wide receiver.

"I remember Bobby saying to the coaches once, 'You know, I have two sons on this team. I don't want you to show them any favoritism. But if they're good enough to play, I don't want you to hold it against them, either.' I thought that was a good way to put it."

Terry's marginal success on the field was offset by a raft of honors in the classroom. He earned the best grades on the team, graduated magna cum laude, spent a summer studying at Oxford and was awarded a degree from the Florida State School of Law. But instead of earning his livelihood in a courtroom, Terry wound up in the family "business "--coaching.

The Bowdens are a prominent presence on the college scene today. Besides Bobby and Terry--the first father-son act to simultaneously coach Division I programs--there's Jeff, who works as his father's receivers coach at Florida State, and Tommy, who served as his brother's offensive coordinator at Auburn until accepting the Tulane University head coaching position following the 1996 season.

Terry Bowden's Auburn staff also features Jack Hines, a defensive back during Klausing's tenure at West Virginia. His connection to the clan? Hines is married to Bobby and Ann Bowden's daughter, Robyn.

The Smoking Gun

While at WVU, Bobby Bowden occasionally received phone calls from Herman Moses, the school's dean of men. Not to exchange pleasantries--to complain about football players causing mischief.

"He was always calling Bobby up. One night he called him and said, 'Your football players are shooting guns off in the dorm.' So Bobby called me and asked me to go out there with him.

"We met Herman in the lobby and everything was calm. No noise, nothing going on. Bobby's going to Herman, 'See, you got me out here for nothing.' All of a sudden we hear 'bang, bang.'

"Bobby tells me to take the elevator up to the top floor and start working my way down. He and Herman start on the first floor and work their way up. We met about the fifth floor. All of a sudden we hear 'bang, bang' again.

"This was a circular dorm, so they start running to the left and I start running to the right. I come around the bend just as Bobby and Herman come around the other way and we see a football player of ours, who shall remain nameless, standing there with a smoking gun in his hand.

"He looks at Bobby and he says, 'Coach Bowden. Did you see that guy run who shot the gun and handed it to me?' "

Golfing with the Pros

Because Klausing took pains to befriend a youngster at a football camp operated by the WVU coaches, he had the pleasure of meeting two golfing greats.

"I'm running a camp down in Greenbrier County, W.Va. We had about 150 kids there. Well, there's a little 7- or 8-year-old with big crocodile tears having problems and he wanted to go home after being at the camp for about 30 minutes.

"I called the boy's father and told him the story. The father begged me, 'Please, keep him there, see what you can do. He's a momma's little boy and he needs to be away from home and make some friends."

Klausing spoke with the youngster, smoothed things over and spent the week plying him with chocolate and giving him extra attention. The lad wound up thoroughly enjoying his stay, to the delight of his father.

"His dad came in to pick him up and take him home. He thanked me for looking after his son. He asked if I ever played golf. I told him I had my clubs in the car, that myself and three other coaches were gonna stop at a public course on the way home and play a round.

"He says to me, 'I'm the starter at Greenbrier Country Club and if you'll come there around noon, I'll give you golfing privileges and you'll have the chance to play one of the greatest courses in America.'

"So the four of us stop and he's waiting for us. He says to our caddies, 'You take care of these gentlemen. Don't you take any tips off of them.' And he throws each of us three brand new golf balls. Boy, I'm the king of the hill with my fellow coaches.

"We go out and we play and there's a twosome coming up behind us. And, boy, are they long-ball hitters. We're on a par-4 hole and we wave them ahead. Their drives are like our two good hits.

"Anyway, my ball's laying in the rough about 150 yards from the hole. These two guys come up in a golf cart and one guy's ball is right next to mine. He says, 'I'm gonna show you how to hit this thing. You have some heavy rough there and you really have to zip your club.'

"This guy hits the ball and it rolls within a yard of the hole. He says, 'Now you do it.' I don't know why I did so well--I zipped the dang thing and I go right on the green with it. He says, 'That's the way to do it.'

"Turns out the two guys who were playing through were Sam Snead, who was the pro at Greenbrier Country Club at the time, and his nephew, J.C. Snead."

Sam Snead, a native West Virginian, won a record 81 PGA tournaments in his career and was a charter member of the Golf Hall of Fame. J.C. Snead is now a fixture on the PGA Senior Tour.

The $600 Victory

West Virginia forged a winning record--barely--in 1973, winning three of its last four games to finish at 6-5. One of those victories came at a cost--literally.

The Mountaineers had lost four consecutive games entering a

Nov. 2 showdown with Miami at the Orange Bowl. When the team practiced on the eve of the game, Klausing recalls, the players struggled to keep their footing on the artificial turf. Prospects for the next day suddenly seemed bleak.

"It was a completely different type of artificial turf and, boy, our shoes were not right. We're slipping all over the place. There was an equipment man from the Dolphins there in the locker room and I got to talking with him.

"He says, 'Seems that you guys don't have the right shoes.' I said, 'Boy, I really found that out tonight. I don't know what we're gonna do. We're slipping all over that field.' "

The equipment man, a sly grin on his face, excused himself and returned moments later carrying several pairs of turf shoes that would provide proper traction. He knew because they belonged to members of the Dolphins, who were then tenants of the Orange Bowl.

"I looked at them and I said, 'Boy, I wish we had shoes like that. He said, 'I know how you can get them. You tell me what sizes you want and how many pairs you want and I'll rent them to you for $10 a pair.' We had 60 kids so that was $600.

"He told me those shoes cost about $50 a pair, so he wanted $3,000 in cash to make sure he got the shoes back. Well, I went to a coal operator from West Virginia who was at the game and told him my problem."

It wasn't a problem for long.

"He gave me the $3,000, we played the game and we returned the shoes. The equipment man made his $600 and I got the $2,400 back for the coal operator."

Most important, the Mountaineers prevailed, 20-14. That victory made the difference between a winning season and a losing one.

Final Rehearsal

The record shows that Bobby Bowden coached 68 games while at West Virginia. Bowden actually coached twice that many--half on the field, half in his head.

He would gather his coaching staff around him on the eve of every game and, usually while chomping on an unlit cigar, mentally play the next day's opponent.

Those rehearsals, Klausing maintains, are one of the keys to Bowden's long-standing success.

"The thing that impressed me most about him was his visualization the night before a game. He played every situation and every play of the game the night before.

"He would ask the coaches what they were gonna do right after the kickoff. What would they do if they were backed up, what would they do if they had good field position? He would play out the whole game--offense, defense and special teams.

"So many times we came to that situation in the game. And because we had rehearsed the night before, we knew just what to do."

Toasted Pigskin

Jack Duffy, one of Klausing's hometown friends, will never join Thomas Edison in the inventors' hall of fame.

Duffy's son, Jack, was a manager at West Virginia during Klausing's tenure with the Mountaineers. One rainy afternoon poor Jack couldn't keep the footballs dry. His plight inspired the elder Duffy to search for a solution.

"His dad came up with the first mechanical ball dryer I ever saw. He had like a toaster sitting inside of a breadbox and he had cut holes in the breadbox.

"You would slide the football into this breadbox and the toaster would dry the ball. You would push a wet ball in and a dry ball would come out. He thought he was gonna be able to market it and make a fortune, but I don't think it ever went."

The Break-in

More than 20 years after the fact, Klausing can't suppress a laugh when he thinks of West Virginia's secretary of state crawling through a tiny window like a prisoner making his escape.

Only A. James Manchin wasn't breaking out. He was breaking *in*--to a football game.

"He was quite a character. He was always calling me because I was the guy who handled the complimentary tickets. He calls me the week of the Pitt game, wanting some tickets. I said, 'Aw, A. James, the game's a sellout and I've already given out all my tickets.' "

Being a politician, Manchin wasn't accustomed to being rebuffed. He refused to take no for an answer.

"I finally said, 'Well, there's a back door to our office. If you come early I'll have a graduate assistant take you in through the back door and you can get into the stadium that way.

"What happened, we had a new athletic director, Leland Byrd, and he came and had a padlock put on the back door that week because he knew a lot of people were getting in that way. I said to the grad assistant, 'What are we gonna do?' And he pointed at the window.

"The window in our office was about six feet off the floor and it had a wire grate over it. The grad assistant said he'd bring a crowbar, open up that window and pull the grate off and A. James could climb through the window.

"We were expecting A. James and three or four other guys. Well, A. James comes with his wife and daughter, maybe 20 people altogether. The grad assistant had to go get a stepladder. People had to climb the stepladder and squeeze through the window into the end zone stands.

"I'd already gone down to the field when one of the other assistants, George Henshaw [now offensive coordinator for the New York Giants], who knew of my problems with A. James, walks up to me. He says, 'I see your friend A. James got here.' ' Where's he at, up in the end zone?' 'No, he's right on the 50-yard line--sitting on the steps.' "

Mirage in Morgantown

Franco Harris scored one of the most remarkable touchdowns in NFL history when he caught a deflected pass and raced for a last-second touchdown to give the Steelers a dramatic 13-7 victory over the Oakland Raiders in a 1972 playoff game at Three Rivers Stadium.

One year before and 60 miles to the south, Harris scored another remarkable touchdown. Remarkable because when he crossed the goal line, the ball was 10 yards behind him.

"One of the oddest plays I ever saw was a blown call by an official in a Penn State-West Virginia game. Franco Harris and Lydell Mitchell were in the backfield for Penn State, so this had to be in 1971.

"Franco goes into the line on a dive play at about the 5-yard line and the ball gets stripped. It's laying on the 10. Franco's momentum without the football carries him into the end zone and, as he goes over the goal line, an official signals touchdown.

"The other officials, they're shaking their heads. They don't know what to do. The officiating rule is if even one guy calls a touchdown, it's a touchdown. This official claims he saw Franco go across that line with the football.

"I'm up above in the press box and Bud Wilkinson is the color man on TV in the booth right next to me. He shows me the replay. You could see the ball never went past the 5-yard line.

"I called down to Bobby Bowden. I told Bobby, 'Go out and put your foot on the football and tell the officials you're not gonna leave until they give us the ball.' But it was to no avail. The touchdown stood. It was the oddest play I've ever seen."

Penn State scored four other times by more conventional methods to post a 35-7 victory.

Persistence Pays Off

David Van Halanger's prospects of making the WVU football team, it seemed, ranged somewhere between slim and none.

But his persistence--and his father's--ultimately paid dividends. Not only did he play at WVU while Klausing was there--he captained the team as a senior.

"When he was between his junior and senior years in high school his dad came to me and said, 'Look, I want my son to get a football scholarship. He's a pretty big boy. What can you do to help me?' I said, 'Well, why don't you have him come to our football camps and we'll see what we can do.'

"He was a tall boy with a lot of baby fat. He wasn't even a regular on his high school football team as a junior. He went to camp and got a little bit interested in weightlifting--he had never lifted before.

"After his senior year his dad called me up again. 'Are you gonna give David a scholarship?' I said, 'Mr. Van Halanger, he was lucky to play for his high school team. There's no way that we can give him a scholarship.'

"And he said, 'Well, what can you do further to try to get him a football scholarship?' I said, 'Well, one of the things I would recommend is for David to spend a fifth year in prep school. There's one at Greenbrier Military School that might be able to help develop him.'

"So he goes to Greenbrier and he wasn't even on the first team. His dad calls me again after the season and says, 'Are you gonna give him a scholarship to West Virginia?' I said, 'Mr. Van Halanger, there's no way I can do that. He couldn't even play regular at Greenbrier.'

"He finally begged me to look at a film. He'd cut out David's 25 best plays. Sure enough, he showed some things in these 25 plays. I showed the film to our line coach, Jerry Bruner. Jerry says, 'You know, he has some things that we can't teach. He's 6-foot-6; we can't teach him to be tall. He's 250 pounds; we can't teach him to be that big. And we do have a scholarship open.' "

The clincher came when Klausing dragged Bobby Bowden to a basketball game at the Coliseum in Morgantown.

"Bobby hates to watch basketball, but I got him to go to a game between Greenbrier and the West Virginia freshmen. David was Greenbrier's center. He wasn't a very good player, but he ran up and down the floor pretty good.

"Bobby finally turns to me and says, 'Chuck, if you want to give him a scholarship, go ahead.' "

The persistence of the Van Halangers--father and son alike--had paid off. Van Halanger enrolled at WVU, lettered three seasons as an offensive tackle and played on the victorious Peach Bowl squad in 1975.

Van Halanger, as Klausing once did, now works under Bowden. He serves as Florida State's strength coach.

The 1940-41 Wilmerding High School basketball team. Chuck Klausing sits at the bottom left.

Coach Leo Houck's 1943-44 Penn State boxing team, which featured freshman Chuck Klausing (first row, far left)

The Penn State Marines, massed in front of Old Main on campus in 1944. Klausing is pictured in the back row, third from right.

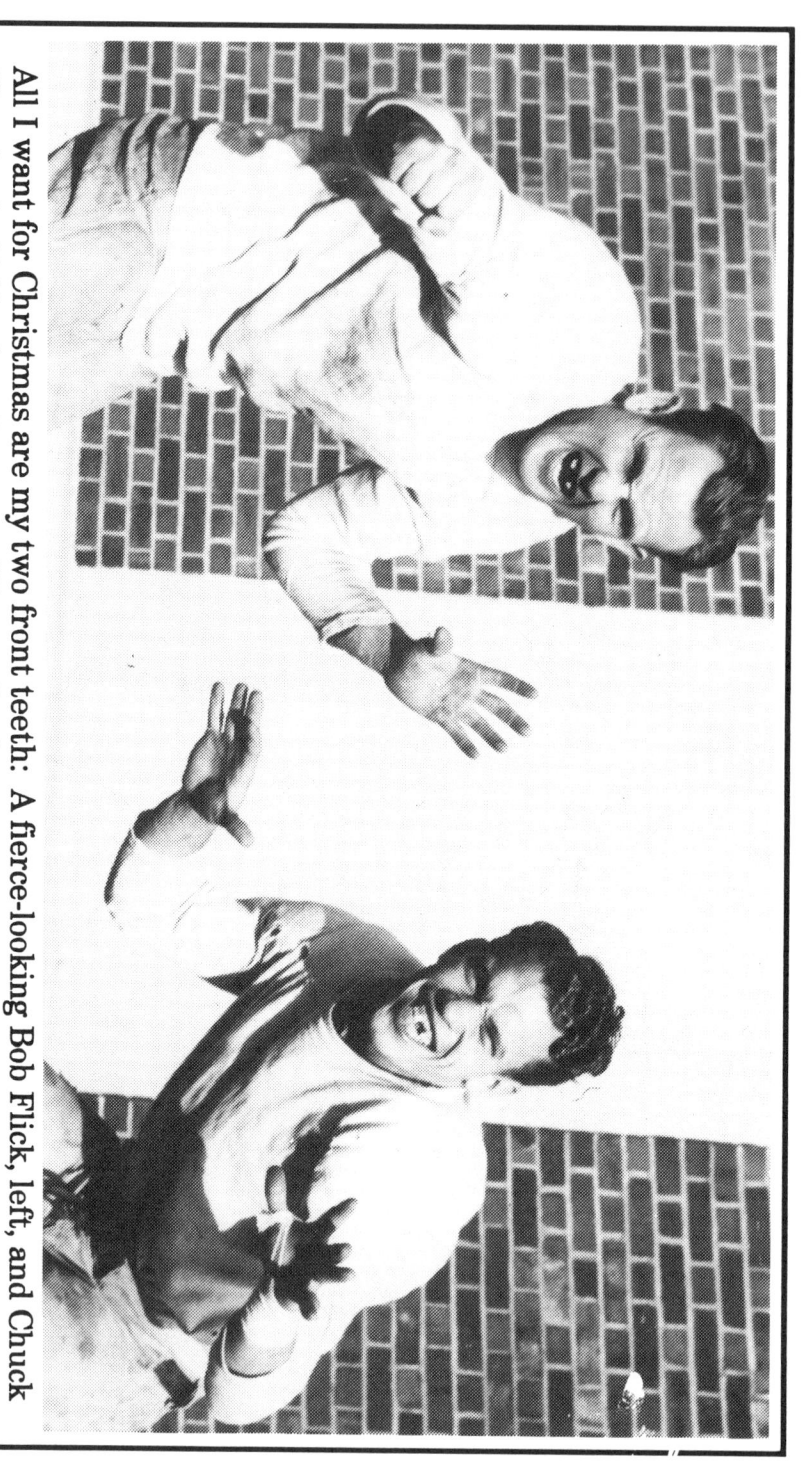

All I want for Christmas are my two front teeth: A fierce-looking Bob Flick, left, and Chuck Klausing in 1946, when they were Slippery Rock teammates. Both later coached in Saltsburg, Klausing at Kiski School and Flick at Saltsburg High School.

Chuck Klausing snapping to Slippery Rock roommate Paul Uram during the 1946 season.

The 1946 Slippery Rock football team, featuring center Chuck Klausing, third from right in the front row.

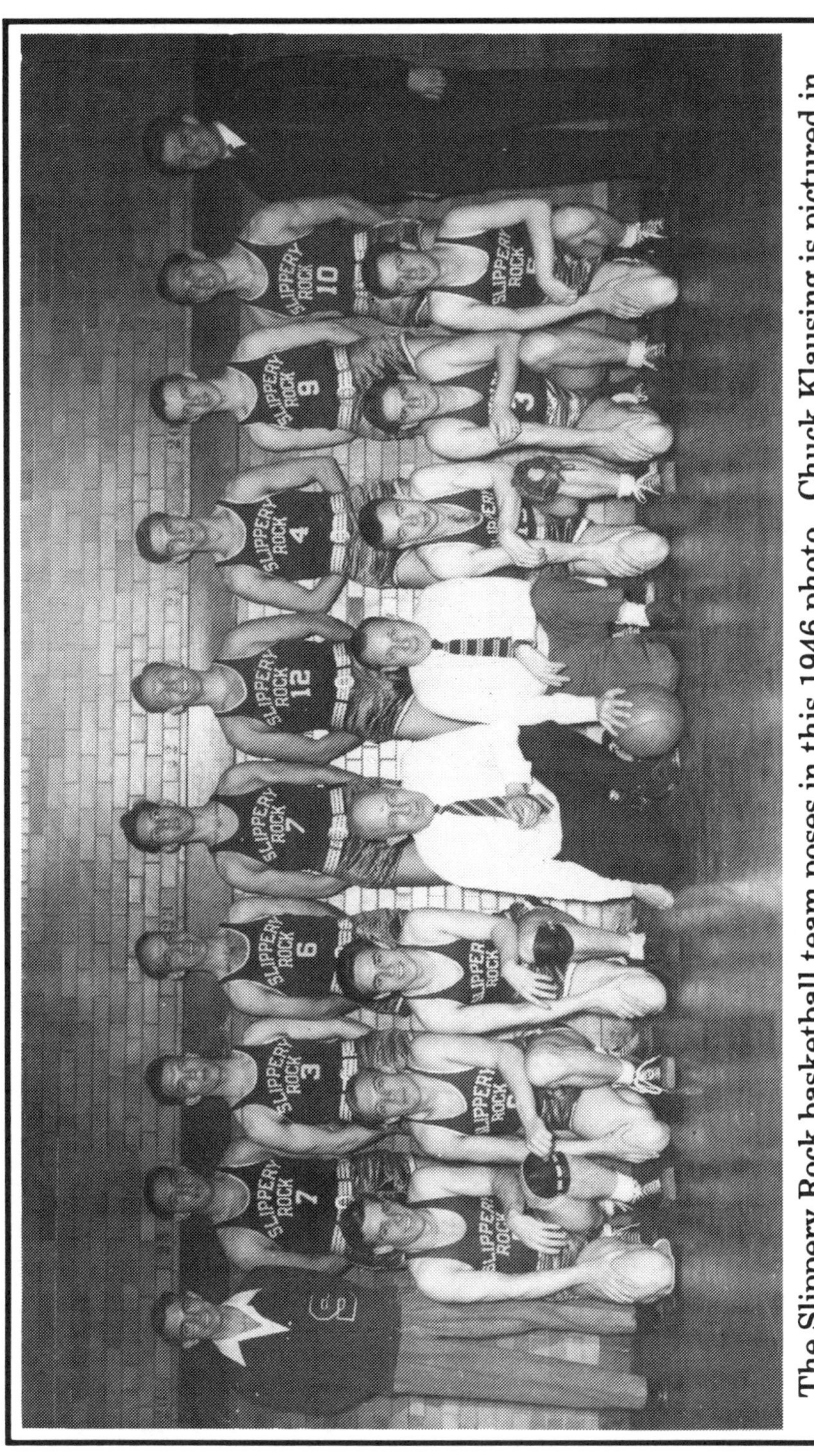

The Slippery Rock basketball team poses in this 1946 photo. Chuck Klausing is pictured in the second row, third from left.

The Wilmerding YMCA basketball team, which won the state YMCA championship in 1948 and placed third in the national tournament. Pictured are, first row, left to right, manager Bill Lewis, Joe Leonatti, Chuck Klausing, George Kerr and Bob Wilkie; second row, Pete Evanovich, Milos Adjia, John Galagaza, Bernie Leech and Wayne Berkoben.

Players, coaches and cheerleaders pose for a photo during Pitcairn High School's 1950 football banquet. Coach Chuck Klausing is pictured in the second row, far left.

Chuck Klausing's 1951 Pitcairn High School football team, which finished 8-1, the Railroaders' best record in his six seasons as head coach. Klausing stands in the middle of the back row.

Head coach Chuck Klausing, front row, far left, poses with his 1952 Pitcairn High School football team. Assistant coach Pete Antimarino sits at the opposite end of the first row.

BRADDOCK HIGH SCHOOL TIGERS
CLASS A CHAMPIONS 1955

The 1955 Braddock High School football team, which finished the season with a perfect record and the WPIAL title trophy. Coach Chuck Klausing is pictured in the top row, far left.

The 1958 Braddock High School football team, which claimed WPIAL championship No. 5 for coach Chuck Klausing

Chuck Klausing's last Braddock High School team, which won the 1959 WPIAL Class A championship and was the subject of a *Sports Illustrated* feature. Klausing is pictured in the back row, second from right.

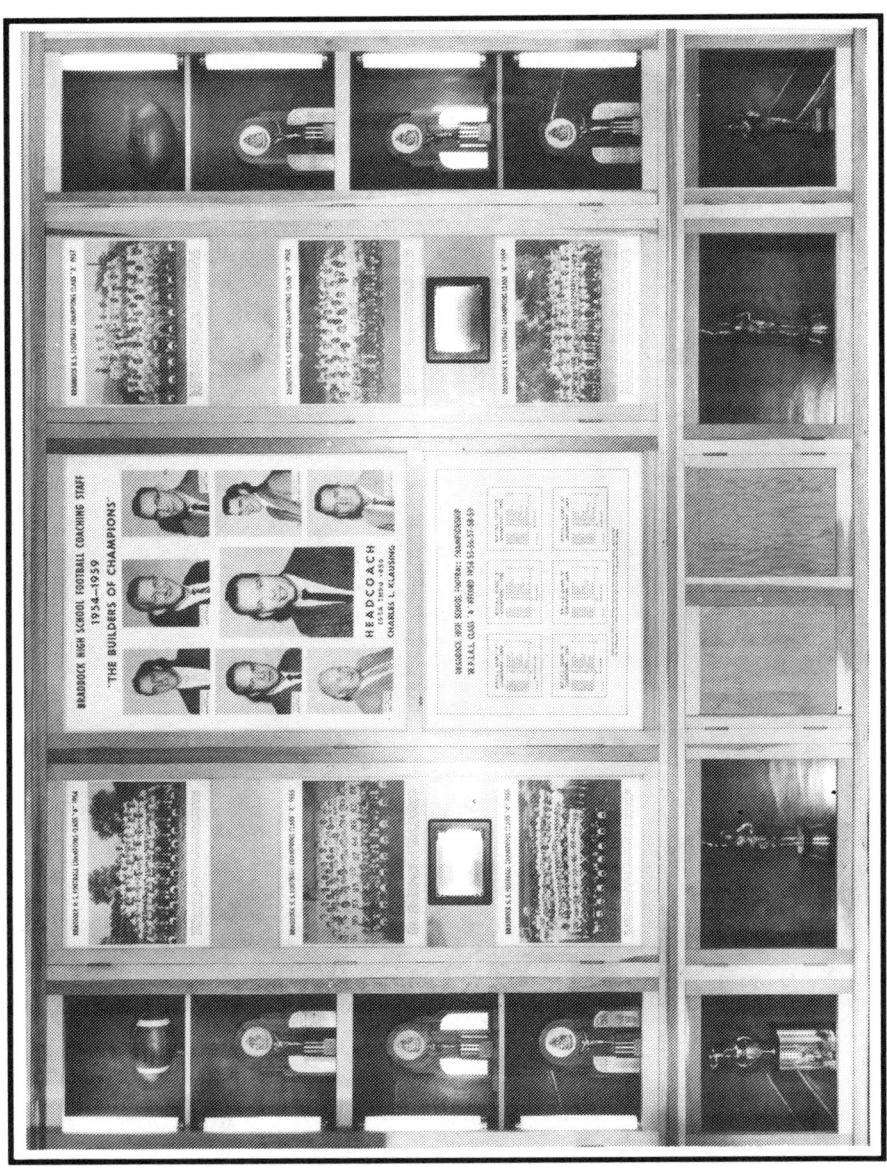

The Braddock High School trophy case, which honored Chuck Klausing's six WPIAL championship teams.

Head coach Chuck Klausing speaks at a Braddock High School pep rally in 1959. That was the year the Tigers captured the school's sixth consecutive WPIAL championship and shattered the national record for the longest unbeaten streak.

A family portrait from 1959, when Chuck Klausing was closing out his record-breaking run at Braddock High School: from left to right, Marylou, Joann holding Kathy, Patti, Chuck holding Nancy, and Tom.

Chuck Klausing at Kutsher's Country Club (he's standing under the K in the sign), located in New York's Catskill Mountains, in the late 1950s. Also pictured are long-time Penn State football coach Rip Engle (fifth from left), former Los Angeles Lakers great Fred Schaus (to Klausing's left), University of California basketball coach Pete Newell (to Klausing's right) and Earl D. Edwards (sixth from right), Klausing's position coach when he played football at Penn State during World War II.

Chuck Klausing talks shop in 1961 with another football legend, long-time Florida A&M coach Jake Gaither, a member of the College Football Hall of Fame. Both were in Pittsburgh to speak at a clinic.

Dale Hall's 1961 Army coaching staff, which featured assistant Chuck Klausing (standing, far right). That was the first of Klausing's three seasons at West Point.

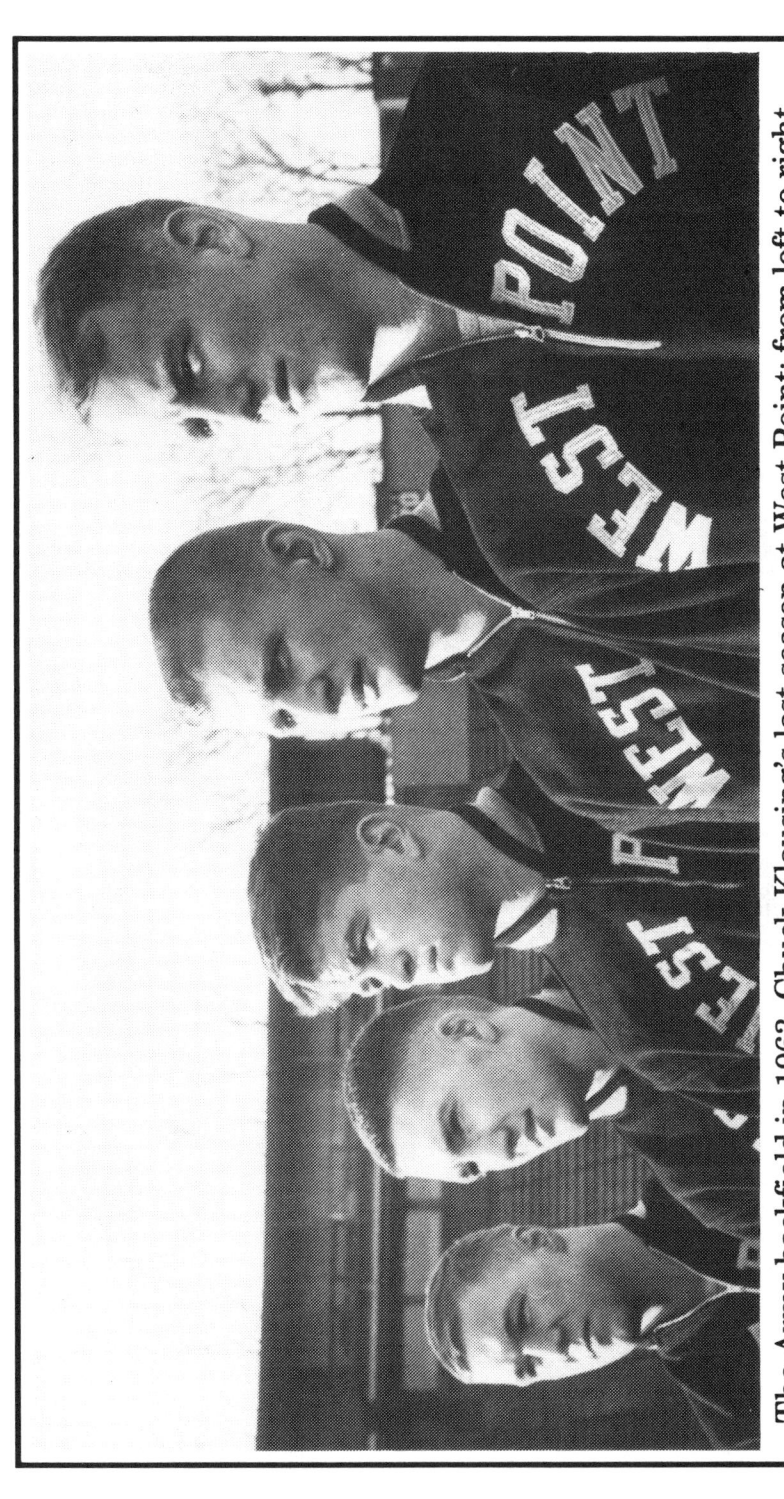

The Army backfield in 1963, Chuck Klausing's last season at West Point: from left to right, Ray Paske, Curt Lindler, Don Parcells (whose brother Bill now coaches in the NFL), Ken Waldrop and Rollie Stichweh.

Chuck Klausing with quarterback Wally Blucas, left, and defensive back Paul Neatrour, two of IUP's key performers during the 1966 season.

IUP's 1967 team, which finished 8-1. Coach Chuck Klausing stands in the second row, far right.

Chuck Klausing regularly recruited big names to work his summer football camps at IUP. Pictured, left to right, are Chuck Scales of the Cleveland Browns, Ted Marchibroda of the Baltimore Colts (now coach of the Baltimore Ravens), Klausing, Dick Van Raaphorst of the Los Angeles Rams and Jim Bradshaw of the Pittsburgh Steelers.

Paul McGregor, right, presents IUP coach Chuck Klausing with a check to be used toward scholarships at a banquet in 1968. Looking on are, from left, long-time Westinghouse High School football coach Peter Dimperio, former Pittsburgh Pirate outfielder Frank Thomas and IUP President Dr. Willis Pratt.

IUP's Boardwalk Bowl team, which won all nine of its regular-season games before bowing 31-24 to powerful Delaware in the final seconds of a thrilling showdown at Atlantic City's Convention Hall in 1968. Coach Chuck Klausing stands in the back row, far left.

Joann and Chuck Klausing flash the "V for victory" sign in front of their Indiana home in 1968 after IUP accepted a bid to play Delaware in the Boardwalk Bowl at Atlantic City, N.J. Victory eluded the Indians when Delaware scored a touchdown with 15 seconds remaining.

WESTERN UNION
TELEGRAM

CLASS OF SERVICE

This is a fast message unless its deferred character is indicated by the proper symbol.

SYMBOLS
DL=Day Letter
NL=Night Letter
LT=International Letter Telegram

The filing time shown in the date line on domestic telegrams is LOCAL TIME at point of origin. Time of receipt is LOCAL TIME at point of destination

PA145

P LLM218 (L BHA216) NL PDB FAX BEVERLY HILL CALIF 11
COACH CHUCK DLANSING, INDIANA UNIV OF PENNSYLVANIA, FOOTBALL
TEAM SHELBURNE HOTEL
ATLANTIC CITY NJER
CONGRATULATIONS TO YOU AND THE TEAM ON YOUR SELECTION BY THE
NCAA. BEST WISHES FOR A VICTORY SATURDAY NIGHT
JIMMY STEWART
(501).

A telegram Chuck Klausing received prior to IUP's appearance in the 1968 Boardwalk Bowl from Indiana's favorite son, Oscar-winning actor Jimmy Stewart. Stewart attended elementary school in a building that is now part of the IUP campus.

Chuck Klausing and his captains are the picture of dejection as they accept the runner-up trophy moments after IUP's heart-breaking 31-24 loss to Delaware in the 1968 Boardwalk Bowl. Pictured, left to right, are Bob Tate, Jack Henry, Al Dellavechio, Klausing, Ernie Casale, Chairman of the NCAA's Atlantic Region, and NCAA representative Jon Foley.

(Photo courtesy of IUP Sports Information Department)

IUP's 1969 team, arguably the best of the six Chuck Klausing coached at the school. The Indians finished 8-1, the lone setback a 23-21 heartbreaker against Klausing's alma mater, Slippery Rock. Klausing stands at the center of the back row.

Chuck Klausing chats with IUP President Dr. Willis Pratt at a going-away party given in Klausing's honor following the 1969 season. Klausing had accepted Bobby Bowden's offer to work as his top assistant at West Virginia University.

Chuck Klausing at West Virginia in 1974, his fifth season as an assistant under Bobby Bowden.

Three members of the West Virginia coaching staff talk football with U.S. Senator Robert C. Byrd, D-W.Va., in Washington, D.C. Pictured, left to right, are Hayden Buckley, Byrd, Chuck Klausing and Bobby Bowden.

Chuck Klausing visited Steelers training camp in Latrobe along with several other West Virginia assistants in 1975, six months after Pittsburgh won the first of its four Super Bowl trophies. Pictured, left to right, are Mike Working, Paul Moran, Greg Williams, Klausing, Steelers scout Bill Nunn, Frank Cignetti, Don Young and George Henshaw.

Chuck Klausing poses with his former Slippery Rock teammate and roommate Paul Uram at Steelers training camp in Latrobe. Uram was then serving as Pittsburgh's strength and flexibility coach.

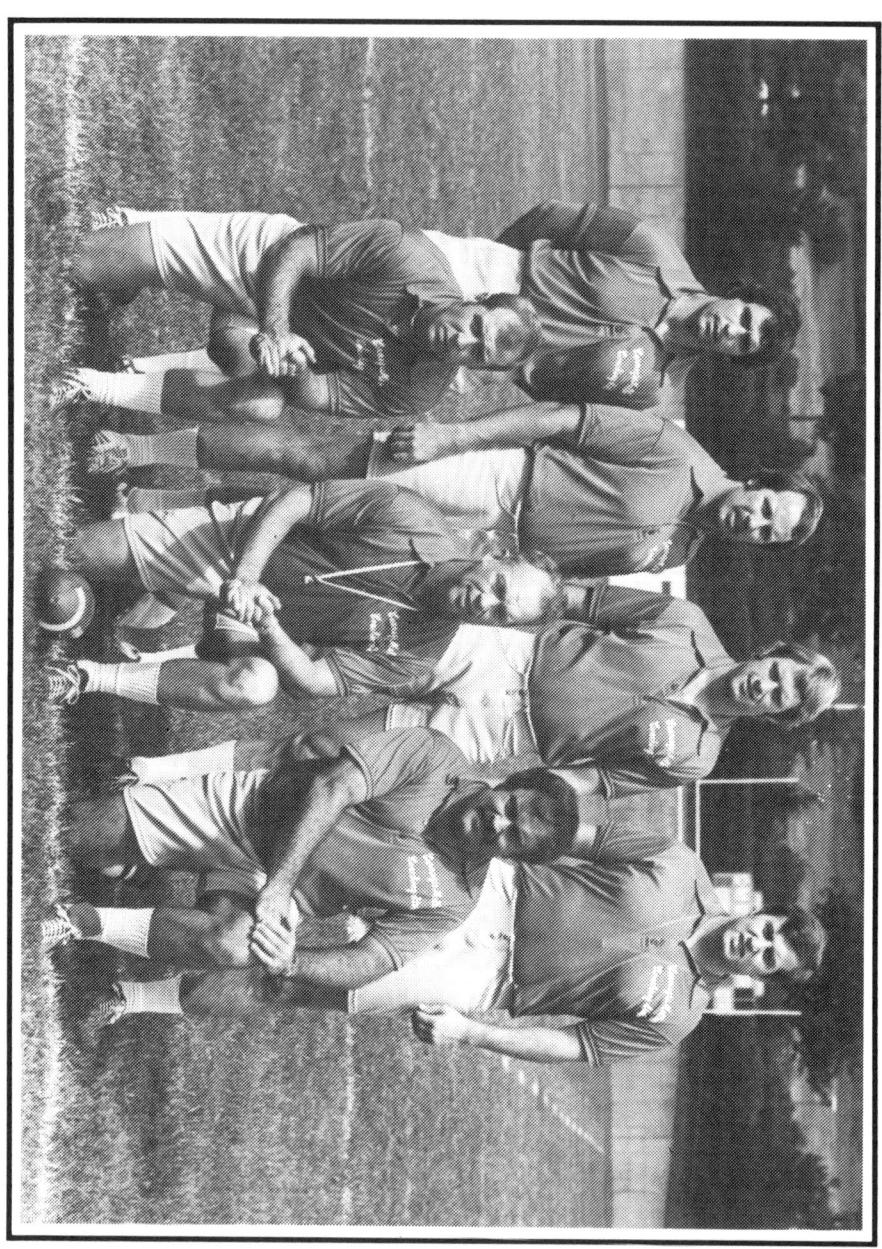

The Carnegie Mellon University coaching staff in 1976, Chuck Klausing's first season as head coach of the Tartans. Pictured are, first row, from left, Moe Smith, Klausing and Jerry Mancini; second row, Denny Morabito, Bob Lyerly, Bill Englert and Dave DeCammila.

Chuck Klausing with basketball Hall of Famer Julius (Dr. J) Erving during a banquet at Three Rivers Stadium in Pittsburgh.

Carnegie Mellon running back/co-captain Jim Morrison with head coach Chuck Klausing in 1981.

Chuck Klausing being interviewed on national television in 1985 following a Carnegie Mellon playoff game.

Chuck Klausing on the sidelines with head coach Mike Gottfried in 1986, when he served as a Pitt assistant.

Chuck Klausing's 1987 team at Kiski School. The Cougars finished 5-1-1 and won the Interstate Prep School League title in Klausing's first year at the helm.

Chuck Klausing's 1988 team at Kiski School. No. 12 is quarterback Dan Freiburger, who went on to a distinguished career at Southern Methodist University.

Chuck Klausing's 1990 team at Kiski School, which won the Interstate Prep School League crown. One of Klausing's linemen that year, Scott Paterno (fourth row, fifth from left), is the son of Penn State coach Joe Paterno.

IPSL Football Champions

The 1993 Kiski School team that captured the Interstate Prep School League championship in Chuck Klausing's final year of coaching. No. 10 is quarterback-safety Jeff Simmons, Klausing's grandson.

Chuck Klausing delivering a halftime speech during a Kiski School game early in the 1993 season.

Chuck Klausing exhorts his Kiski School team at halftime of his final game--Nov. 6, 1993. The Cougars capped the Klausing era with a 33-8 victory over Shady Side Academy to wrap up the Interstate Prep School League title.

Chuck Klausing speaks with his Kiski School team at the close of his final game, the 310th victory of his career as a high school and college coach.

The 1995 inductees to the Pennsylvania Sports Hall of Fame. Chuck Klausing is pictured in the first row, third from left.

The charter class of the IUP Athletic Hall of Fame, which was inducted Sept. 14, 1996. Chuck Klausing is standing, third from left. Current IUP football coach Frank Cignetti, who was a member of Bobby Bowden's West Virginia staff along with Klausing, is pictured in the second row, fifth from right.

(Photo courtesy of IUP Sports Information Department)

CHAPTER 7
The Pride of Pittsburgh

Chuck Klausing coached at two high schools, six colleges and one prep school during his 46 years in football. He did arguably his best work at Pittsburgh's Carnegie Mellon University (1976-85), turning the Tartans into national championship contenders despite antiquated facilities, a lack of athletic scholarships and rigorous academic standards that scared off many a potential prospect.

"I felt I never accomplished so much with so little," Klausing says today.

Under his stewardship, CMU posted a 77-15-2 record, made four trips to the NCAA Division III playoffs and won the 1979 Lambert trophy as the premier Division III team in the East. Klausing earned Division III Coach of the Year awards in 1979 and 1983 and finished with a winning percentage of .830, which placed him second nationally among active Division III coaches at the time of his departure.

They were spectacular achievements given the school's emphasis on the academic, not the athletic. Players tackled courses such as Experimental Techniques in Genetic Molecular Biology, Advanced Chemical Engineering Thermodynamics and Fluorescence Spectroscopy in Biological Research, were more likely to read *The Wall Street Journal* than *The Sporting News* and were often tied up in science labs that ran till 4:30 p.m., leaving Klausing precious little time to prepare for games. Especially late in the season, when darkness fell earlier.

"We had some of the shortest practices in America," he recalls. "Because of late labs we would practice late. And we didn't have lights, so we couldn't practice too long."

What's more, Klausing didn't have blue-chip prospects at his command like he did at prior coaching stops. In a 1979 preseason interview, Klausing said of the Tartans, "We're not a physical team--we're slow and we're small." He touched on a similar theme later that season when CMU was about to tangle with Ithaca in the national semifinals. Upon learning that an Ithaca back ran a 9.8 hundred, Klausing cracked, "I don't have anyone who runs a 9.8 *40*."

But that didn't stop him from leading the Tartans to national prominence, much as he had a rag-tag group of high school players at Braddock two decades before.

Following a decade at CMU, Klausing moved less than a mile down Fifth Avenue to Pitt, where he served on Mike Gottfried's staff during the 1986 season. It was his last year in the college ranks.

The Tartan Turnaround

The renaissance at Carnegie Mellon did not occur by happenstance. The administration resolved to beef up the program, which meant turning the reins over to a full-time coach for the first time in school history.

Joe Gasparella, a former Notre Dame and Pittsburgh Steeler quarterback, had guided the Tartans since 1963, but he couldn't devote all his energies to the program. Not with a full-time job off campus.

"The poor guy before me didn't have time to recruit or anything. He was a very bright, knowledgeable guy, but he ran an architectural firm all day long and then came over at 3 o'clock to coach the football team.

"I was able to go to work in the morning. I recruited, I counseled my players, I made preparations. I just had the opportunity to coach football 24 hours a day, 365 days a year. The guy before me didn't have that opportunity."

Working full-time, Klausing was able to effect a rapid turnaround. CMU finished 6-1-1 in Klausing's first season, the school's best record since 1959. A year later the Tartans finished 8-1 to set a CMU record for victories in a season.

Klausing's third team went 9-2 and participated in the NCAA playoffs, the school's first postseason appearance since the 1939 Sugar Bowl. And in year No. 4, the Tartans came within a minute and a half of reaching the national championship game. For the third year in a row, CMU set a school record for wins (10).

The Con Man

The glowing records cited above suggest that Klausing's tenure at CMU was all smooth sailing. That's a myth, as the tale of the con man illustrates.

In 1980 Klausing received an offseason visit from a prospect who was more--and less--than he seemed.

"What would you do if you're a college football coach and you're supposed to go home at 4 o'clock and at one minute to 4 a prospect walks into your office? He had been to the admissions office and they sent him to me because he told them he was a football player. He wasn't a bad-looking kid physically. And, oh, boy, did he have all the right answers.

"He said he was from Kansas City and had won the state 100-meter championship in Missouri. He had good numbers. Scored 21 touchdowns his senior year in high school, No. 2 student academically in his class, had a 1,300 on his SATs.

"I started to say to him, 'You know, it's awfully expensive to go to school here.' He says, 'I'm an orphan and I think I can qualify for full financial aid.' Well, I started getting real interested. I thought I had one that came out of heaven.

"It was too late for me to do the things I had to do as far as getting him admitted to school and meeting with the financial aid people to see if he qualified, which it sounded like he would. So I called a fraternity house and some fraternity kids came over.

"I said, 'Can you put this boy up for the night?' 'Oh, ya, Coach, we always have an extra bed.' 'OK, give him a meal and give him breakfast. Here's $20 to take care of things.' So I go home and all night I'm thinking, Boy, am I ever lucky. I've got this great prospect. I can't wait to get in there tomorrow morning and take care of things.

"I'm driving in the next day and I thought, You know, this is too darn good to be true. And I remember there was a coach who used to be at North Allegheny--in fact, he's [former Pitt All-American and Steeler assistant coach] Joe Walton's brother--who was coaching at a high school in Kansas City. The same high school this boy told me he was from.

"So I call Joe's brother and I ask him about the boy--let's call him John Doe. 'What kind of player was John Doe?' He says, 'Chuck, I've been at this school for five years and I've never heard of him. I'll call the athletic directors from some other schools in Kansas City to see if they know him.'

"Well, none of them ever had a boy of that name. I said, 'Maybe the kid's lying about being a player. Maybe he's a good student and he's doing this to get into school. How about checking the guidance office to see what kind of student he was.' Well, they never had a student by that name. And I go, 'Uh-oh.'

"I call the police department at Carnegie Mellon, tell them the story and they run over to the fraternity house. Here the kid and another boy had a van and they were unloading TVs and computers and everything out of the fraternity house. They were con artists who would use this method all around the country.

"They'd go to colleges and prey on the football coach. They knew the right things to say and the right time to get there--late in the day when all the other offices were closing, realizing that the coach would find a way to put them up for the night.

"Then, when all the other fraternity students had gone to class, they'd clean them out."

The Doctor and the Robot

Klausing had better luck with a CMU prospect named Tony DeGioia, who developed into an all-conference tight end and, more importantly, a pioneering orthopedic surgeon. DeGioia is the director of Shadyside Hospital's Center for Orthopedic Research and co-director of CMU's Center for Medical Robotics and Computer Assisted Surgery.

"After Tony graduated [in 1979], he got a Masters in bio-medical engineering. He was accepted to Harvard Medical School, did real well, graduated and became an orthopedic surgeon. I read an article recently in the Carnegie Mellon alumni magazine that said Dr. Tony DiGioia had invented a robot that he uses in hip replacement surgery."

Robodoc by name.

"In the past, orthopedic surgeons had to go in there with a mallet and chisel and chisel out the socket. But this robot adjusts a milling machine that mills a perfect socket for hip replacements. Tony has a camera attached to the robot so he can see what's going on."

A quarter-million Americans undergo total hip replacement surgery each year. When the smooth cartilage surrounding the hip socket and the ball of the femur--the thighbone--is worn down, bone rubs on bone, causing persistent pain. In years past, the worn femoral ball was removed and an implant held in place with cement. But doctors found that the cement would inevitably loosen after 10 or 15 years, necessitating another operation.

Cementless implants are now gaining in popularity, although there's a hitch: A tight fit is imperative, for gaps between the implant and the bone hinder the healing process. What's more, the implant must remain completely stable.

DeGioia's invention answers the call on both counts, drilling perfect holes in the thighbone and milling perfect sockets while the surgeon monitors the operation on a video screen. According to the story in *Carnegie Mellon Magazine*, Robodoc "is the first robot ever to actively perform part of an operation."

The Giant Killers

When the NCAA matched the Tartans with Dayton University in the first round of the Division III playoffs in 1978, Klausing acknowledged the overwhelming odds against his team. He likened himself to "David looking for sharp stones."

The Flyers were truly Goliaths that season. They brought a 7-1-1 record into the game, the loss handed them by Division I-AA Eastern Kentucky (18-17) and the tie coming against Division I Miami of Ohio.

Dayton itself had been a Division I team until a de-emphasis movement two years before. Consequently, the Flyers were hardly a typical Division III program. In fact, their juniors and seniors were still playing with athletic scholarships awarded them when the school held membership in Division I. That gave Dayton an enormous advantage in the non-scholarship world of Division III.

Given the circumstances, CMU (8-1) should have been hopelessly overmatched. But Klausing had a knack for inspiring underdogs in big games, as Delaware discovered 10 years earlier in Atlantic City.

"We went out and we played a great game. We actually had the better of them. We were ahead 14-0 going into the last quarter, but they came back throwing the ball and tied us, 14-14."

Which set the stage for the first overtime game in CMU history. Unlike the NFL, which operates under a sudden death system, NCAA overtime guidelines ensure both teams an equal opportunity. Each team begins overtime at the opposition's 25-yard line (the starting point back in 1978 was the 15) and maintains possession until running out of downs, turning the ball over or scoring. If the game remains tied after each side has its opportunity, a second overtime period follows, with the teams reversing order.

"In the first overtime they scored first and then we scored. So now we have the ball first and they hold us to a fourth-and-five situation and we kick a field goal [a 27-yarder by Denny Postufka]. Now all Dayton has to do is advance the ball 15 yards and score."

But the Flyers never reached the end zone. Linebacker Rich Lackner, who succeeded Klausing as CMU's head coach in 1986, stripped the ball from Dayton running back Brian Dorenkott and Gregg Gailey recovered to end the game and send the spectators at Tech Field into a frenzy. Even Pitt fans were moved by the Tartans' stunning 24-21 victory.

"Pitt was playing a home game that day a mile across town. I was told that when the score of our game was announced at Pitt Stadium, 50,000 people gave us a standing ovation. It might have been the biggest upset that I've ever been involved in."

Working Overtime--Again

The Tartans were understandably overcome by a sense of deja vu in 1979. Here they were, back in the NCAA playoffs, back in overtime.

And back in the semifinals after posting a 31-25 victory over Minnesota-Morris. According to *The Pittsburgh Press*, the team's "heart-stopping win was something right out of CMU's drama school." It was dramatic, all right, given that the Tartans trailed 25-14 with 7:24 remaining. Klausing recalls the game not only for the stirring comeback, but for two coaching decisions that came under scrutiny.

"We were losing by 11 points with a possibility of having two more possessions. The first possession we come up fourth-and-15. A lot of people doubted our strategy, but we kicked a field goal."

Denny Postufka's 34-yarder sliced the deficit to eight points. The Tartans then held Minnesota-Morris, regained possession and marched for a touchdown, Bob Gasior bulling over from the 2-yard line. Bob Kennedy's ensuing two-point conversion pass to Pete Recchia tied the score.

"Minnesota-Morris has the ball first in overtime and we hold them without a score [thanks to Tom Frost's interception]. So now we get the ball on the 15-yard line. Well, I have a great placekicker so I decided to try a field goal."

On first down. Unfortunately, Postufka's kick sailed wide.

"A lot of people doubted my strategy. They asked, 'Why didn't I try to run?' I was afraid of a fumble. We'll score a touchdown from there maybe 50 percent of the time, but we'll make a kick from that position 90 percent of the time. It's almost a sure-fire thing. I was just figuring the percentages, but it backfired.

Gasior took his coach off the hook moments later, sending CMU ahead 31-25 on a 1-yard run. Postufka's extra point attempt was blocked, leaving Minnesota-Morris a window of opportunity, but the Cougars never budged from the 15-yard line. A first-down run that went nowhere was followed by three incomplete passes.

For the second year in a row, Carnegie Mellon had advanced to the national semifinals by working--and winning in--overtime.

Lucrative Benefits

Klausing took part in 310 victories during his career, led his teams to dozens of championships and earned two national coach of the year awards. But he probably takes more pride in the two benefits he organized at CMU, for Jimmy Starr and Moe Smith.

"My wife thinks those are the two greatest things I've ever done."

Few would dispute Joann Klausing on that point. People in Pittsburgh still talk about her husband's generosity, both with his time and his money.

Starr played tight end for the Tartans, which was a story unto itself. He had led Peabody High School to a Pittsburgh City League championship as a quarterback, but when he arrived at CMU, the position he coveted was held by a veteran. Rather than bemoan his fate, Starr volunteered to play elsewhere.

"Most people would've quit. It was amazing how he became an offensive end. But Jimmy only knew how to play one way--hard."

He became an inspirational force in the Tartans' lineup, which is why his death, at age 20, hit everyone at CMU so hard.

"The summer before the football season of 1979 I get word that Jimmy had been killed in an automobile accident. His teammates got together and wanted to set up a scholarship in his name. I asked them how they were gonna do it. They said they were gonna all contribute $50 or something like that.

"I said, 'Well, that might be enough for a scholarship for one year, but let's try to have a benefit for him and maybe we'll raise enough money that we can use the interest to give a scholarship every year.' So we had this benefit in our gymnasium.

"More than 3,000 people came. We had sports celebrities there, we had all kind of auctions and raffles--everything was donated. We didn't have to spend a nickel. It was all clear profit."

Houston Oiler coach Bum Phillips sent his 10-gallon hat to be raffled off. Klausing donated the $2,500 he'd been awarded as the Division III Coach of the Year for 1979. Contributions poured in from across the country. The CMU players had hoped to raise $10,000 for the Jimmy Starr Memorial Scholarship Fund, but their estimate was way off.

"I think we made $40,000 that night. We had to clean up right afterwards to leave the gym in perfect condition. My wife and I got home about 4 o'clock in the morning. I was just exhausted. She said to me, 'That's the nicest thing you've ever done. But don't ever do it again.' "

Unfortunately, Smith was diagnosed with pancreatic cancer less than a year later. Klausing again sprang into action, organizing another benefit at Skibo Gym for his former defensive coordinator (1976-79), who had since joined the staff at Southern Illinois, where Rey Dempsey--Klausing's former quarterback at Pitcairn High School--was head coach.

Smith, who played under Klausing at IUP, had been the exuberant ringleader of Moe's Maniacs, the defensive units that served as the backbone for CMU's success in the late '70s. The Tartans led Division III in scoring defense (4.9) in 1979 and surrendered only 7.4 points per regular-season game during his tenure.

When Klausing learned that Smith needed help, he recalled his wife's gentle admonition the night of the Jimmy Starr benefit. He hesitated--for all of two seconds--before volunteering his services.

"We found out that he had taken all his retirement money and used it in the move to Southern Illinois. He had no health insurance. There he's dying of pancreatic cancer, a wife and a child, and he has no money at all.

"So two ladies who had helped with the Jimmy Starr benefit came to see me and said, 'You've got to do it again for Moe.' And we did. We raised $40,000 to help pay for a lot of his expenses."

The benefit was held May 3, 1981. Celebrities again jammed Skibo Gym, a Willie Stargell bat was auctioned and a Pitt jersey worn by All-America defensive end Hugh Green--the runner-up for the Heisman trophy the year before--was raffled off.

Seven months to the day later, Smith died at the age of 35. At his funeral, Klausing delivered the following eulogy:

"I have seen a young man visit a college campus
    and I know what hope is.
I have seen him enter school

and I know what anxiety is.
I have seen him earn his position
and I know what satisfaction is.
I have seen him lose a game
and I know what disappointment is.
I have seen him cheer his teammates on in Atlantic City
and I know what caring is.
I have seen him pay his dues as a part-time coach
and I know what want is.
I have seen him married to Cyndy
and I know what love is.
I have seen him receive his job at CMU
and I know what happiness is.
I have seen him build his defenses
and I know what teamwork is.
I have seen the love of his players
and I know what respect is.
I have seen him lose his father
and I know what sadness is.
I have gazed into the eyes of Lindsay
and I know what faith is.
I have seen him contract a dreadful disease
and I know what fear is.
I have seen and felt all these things
so now I know what Moe Smith is."

An Alternative Approach

Klausing first experienced two-platoon football as an Army assistant coach under Paul Dietzel, who demoralized opponents by continually running fresh troops into a game.

The strategy succeeded at West Point. Why, Klausing wondered in 1978, couldn't it succeed at CMU? He was blessed with two gifted quarterbacks and two offensive units of nearly equal ability, wasn't he?

So Klausing decided to unveil a two-platoon attack in the season opener against California.

"My second team was almost as good as my first team that year.

I had told my second team that at the end of the first quarter, I was gonna put them in for a series. If they did all right, I'd keep them in. But if they didn't do well, I was gonna take them out."

The first team, directed by quarterback Bobby Kennedy--a predecessor of Dan Marino's at Pittsburgh Central Catholic High School--sputtered offensively during the first quarter and failed to score.

"Well, at the end of the first quarter I turn around and there's my second team ready to go in the game. I had forgotten my promise. So I put them in and right away they score a touchdown."

Backup quarterback Rich Brown, who practiced with a sophomore-dominated unit, marched the Tartans 80 yards to finally get CMU on the board. He didn't stop there.

"They get the ball again late in the second quarter and they drive and score another touchdown. So we go in at halftime and, boy, the first unit is really steaming. They haven't played very much."

Klausing reinserted his starters in the third quarter, but again they failed to muster anything offensively. The second unit returned in the fourth period and helped run out the clock, sealing a 14-3 victory.

"We have a meeting on Monday and I tell the team, 'From now on we're going to play interchangeable units. But if you get in the game and you score, you're gonna stay in the game. If you don't score, the other team comes in.' I think it made it a real competitive situation."

The Railroad Engineer

Like the fabled Casey Jones, Klausing gained fame as a railroad engineer--even though he never ran a locomotive.

"Carnegie Mellon's a great engineering school. In fact, engineering's the most popular curriculum. But you had to be a great student to get admitted--you had to be in the top 10 percent of your class, you had to have close to a 700 on the math college boards and at least a 500 on the verbal college boards.

"Well, I wasn't finding enough football players with grades like that. One day I'm playing handball with the dean of engineering and I told him my problem. He said, 'Chuck, you ought to bring them in through the liberal arts program.' I said, 'These kids don't want liberal arts, they want engineering.'

"He explains that every year 20 to 30 percent of the engineering freshmen drop out of school. 'I need replacements in order to keep my faculty working. So if you can bring in freshmen who are in liberal arts and get them to take physics and calculus as part of their freshman curriculum, and if they get decent grades, they can apply to engineering and come in as sophomore engineering majors.'

"So I started to encourage kids to do that. We would have 10 to 12 kids every year come in through the liberal arts program, take engineering subjects their freshman year and then apply to the engineering school. And a great number--a high percentage--got accepted. The kids used to call me the dean of the school of railroad engineering because we sort of railroaded them in."

Afternoon Soap

Throughout his career, Klausing observed one rule with regard to swearing: If a player uttered an expletive, he ate soap as punishment. The rule applied to coaches, too--even Chuck Klausing.

When Klausing uncharacteristically let a four-letter word slip during a CMU practice session, he marched into the locker room, grabbed a bar of soap and chomped down on it in the presence of his players.

"That was the only time in my career I swore. In fact, it was a little bit premeditated. I sort of felt that I had to get my team turned around. It was effective in the short run, but not in the long run. I wish I never would have done it."

Besides, the taste of soap lingers. Any number of Klausing's former players could have told him that.

The Hijacked Bus

Klausing was in no mood for an argument in 1979 after his team surrendered 15 points in the final 1:25 to lose an NCAA semifinal game to Ithaca, 15-6. The host Bombers scored on an intentional safety, a pass play and an interception return to steal a victory from CMU and land a berth in the national championship game, which they won a week later.

"We had lost a tough, hard game. Afterwards we loaded our buses, which were to take us to the airport. We were to fly a chartered plane back to Pittsburgh.

"Well, no one had made any arrangements for us to eat. The game started at 12 o'clock, so we had had breakfast at 9. Here it is 3:30, 4 o'clock in the afternoon and we're hungry. There was gonna be no food on the plane--no food until we got back home to Pittsburgh.

"So I said to the bus driver, 'I see a Wendy's up ahead. Pull the bus in there.' He told me he had orders to take the bus straight to the airport. Well, I pretended I had a gun. I said, 'Look, I'm commandeering this bus. You pull into Wendy's.' He did and I fed my team."

The bus driver didn't grumble much about the detour, but Joann Klausing sure did.

"The person who got the maddest about it was my wife. She was waiting for us at the airport. There wasn't any food there, so all she had for dinner was cashew nuts."

Casualty List

The trainer's report for Carnegie Mellon's season finale against Hiram in 1981 showed the usual bumps and bruises and one participant with a torn knee cartilage. The head coach.

While running onto the field to protest a penalty, Klausing slipped and injured his knee. Despite the pain, he gamely hung in until the Tartans' 7-6 victory was in the books.

"There was a rule at that time that you could take a timeout and debate the official and correct the call. You couldn't debate whether there was holding or not or anything like that, but you could debate a rules interpretation.

"As I remember it, I moved so fast that I tore the cartilage in my knee. But I got the timeout and debated the official and had the play changed. It was something about half the distance to the goal. We had clipped on the 19-yard line and he marched off 15 yards from the spot of the foul and put the ball on the 4. I wanted the ball on the 9½."

Klausing won the argument, although the victory came at a cost.

Less than a week later he underwent surgery to repair the damage to his knee.

A Hoops Homecoming

When Klausing lugged his gear up Fifth Avenue in 1986 to begin a new job at the University of Pittsburgh, he celebrated a homecoming of sorts. He had played at Pitt Stadium 44 years before--basketball, not football.

Klausing's Wilmerding High School team split a pair of WPIAL playoff games at Pitt Pavilion, a court tucked into the bowels of Pitt Stadium that, long ago, served as the Panthers' basketball home and hosted scholastic tournaments. He revisited the glory days of Pitt Pavilion during his year with the Panthers.

"The interesting thing, when I coached at Pitt, we would have pickup basketball games at noon among the football coaching staff. I guess I'm 61, 62 years of age and here I am playing in the Pitt Pavilion--again."

Memories of the 1942 WPIAL playoffs came rushing back every time Klausing stepped onto the floor.

"I remember once I had what was considered a pretty good night. I think I scored nine points or something to that effect. And I did something I wasn't allowed to do. We were only allowed to take three types of shots--we could take a two-handed set shot, we could drive and shoot a layup and we shot an underhanded foul shot.

"Well, I had been to a YMCA camp near Youngstown and I had learned a one-handed shot. I guess I really amazed people. I think I made four one-handed shots in that game. It caught the eye of the fans, but my coach didn't like it. He told me at halftime, 'You made four-for-four. The law of averages is gonna catch up to you, so don't take any more shots.' "

The Pitt Pavilion soon faded into obscurity and ceased to exist altogether several years ago. Weight rooms and an office complex now occupy the space where Klausing played basketball as a teen-ager and again as a sexagenarian.

Incidentally, Klausing *did* play football at Pitt Stadium once. He was a Penn State center and linebacker when the Nittany Lions closed out the 1943 season with a 14-0 victory over the host Panthers.

The Taxi Squad

Craig "Ironhead" Heyward finished his career at Pitt with 2,950 yards rushing, second only to Tony Dorsett on the school's all-time list. But where Dorsett was sleek and elusive, Heyward was hulking and ponderous.

Just walking up hills was a grueling experience for the 260-pound Ironhead--especially "Cardiac Hill," the precipitous slope on which Pitt Stadium is perched. So Heyward found a less taxing means of getting around, as Klausing discovered one day in 1986.

"I had some business down at the Cathedral of Learning. It was a pleasant day, so I walked. I'm coming back up the hill and a taxi cab pulls up and stops and a guy in the back seat says, 'Coach, c'mon, jump in. I'm going up to practice.' Here it's Ironhead.

"He says to me, 'Coach, do you need a ride like this every day? I take a cab to practice every day.' I think he was paying about $2 just to ride four or five blocks up the hill from his dormitory."

Despite his aversion to exertion, Heyward went on to play professionally with the New Orleans Saints, Chicago Bears and Atlanta Falcons.

Hurricane Signals

The University of Miami Hurricanes arrived at Pitt Stadium in 1986 ranked first in the nation, proud owners of an 8-0 record and a roster packed with future NFL standouts: Michael Irvin, Melvin Bratton, Jerome Brown, Brett Perriman, Alonzo Highsmith, Brian and Bennie Blades and eventual Heisman trophy winner Vinny Testaverde, to name a few.

Penn State coach Joe Paterno, whose Nittany Lions later faced Miami in a gripping Fiesta Bowl showdown, called the Hurricanes "as good a college football team as ever played the game."

All the signs pointed to a Miami rout that day at Pitt Stadium. Fortunately for the Panthers, Klausing had figured out all the signs.

"The key to breaking the Miami code was knowing the indicator. I remember their coach would give all kind of signals, like a catcher with a runner at second base. If you knew the indicator, you knew the call. Well, I noticed he gave a hand salute when he was giving all those signals. The signal right after the hand salute was the actual play."

Thus forewarned, the Panther defense bottled up the vaunted Miami running game, allowing only 36 yards on 32 attempts.

"They had a great rushing attack. They were averaging over 200 yards a game, but we just completely shut down their running plays."

Jimmy Johnson, whose team was clinging to a 14-3 halftime lead, responded by opening up his offense in the second half. Even without a complementary ground game, Testaverde threw for 291 yards and four touchdowns, powering the Hurricanes to a 37-10 victory.]

"I was a little perturbed because we knew every pass play that was coming, but we didn't defend them. We were able to get into double coverages to stop the pass plays, but our kids didn't do a good job--or maybe I didn't do a good job--with Vinny Testaverde checking off at the line of scrimmage. Of course, their talent was fantastic."

But it did not yield a national championship. Paterno's Nittany Lions upended Miami 14-10 in the Fiesta Bowl two months later to claim that honor for themselves.

A Fighting Chance

Klausing has long considered Paterno a respected colleague, yet they nearly came to blows during the 1986 Pitt-Penn State game. He shudders today to think of the repercussions had he duked it out with a legend--on national television, no less.

"I'm not exactly proud of that. Early in the game, after Penn State had scored, one of our defensive backs hit their guy late in the end zone and a scuffle broke out on the Penn State side of the field. Joe rushed down and sort of helped break up the fight.

"Later in the game a worse scuffle breaks out on our sideline. It was a pretty good one--it was 11 vs. 11 practically. I'm doing everything I can to break it up. I'm grabbing kids and holding people back and everything else. And I see Joe coming all the way across the field."

Paterno took some heat from the media afterwards, several critics contending that his sprint to the Pitt bench could easily have been misinterpreted and might well have escalated the hostilities.

"You know, I have great respect for Joe Paterno, but I don't think he should've come across the field. I thought to myself, I'm gonna step out--he and I are about the same age and my boxing experience at Penn State never hurt me. And I was ready to challenge him."

Fortunately, Klausing resisted the impulse.

"I knew this was gonna be my last college football game. I didn't want it to go down that way. Instead of 11 against 11 I think it would've been 100 vs. 100 if I'd done what I was tempted to do. But I'm glad that I kept my composure and kept trying to break up the fight rather than start a big one."

Paterno survived the afternoon unscathed and so did his team. The Nittany Lions won, 34-14.

CHAPTER 8
On the Road Again

Like Willie Nelson, Chuck Klausing is no stranger to the road. In fact, it's where he's done some of his best work.

Long regarded as a master recruiter, Klausing scoured the fertile fields of his native western Pennsylvania during his 27 years as a college coach, rounding up prospects to play at Rutgers, Army, IUP, West Virginia, Carnegie Mellon and Pitt.

With his low-key but persuasive approach, he won over scholastic stars who hadn't even considered Klausing's school until he showed up at their door and turned on the charm.

"I was already signed, sealed and delivered to Westminster," recalls Wally Blucas, who quarterbacked IUP's Boardwalk Bowl team. "One day I came home from school and Chuck was sitting in the living room chatting with my folks. Two hours later I called Westminster and told them I wasn't coming."

No destination was too remote or too perilous for Klausing. He ventured into crime-ridden urban neighborhoods, into mill towns and coal towns, into communities so tiny that Rand McNally doesn't even acknowledge their existence. He missed mealtimes and bedtimes and spent weeks away from his family, sometimes with nothing to show for the effort.

Fortunately, successes outnumbered failures in Klausing's years as a recruiter. He consistently landed top-notch prospects with his salesmanship, his honesty, his common touch--even a promise of white lightning.

The Moonshine Recruit

Some football coaches will go to extraordinary lengths to legally land a recruit. Why, they'll even supply moonshine. Or at least a passable imitation.

That's how Klausing reeled in one prospect during his six-season stint as Bobby Bowden's assistant and head recruiter at West Virginia.

Klausing had access to a private plane owned by Harold Sargent, president of the Fairmont Construction Company. In one instance, Sargent tagged along on a recruiting trip and was instrumental, through a bit of deception, in persuading a promising player to attend WVU.

"This kid was a great-looking prospect--about 6-6, 270 pounds. His dad was an invalid, but he was always drinking. We'd go into the home and he'd bring out a bottle. You had to drink with him, too, because if you didn't you weren't gonna get his son.

"We're getting close to closing the deal, but the kid won't commit. I finally asked him, 'What's keeping you from signing a letter of intent to go to West Virginia?' You're really dealing with the dad. And the father says, 'If I had a bottle of Lewis County white lightning I would sign that contract today.'

"Mr. Sargent goes, 'I have a bottle of that. You know, they don't make it anymore, but I've had it stored down in my basement. I only bring it out when good friends come in or something like that.'

"So the father says, 'Well, you bring that white lightning from Lewis County and I'll sign the letter of intent for my son to go to WVU.' We're flying back in the plane and I go to Mr. Sargent, 'How in the heck are we gonna do this? You don't have any of that stuff.'

"He says, 'Chuck, I'll show you.' So we go back to his house and we go down in his basement and he has an empty bottle, real dusty. He takes some other liquor, pours it into that bottle and puts a cork on it.

"A couple days later we go over to see the recruit and Mr. Sargent hands the bottle, which is still pretty dirty, to the father. And the old man says, 'Just a minute, I'm gonna test you, see if you got the right stuff.' He wipes the top off and he takes a big swig, smiles and says, 'That's pure Lewis County white lightning.' And he signed the letter."

'Goldilocks' Loses Out

Resorting to extraordinary measures does not always guarantee success in the recruiting wars, as Virginia Tech's Charlie Coffey learned while battling Klausing and West Virginia for a prospect.

Like Goldilocks, Coffey slept in someone else's bed. All he got for his trouble was 40 winks.

"We were recruiting a great middle linebacker from Ferrum [Va.] Junior College named Billy Joe Mantooth. Everybody wanted him. We were playing a 4-3 defense at West Virginia and you can't have a good 4-3 defense without a great middle linebacker. Well, Mantooth was it.

"I'd recruited him out of Ferrum. Coffey was the new coach at Virginia Tech, which was 20 miles from Ferrum. He had the guy who was the head coach at Boston College for the last few years [Dan Henning] on his staff along with Charlie Pell, the guy who was head coach when Florida got into trouble. The three of them were recruiting Mantooth and they thought they had him locked up.

"We thought we had him locked up, too. I couldn't be everywhere, so I had a young graduate assistant named George Henshaw, who's now the offensive coordinator of the Giants, keep an eye on him.

"They go out together the night before the national signing date and Henshaw takes Billy Joe back to his hotel room. Coffey, meanwhile, thought he was smart. He slept in Mantooth's bed in his dormitory. Coffey figures the kid will be out till 12, 1 o'clock, and when he comes in, he'll take care of him for eight or nine hours until the signing time.

"Coffey slept and Mantooth didn't show up till about 10 o'clock the next morning. He says, 'Well, Billy Joe, you ready to sign?' Mantooth says, 'No, I signed with West Virginia.' They say that Coffey never lived that down."

No wonder. Mantooth developed into an outstanding collegiate linebacker and later played in the NFL with the Philadelphia Eagles and Houston Oilers.

Passing on Montana

The recruiting process entails gazing into a cloudy crystal ball and trying to predict which high school players will blossom into collegiate stars.

Not even veteran coaches are infallible when it comes to evaluating talent, as a tale involving Klausing, fellow WVU assistant Frank Cignetti and a quartet of quarterbacks shows.

"There were four great quarterbacks available [in the tri-state area] this one year. None of them wanted to go to the same school. When Matt Cavanaugh signed with Pitt, none of the other three was gonna go there. When Chuck Fusina signed at Penn State, neither of the other two was gonna go there. So we sort of felt we had a choice between Chuck Fiorante or Joe Montana."

Fiorante had distinguished himself at New Castle High School, a Quad-A power. Montana played at little Ringgold High School in Monongahela.

"We had a real good chance to get Montana. Frank wanted him. But most everybody else thought that Fiorante was the best quarterback to ever come out of western Pennsylvania. Frank and I argued long and hard on this one and I won out."

Or lost out, as the case may be.

Montana wound up at Notre Dame, where he led the Fighting Irish to a pair of Cotton Bowl victories and a national championship in 1977. Montana, you'll recall, also enjoyed some success at the professional level.

And Fiorante? He played two seasons at WVU and did not leave a lasting impression as Montana, Cavanaugh and Fusina did at their schools. A torn rotator cuff ended his collegiate career before it really got started.

Super Slip-up

The West Virginia coaches also miscalculated on Steve Courson, who later started at guard for two Steeler Super Bowl teams. Courson was a high school senior in Gettysburg when Klausing passed through, trolling for prospects.

"I go into this high school gym class and they were playing a game that they called war. It's sort of like dodge ball. You divide the class in half, get about 20 balls and throw the balls at each other. If you get hit, you sit down. The last team with anybody left wins.

"This one athlete--he was about 6-1, 225 pounds--no one could hit him. He was just so agile. I brought some film back of him as a high school player, but the coaches at West Virginia turned him down because he was only 6-1. They thought he was gonna end up 6-1, 265 pounds and fat."

They were two-thirds correct. Courson ended up 6-1 and 260, but with the kind of physique that line coaches swoon over. He played at the University of South Carolina and was drafted in the fifth round by the Steelers, for whom he toiled from 1978 through 1983.

Two of those seasons culminated with Pittsburgh victories in the Super Bowl.

Laying Rubber

Klausing spent a considerable amount of time in his car during his recruiting days. In fact, he almost spent the night there once. Not by choice--by necessity.

Klausing was trying to land prospects for Rutgers when he ventured into rural western Pennsylvania in the dead of winter, when country roads are at their most treacherous.

"I was recruiting a guy from Moniteau High School up in Butler County. I can still remember his name--Pat Stone. It had snowed in the morning, but they had plowed during the day so I was able to drive out to his home, which was a farm home. I talked with him and his parents into the early evening--maybe 6:30 or 7 o'clock. I know it was dark outside.

"I started back towards Butler and I'm driving through farm area. The snow had drifted back onto the road and it was hilly. I had a stick shift car at the time. I'm trying to make it up this hill, but I just couldn't do it. I figured I was gonna have to stay there the rest of the night."

Klausing might have done just that had he not realized that the solution to his predicament was right there at his feet.

"I finally took the rubber floor mats out of my car and I put one under each rear wheel. I would inch the car forward maybe five feet before the mats would slip and fly. I'd have to put the brake on and go back, find the mats and put them underneath the wheels again. It was really frustrating to work that hard."

Fortunately, Klausing's hard work was not in vain. Stone signed with Rutgers.

Oh, Brother!

Klausing recalls a memorable recruiting trip he made to Shelby, N.C., during his tenure at West Virginia. Not so much for the player he signed, but for the two he didn't.

"We were recruiting a kid by the name of Marcus Mauney. While I was down in Shelby I met his neighbors--the Bibby brothers. One was a basketball player at UCLA and the other was a baseball pitcher.

"This kid we were after, everyone said he was the best athlete to ever come out of Shelby. I said, 'If he's as good as the Bibby brothers, I'm getting a great athlete.' And he was a great football player."

Mauney just didn't quite measure up to what the Bibbys accomplished. Henry played on three consecutive national championship teams as an All-American at UCLA (1970-72), celebrated another title as a rookie with the New York Knicks and played nine seasons all told in the NBA. Jim spent 12 seasons in the major leagues. He pitched for the world champion Pittsburgh Pirates in 1979 and threw a no-hitter against Oakland in 1973 while a member of the Texas Rangers.

Guilty of Kidnapping

One of the favorite techniques of college recruiters is referred to--affectionately, of course--as kidnapping. And one of the coaches guilty of kidnapping was Charles L. Klausing.

He recalls one such incident from his days at WVU.

"We had a great junior-college football player that we wanted by the name of Brian Chiles. We needed a big fullback and Brian was the best fullback prospect in the country. We had him convinced to go to West Virginia.

"Garrett Ford, one of our assistants, did what we called

kidnapping. For two days before the national signing date, Garrett put him up in his hotel room in the town where he was going to school [Dover, Del.] and registered under an assumed name.

"The main competition for Brian was Georgia Tech. The Georgia Tech coaches were looking all over for Brian. His teammates told the Georgia Tech coaches that a West Virginia coach had him hidden at a hotel in town.

"They called all the hotels in town, but there was no Garrett Ford registered, no Brian Chiles registered. The Georgia Tech coaches weren't dumb, so they called Garrett's wife back in Morgantown. They told her they needed a new running backs coach at Georgia Tech, that they were interested in Garrett and that they needed to get in touch with him."

It was a devious ploy to locate Ford and, hence, Chiles. The Tech coaches were only 50 percent successful in their mission.

They found Chiles, all right, but they didn't sign him. He wound up lugging the football at West Virginia--just as Ford had done several years before.

Big Problem, Small Solution

The Mountaineers landed wide receiver Danny Buggs--a future WVU All-American--with a little help. Emphasis on the word little.

Klausing and Bowden had stopped off in Sumter, S.C., to make a last-ditch effort to recruit quarterback Freddie Solomon, who ultimately signed with the University of Tampa. They planned to fly to Atlanta on a private plane the next day to sign Buggs.

"We get up the next morning and I run down to our rental car, put our suitcases in the trunk and close the trunk. I run around to the front door and I realize I have no keys.

"I go back up to the room and I said, 'Bobby, I pulled a boner. I locked the keys in the trunk of the car.' This is like 6 a.m. and we're to sign Danny Buggs at 8 a.m. in Atlanta. It's about an hour by plane from Sumter to there."

Bowden moaned and decided to return to bed before his day got worse.

"I go over to the lobby of the hotel where we're staying and I'm telling the desk clerk my problem. A bellboy comes up and says he could get the keys out for me. He takes a hangar from the coat rack, we go out in the parking lot and in five seconds he has the car door open. He jumps in the back seat and he starts pulling all kind of padding out.

"Finally, he says, 'Uh-oh. There's bars in the back seat. I can't reach the keys.' Then he says, 'Don't worry, I have a buddy who'll get them for you.'

"He goes over to Room 101 and he knocks on the door and out comes a midget--a dwarf--about three feet tall. He goes over to the car, gets in, squirms his body, gets between the bars and grabs the keys.

"At 6:15 I'm waking Bobby up and saying, 'Let's go, we can still make the appointment with Danny Buggs.' "

The Mountaineers signed Buggs a few hours later--thanks to a big assist from a little helper.

Desperately Seeking Solomon

Klausing had visited Sumter several times before the memorable keys-in-the-trunk incident. He was hot in pursuit of Solomon, "the greatest high school quarterback I've ever seen."

Klausing had been tipped off by South Carolina coach Paul Dietzel, under whom he had worked at West Point.

"I went to a Sumter High School game early in the season and there were about 2,000 fans in the stands. I went to a game later in the year and every seat was taken. There were about 12,000 people in the stands.

"Everybody was telling me, 'Come see Freddie run. See Freddie run.' When he dropped back to pass his coach would hope that everybody would be covered because Freddie would scramble and no one could get him. He was one of the greatest scramblers I've ever seen.

"Bobby and I thought we had Freddie coming to West Virginia. He had promised me he was gonna sign, but I guess someone from Tampa had influenced him and he was gonna go there instead. Freddie told us he was gonna spend a year or two at Tampa and then go to the Canadian Football League and make a lot of money."

He did make a lot of money, but not in the CFL--and not as a quarterback. The Miami Dolphins drafted Solomon in the second round in 1975 and converted him into a wide receiver. He spent 11 seasons in the NFL, the last eight with the 49ers, for whom he played in Super Bowls XVI and XIX, both San Francisco victories.

On a Wing and a Prayer

Given all the trips--by highway and by air--that Klausing made in his years as a recruiter, some missed connections were inevitable. For example, he'll never forget a flight he made to Welch, W.Va., a town at the extreme southern end of West Virginia, during his time at WVU.

Klausing and his pilot, Raymond Dellagatti, never reached their destination. In fact, they wound up in another state.

"Probably 250 days out of 365 there's fog in southern West Virginia. We're flying down to Welch to sign a boy and we're close to Welch, but the fog is so bad Raymond can't land.

"Finally he says, 'Chuck, there's no way we can get into Welch. Where do you want to go?' I said, 'Well, what are our options?' 'It's either Charleston or Roanoke, Va.' I said, 'Which is closest to Welch?' He says 'Charleston.' So I said, 'Let's go to Charleston.' "

Dellagatti swung the plane back north, toward Charleston, 65 miles away. A few minutes later he relayed more bad news to Klausing.

"He says, 'I just got Charleston on the radio and they have fog. We don't have instruments to land. We're not gonna be able to go there. And now I'm running out of fuel.' I said, 'Well, let's go to Roanoke.' "

Dellagatti again changed direction and headed for Roanoke, about 95 miles to the east.

"We're flying toward Roanoke and it's getting sunny and we're gonna have no trouble getting in. I finally asked Raymond, 'What if we had gone all the way to Charleston and it was foggy and we couldn't get in and we would've run out of fuel. What would we have done?'

"He said, 'I would've got on the radio and asked for instructions.' I said, 'You told me you didn't have instruments. What kind of instructions could they have given you?' And he said, 'They would've told me this--repeat after me: Our father, who art in heaven . . .' "

Technical Foul

Perhaps the most dazzling player Klausing ever tried to recruit became another in a line of outstanding running backs at Syracuse University. Unfortunately, Klausing was then recruiting for Army.

He thought he had Floyd Little locked up, having persuaded him to attend West Point through the assistance, oddly enough, of several baseball Hall of Famers.

That Little wound up playing *against* Army rather than *for* Army was due to a technicality--a technicality that Klausing likely cursed every time Little victimized the Cadets with a long run.

"Floyd Little was a great high school player out of New Haven, Conn. He did not have the grades to get into college from high school--actually, he was too old to play his senior year--so he went to Bordentown Military School in New Jersey and had a great season there.

"Then he took a postgraduate year and had another great season. He was the top recruit in the country at that time. I had New Jersey in my recruiting responsibility so I went down and visited Bordentown. I knew the coach there, Al Verdell.

"When I visited with him he told me Floyd Little was off limits. He had other guys that I could recruit, but he said Notre Dame had paid the way for Floyd to go to prep school and he was protecting him for Notre Dame. So I honored his wishes.

"When I went back to West Point we had a recruiting meeting and I talked about my prospects in New Jersey. When I finished, [head coach] Paul Dietzel asks why I was avoiding the best prospect in the country, Floyd Little. And I explained to him what Al Verdell had told me.

"He told me to go home and pack my bags and to spend the rest of the recruiting season trying to recruit Floyd Little, because he was the most important recruit we had. So I went back to Bordentown and I did some research. I found that there was a retired West Pointer on the staff and I went to visit him at his home and told him my problem.

"He said he would ask Floyd over to his quarters and I could talk to him there, which I did. The boy was very polite, but he didn't seem to show any great interest in West Point."

Klausing's hopes of landing Little were fading. But his ears perked up when the retired colonel mentioned that Little hitchhiked home to New Haven each weekend when he was dismissed Saturday at noon. Klausing could pick up the prized recruit and drive him to Connecticut, all the while extolling the virtues of West Point. As Little's weekend chauffeur, he was guaranteed a captive audience.

"This was legal at the time--today that would be an illegal contact. So I started getting closer to Floyd, started to understand some of his problems. But I needed something to get me over the hump.

"I remembered a man from Pittsburgh by the name of Mal Goode, who was the former editor of the *Pittsburgh Courier* [a nationally prominent black newspaper]. At that time he was a United Nations correspondent, I think for NBC.

"I told Mal my problem and he wanted to help me. He told me to bring Floyd to the Americana Hotel in New York City that Wednesday because the baseball writers were having their convention there. So I made plans to take Floyd to New York City to meet Mal Goode.

"We get there and he says, 'C'mon, we're going up to Branch Rickey's room. We get up to the room and who do we meet but Jackie Robinson. Jackie says to Floyd, 'You know, I broke the color line in baseball. It would be great if you would break the color line at West Point--be the first black football player.'

"Then Floyd met Elston Howard, the Yankee catcher. Elston told him how proud he was to wear the Yankee pinstripes and how great it would be for Floyd to wear that Army gray uniform, that he would be so proud, too. So with the help of Branch Rickey, Jackie Robinson, Elston Howard--Ernie Banks and Hank Aaron were helping me out, also--they talked Floyd into coming to West Point."

Klausing was ecstatic. He had apparently nabbed one of the most sought-after prospects in the land.

"We filled out the application papers, he took the physical exam and when he took the physical aptitude test, he broke the record for the highest score ever by a cadet entering West Point, set by Glenn Davis [the 1946 Heisman trophy recipient]. We got an appointment for him from a congressman and it looked like Floyd was going to be a West Pointer."

But bad news was forthcoming. News that would send Little on to another New York school instead.

"When we got his papers back from Washington, D.C., his appointment was denied. The reason: He was too old. You had to be less than 21 years of age. The class at West Point enters on the first Monday after the Fourth of July. Well, Floyd was born on the Fourth of July. And that Fourth of July was his 21st birthday."

So Little went to Syracuse, where he scored 46 touchdowns in 30 games and became a three-time All-American. He spent eight years in the NFL with the Denver Broncos and rushed for 6,323 yards--still the franchise record.

The Breakfast Guest

Klausing lost a recruit while at Army in 1963. He was lucky he didn't lose his life.

This unnerving incident took place at the Hotel Thayer in West Point, situated on the palisades overlooking the Hudson River.

"I took a recruit there. This particular morning he was to get a medical exam at the West Point hospital, so we went to the Thayer at 7:30, 8 a.m. for breakfast.

"I wanted to get a seat where you could look out at the Hudson through the picture windows. The maitre d' met me when we were coming in. He tried to put us in the back. I said, 'Look, I want this boy to get a nice view of the Hudson. Please take us down front.' "

If Klausing hadn't spoken up, he might never have come face to face with a gunman.

"We're sitting down front and a man came up--he wasn't dressed very neatly--and said to me, 'I'd like to have breakfast with you.' And I said, 'I'm talking business with this young man. It's a private affair and I don't think you'd want to be involved.'

"He goes back to his table and a moment later he comes back--he had a plate of eggs and he had a .45 revolver in his hand. He puts the revolver up to my head and again he said, 'I'd like to have breakfast with you.' I said, 'Sit down, you can have all the breakfast you want.'

"He puts the revolver down between he and I. I'm thinking to myself, Do I grab that? He was younger and bigger than me. I was afraid we'd get into a scuffle and someone might get hurt.

"Just about that time, I looked out the door. The waitress must have noticed something funny about this guy. There were about five military policemen ready to attack. They rushed in and they put the three of us up against the wall and searched us.

"The waitress is trying to tell them, 'Oh, this is Mr. Klausing and one of his recruits,' but they wanted to make sure what they were getting into.

"The military police told me later that there was a U.S. deputy marshal from New York that was delivering subpoenas in upstate New York, got caught in a snowstorm and stopped at the Thayer. The man with the gun made the trip to keep the marshal company.

"This man was mentally unbalanced, but the marshal said he was harmless. He was the kind of guy that hung out around police stations. This was right about the time of the Jack Ruby affair. And wasn't Ruby a guy who hung around police stations?"

Fortunately, the marshal's companion did not pull the trigger as Ruby did when President Kennedy's alleged assassin, Lee Harvey Oswald, was escorted past him in the basement of a Dallas jail on Nov. 24, 1963.

Klausing only lost a recruit. Not his life.

Backyard Bonanza

Klausing gained a reputation as a top-notch recruiter with his very first assignment. After John Bateman hired him at Rutgers University, he was told to search western Pennsylvania--his backyard, so to speak--for available prospects.

He found some, all right. Enough to fill a bus. Which is precisely how Klausing's first batch of recruits ended up traveling to New

Brunswick.

"I accepted the job at Rutgers and had planned to go up and get indoctrinated. But John suggested I stay back in Pittsburgh and recruit out of my home for the month of January. So I went around western Pennsylvania evaluating prospects.

"I picked up a carload of film and drove it to New Brunswick one weekend and the coaching staff looked at the film and approved 35 players from western Pennsylvania. Bateman said, 'Chuck, go back and arrange flights for those 35 boys to come in here for a visit.'

"One of the veteran coaches spoke up and said, 'John, we have a recruiting budget for five airplane trips.' We didn't have the money to fly them all to the university. So I made a suggestion. I told them there was a bus company in my hometown and, for the amount of money it would cost to fly in five recruits, they could bus these 35 players."

So the prospects crowded onto a Bacco Bus Line charter and endured a bumpy 300-mile trip to New Jersey. The travel accommodations were hardly luxurious, but they didn't seem to mind: 21 eventually signed with Rutgers.

Valley Boy

Klausing helped land his first college recruit even before he landed his first college job. He was coaching at Pitcairn High School in the early 1950s when Jack Hennemier, a Maryland assistant, came to him, pleading for help.

"School was almost out--this was in May--and he said, 'Chuck, I need a linebacker badly. Do you know of anybody?' I said, 'Jack, almost everybody's picked up.' He says, 'I've got to go back with a linebacker.'

"So I told him about a guy I saw when I refereed a game up near Kittanning. I told him he might be available because no other recruiter could find his way to Rural Valley. 'You go up to Rural Valley and there's a guy who's a split-T quarterback and linebacker.' And that's where Jack Hennemier got his lead to recruit Bob Pellegrini."

Pellegrini, overlooked by scouts at little Shannock Valley High School, developed into an All-America center-linebacker at Maryland, which compiled a 27-4-1 record and appeared in two Orange Bowl games--both losses to mighty Oklahoma--during his varsity career.

He wasn't overlooked again. The Philadelphia Eagles selected Pellegrini with the second pick in the 1956 NFL draft. He played linebacker on their 1960 championship team and later spent four seasons with the Washington Redskins.

Pellegrini was a 1996 inductee into the College Football Hall of Fame.

One in a Thousand

Stanley Hindman, who dreamed of a pro football career, was undeterred by odds that suggested his chances of not making the pros were 999-to-1. Not even Klausing could dissuade him. Good thing, too.

"When I was at West Point we recruited a kid from Mississippi by the name of Stanley Hindman. This is about my second year there. He's the biggest kid in the plebe class--6-5, 240 pounds.

"Well, a little first classman just drove him nuts--wouldn't give him anything to eat, disciplines him all night long. He gets tired of it and he gets homesick. He says he's going home.

"So I bring him over to the office and talk to him. I ask him, 'Why do you want to go home? Do you have a good reason?' His good reason was that he really wanted to be a professional football player.

"I gave him these statistics--like, of all the kids that are freshman football players in college, only one of a thousand are ever gonna make it in the NFL--but I couldn't persuade him to stay. He goes home to Mississippi, enrolls at Ole Miss and becomes an All-American [at guard]."

And a hot commodity. The NFL and AFL were then engaged in bidding wars for talent, which sent salaries skyrocketing. Hindman was a beneficiary of the interleague feud.

"He was a first-round draft choice of the 49ers, who signed him, I think, for a bonus of $50,000. So he drops me a telegram. It says, 'Coach, I'm that one out of one thousand.' "

The Academic Misfit

Klausing recruited players who won Rhodes scholarships, who made scientific breakthroughs, who became leaders in the military and in business.

But in 27 seasons as a college coach, he was bound to reel in a dud or two. One of his major college recruits--who shall, for obvious reasons, remain nameless--was as far removed from the players above as Pluto is from Mercury.

What's bewildering is how an institution of higher learning even accepted such an academic misfit.

"One of my experiences recruiting was a great high school quarterback who everbody wanted. But he finished 249 out of 250 in his high school class and scored a 600 on his SATs. I finally looked at something on his transcript that told me I didn't want him: In his senior year, out of 180 days of school, he was absent 89 days and late 91. That told me something about his dependability."

Over Klausing's objections, the player in question was offered a scholarship. He played regularly as a freshman and earned three letters at the school. Suffice to say he was never named to the Dean's List.

The Doctor Operates

When dentists dispense wisdom, it usually involves the value of regular brushing and annual checkups. But one dentist taught Klausing a recruiting lesson that left an indelible impression.

"Dr. [William] Skippy Hughes was an ex-Pitt basketball player who was a dentist and was the head basketball coach at St. Francis College. I got talking to Skippy and he taught me something very important.

"He had recruited Maurice Stokes to go to St. Francis. Stokes was the Most Valuable Player in the NIT tournament [in 1955, when he was a senior], so Skippy recruited a great basketball player."

Fact is, Stokes had his pick of dozens of more prestigious schools. But he settled on St. Francis--a small school located in out-of-the-way Loretto, Pa.--because of Hughes.

"The reason that he was able to recruit Stokes--it taught me a little bit of a lesson--he said a dentist has Wednesdays off. Most dentists play golf on Wednesday. He said, 'I drove every Wednesday to Westinghouse High School in Pittsburgh and I visited with Maurice Stokes. I outrecruited everybody because I showed my personal interest in him."

Stokes helped put St. Francis on the national map, leading Hughes' team to three 20-win seasons and two NIT appearances, including a fourth-place finish in 1955. He scored 2,282 points, at that time a school record.

Stokes spent three seasons in the NBA with the Rochester/Cincinnati Royals before he was struck down by post-traumatic encephalitis, which ended his career.

The Airport Shuttle

Klausing won over a reluctant recruit during his rookie year of college coaching, although he nearly lost his sanity in the process. Small wonder, given what he endured.

Then an assistant at Rutgers, Klausing was intent on delivering dozens of prospects from his native western Pennsylvania. One player was proving especially troublesome.

"I was recruiting a boy from West Deer, who promised to come in for a visit. I sent him an airplane ticket and he was to fly from Pittsburgh to Newark. It was an easy 30-minute drive for me from New Brunswick up to the airport."

But that was the only easy part of what was to be an grueling experience.

"The boy was supposed to come in on a 2 o'clock flight. I wait for the plane and he doesn't show. So I drive back to New Brunswick and tell the head coach, John Bateman, that our prospect hadn't come in. John said, 'Call his high school coach and find out what the problem is.'

"So I call the high school coach and he got the kid out of class. The kid on his own had decided he wasn't gonna go to Rutgers. Both the coach and I were disappointed. I told him, 'Look, I'm on the spot. I've been recruiting the boy and he made a promise to come in--can't you get him to come?'

"Well, the coach eventually talked the kid into coming. He told me the boy would be on an evening flight that would get into Newark at about 9 o'clock. So I drive up to Newark again and I check the board and there's no 9 o'clock flight. The 9 o'clock flight is over in New York City, at Idlewild.

"I realize that the plane's gonna land in a half hour and the drive to Idlewild is a good hour or so. By the time I get to Idlewild, the 9 o'clock flight had come in--I'm there at like 10--so I go up to the gate and check the passenger list. The kid wasn't on it.

"So I call the kid's home. The parents say, 'Well, he realized that that plane didn't come into Newark, so he changed to a flight that was to get into Newark at 11 o'clock. So I drive back to Newark. When I get there I check on the board and it says there's fog around Newark--the 11 o'clock flight couldn't land and was circling. They finally decided they could get into Idlewild. So here I go again to Idlewild."

By that time Klausing felt like the ball in a tennis match, bouncing back and forth.

"I finally picked up the youngster around midnight. I think it's an example of persevering. I learned what you had to do to recruit."

And *win over* recruits. The prospect signed with Rutgers.

CHAPTER 9
Foreign Affairs

Chuck Klausing is a coaching legend in Pennsylvania, but his fame extends far beyond the borders of his home state.

And his homeland, for that matter.

Since 1992 Klausing has made regular trips to Europe, teaching, coaching and conducting football clinics. Players and coaches in Austria, Belgium, the Czech Republic, Germany, Hungary, Italy, The Netherlands and Switzerland have benefited from his expertise and enthusiasm.

"My grandparents were from Germany and Sweden," says Klausing. "I've often wondered, What if they hadn't come to America? I probably would've been in Europe, hoping that some American would come over there to teach me to play football."

That's what motivates Klausing to return year after year. He delights in spreading his vast store of football knowledge overseas, much as Johnny Chapman once spread apple seeds across America. And like Chapman's seeds, football's popularity in foreign lands has taken root--no small thanks to Klausing.

A Tale of Tell

Klausing served as an advisory coach to Switzerland's national team at the European youth football tournament in Berlin during the summer of 1994.

He wound up soothing the spirits of players who had just absorbed a 70-0 thrashing with a story of a Swiss hero.

"When you go in to advise, what they hate is some American coach who comes in there and just tries to completely take over. I think I'm smart enough to know my place. The head coach was also the offensive coach and he didn't seem to want to get much advice.

The defensive coach was a sharp young kid who would take correction and constructive criticism, so I helped more defensively than I did offensively during this tournament.

"In our first game we played Sweden--we were the 10th-ranked team out of 10 and Sweden was probably ranked fourth--and they beat us, 67-0. Our offense never made a first down. The second game we're playing the Germans and, oh, man, are they tough. They're the second-ranked team. We got beat, 70-0.

"Near the end of the game a big German kid hits one of our players high in the face. Our kid jumps right up to him and pushes him back and the official sees the push and throws a penalty flag. So after the game the team meets in the middle of the field and the head coach is talking to the players in German, but I can almost understand what he's saying.

"He points to this little kid who drew the penalty and he says, 'You lost the game--go home.' The kid has to be at least 400 miles from home. He starts walking off the field. Well, the whole team rallies behind him and goes with him. I followed them and got them to stop.

"I told them the Swiss people are very smart. I even said they weren't dumb like Americans, always getting in wars. They liked that. I said, 'You know, I read a story about how courageous one of the noble Swiss people was, a man by the name of William Tell. A man who had so much courage that he put an apple on his son's head--and he loved his son very much--and he shot an arrow through the apple.'

"I told them it was example of great courage, that not many people would have the courage to do that. I said, 'What this young man did was wrong, and he should have kept his poise, but he didn't lose the game.' One of the kids jumped up and said, 'Coach, the only way we'll stay is if you be the head coach.' I said, 'Look, I'm not looking for a coaching job. But I'll stay and help if you stay.' "

The players stayed. And in a dramatic turnaround, the team that was trampled by its first two foes rose up and beat favored Norway in its final game.

The Swiss team, just like William Tell, had come through in the end.

Speaking in Tongues

Through his 46 years as a high school and college coach, Klausing touted the virtues of preparation. Ironic, then, that when he first ventured to Europe, Klausing did not make provisions to learn at least a few phrases of the local language.

In fact, he's had no formal foreign language training whatsoever. Yet when Klausing travels overseas, he packs playbooks, not Berlitz books. He manages just the same.

"In Europe, anyone 30 years old or less has learned English as a second language. Every once in a while there's a player who can't speak a word of English. So they'll go to a teammate and the teammate will explain what I want.

"It's the older players who have the most problems. One of the best players and one of the best coaches in Austria--he's a player-coach--cannot speak English. He's struggled. But I think he makes up for it with his playing ability. He's a leader by respect. He coaches the Salzburg Bulls."

Oddly enough, even those individuals not fluent in English seem to grasp the terminology.

"If I say, 'Defense!' and point over there, all the defensive players will go there. If I say 'Offense!' they'll all come running. Or if I tell them to blitz, they'll know what to do. But some of these same kids, I could say, 'Where can I get a soda pop?' and they won't know what I'm talking about. It's amazing.

"The surprising thing to me, I watched the Swiss team doing calisthenics before practice one day. I thought they would be counting in German: *'ein, zwei, drei . . .'* Instead they're going 'one, two, three . . . ' They copy everything we do."

Which might just explain the burgeoning popularity of American football in Europe.

Four Games a Week

In the United States, football teams generally play once a week, a fact that confounds Europeans. Klausing has been compelled to explain to curious Europeans why U.S. teams play so infrequently.

"A player from the Swiss team asked me, 'Why do you Americans not like to play football?' They played four games in seven days at the tournament. They think we must not like the game because we only play once a week. I think they're copying soccer, because soccer teams play a couple times a week."

Klausing can identify with the European mindset. In his younger days he often played several games a week.

"I loved to play so much--and I'm not the only one that ever did this--that while I was in college I'd play a college game on Saturday and go home and play a sandlot game on Sunday. And then there were teams that played on Wednesday night. I'd go to practice Wednesday afternoon and at 6 o'clock somebody would pick me up and drive me someplace to play on Wednesday evening. So there were times I played games on Saturday, Sunday and Wednesday.

"Some people say you're beating your body up too much when you do that. Actually, I think you get beat up less in a game than you do in practice. In practice a coach is trying to extend you, to tire you out so you're in better condition. Where in a game we rest between plays and at halftime and so forth."

Rest was obviously not a requirement for teams at the European tournament. While their American counterparts customarily have seven days between games, players there made do with one.

On the Trail of Jesse Owens

The highlight of Klausing's experiences in Europe had nothing to do with football, really. His biggest thrill was walking in the footsteps of a great Olympic champion--in track.

Klausing advised the Swiss national team at the 1994 European youth football tournament in Berlin, where Adolf Hitler welcomed the Olympians of the world in 1936. Some of the Olympians, at any rate. He treated certain members of the American contingent like outcasts.

"The games were played at the Olympic Stadium where Jesse Owens won four gold medals. In fact, I walked to the private box where Hitler did his thing."

His "thing" consisted of delivering the Nazi salute and congratulating the gold medalists--that is, until a son of Alabama sharecroppers and grandson of slaves won the 100-meter dash. Hitler snubbed Owens, a member of what the Nazis, with undisguised contempt, referred to as America's "black auxiliaries."

Owens was a thorn in Hitler's side throughout the Games, almost single-handedly refuting the myth of Aryan supremacy that Hitler was so eager to prove before the eyes of the world in Berlin. He followed his gold medal in the 100 with victories in the 200 and the long jump and then ran the lead leg for America's 400-meter relay team, which blew away the field while shattering a world record.

Klausing also swam in the Olympic pool during his stay in Berlin.

"They had big pillars with names engraved on them of past Olympic champions. Gee, Johnny Weissmuller's name was on one of them. I'm saying to myself, here I am, a guy from Pittsburgh and Weissmuller was from Windber, Pa."

Small world. Smaller than you might think, actually. While attending a cocktail party in Pittsburgh, Klausing had the pleasure of meeting Weissmuller, a five-time gold medalist (1924 and 1928) perhaps better known for his movie portrayal of Tarzan.

Chief of the Apaches

Klausing made his first trip to Europe in 1992, indirectly through the assistance of two members of his 1968 Boardwalk Bowl squad at IUP.

The man who once coached the Indians wound up helping to coach the Apaches. Only these Apaches were not led by Geronimo and did not roam the American Southwest--they were based in Florence, Italy. Klausing's involvement with the team came about purely by accident. In December of 1991, while he was head coach and athletic director at Kiski School, Klausing traveled to Toronto to coach in the third All-America Bowl, organized by former IUP wide receiver Dave Smith.

"He had the Florence Apaches come over to play against a Canadian all-star team in a preliminary game. I took Sam Patti, who's from Indiana, along with me. Sam has his doctorate in Italian. I think the Apaches had only one coach, so he and I would help.

"They were a lot of fun to coach. They were an adult team, 20 to 35 years of age. While I was there their owner asked me to come to

Florence and spend some time with them, which I agreed to do."

Klausing flew to Italy the following year. His contributions had an immediate impact on the Apaches.

"They were in the Group II league. Group I is the best league, Group II is the next best and there's even a Group III. The winner of the Group II league moves up to Group I the following year and the last-place team in Group I moves down to II [similar to many European soccer leagues].

"They jumped from a mediocre Group II team to the No. 1 team in the division. They moved up to Group I the next year and held their own there. So that was very satisfying, seeing such improvement in a team like that."

Stealing from the Germans

In a half century of coaching, Klausing has gained a deserved reputation as a thief. He's adept at stealing signals and detecting seemingly insignificant clues that tip off plays.

One of his victims was the German national youth team. Klausing was advising the Swiss squad at the time.

"I watched tapes of the German team and watched them in a game and I noticed their backs were tipping the plays. When they were going to run a sweep to the right, the right halfback cheated up and in to accomplish his block. When they were going to run a play to the left, the left halfback cheated up and in.

"When there was going to be a fullback running play, the fullback lined up deeper. So I knew by their adjustments who was gonna carry the ball and what direction they were going to go. Also, when they were going to have a running play, their linemen would raise their butts and put greater weight on their fingers. But when their linemen were going to drop back to protect the passer, their butts would sit lower. There would be hardly any weight on their fingers."

Thus forewarned, the Swiss defense was able to thwart the Germans much of the time. Unfortunately, Germany was such a superior team that Klausing's detective work alone wasn't enough to save the Swiss from a lopsided defeat.

A Bedtime Story

Klausing's first experience coaching in a foreign country occurred during his 10-year tenure as head coach at Carnegie Mellon University, when western Pennsylvania native Frank Kush enlisted his services.

He headed north of the border for two weeks during the summer of 1981 to help the new Hamilton Tiger-Cats coach, who had earlier transformed Arizona State into a powerhouse.

"The Canadian Football League preseason starts about June 1. They would have the rookies in for a week and then the vets would come in for a week before they started to play some exhibition games.

"Frank told me, 'We're gonna have a hundred rookies in camp and then the 50 vets will come in. I only have three full-time coaches. Will you come in and work for us for two weeks?' I said, 'Aw, I'd be happy to, Frank.' So I went up to Hamilton.

"Frank was very apologetic when I got there. He said, 'Chuck, I can't pay you too much.' I said, 'Whatever you pay me is fine.' I think I was only getting about $250 a week. Anyway, the first week everything goes real fine with the rookies. The next week the vets come in.

"They had a regular playbook and on the first page it said if you miss bed check it's a $200 fine. Frank hadn't taken bed check during rookie camp and the first two nights with the vets he doesn't take bed check. And, boy, the first night there were five vets out; the next night there were 25. And Frank knew it.

"He says to me, 'Chuck, here's a list of everybody's room and here's a pass key. I want you to take bed check. Be as tough and as accurate as you can be.' I go through there and I have 51 people missing bed check. So I give Frank the list.

"At the end of morning practice the next day he makes an announcement. 'Fifty-one of you missed bed check. That's a $200 fine. Coach Klausing is going to be standing outside the door for 15 minutes after practice. Anyone who gives him a $20 bill, the $200 will be forgotten.'

"He let me keep those $20 bills. I made only $500 coaching for two weeks, but I made over a thousand dollars for taking bed check."

Prisoner in Vienna

Klausing was coaching in Austria when he was held prisoner for several hours--by a locked door. He can laugh now at the experience, but mirth--like an escape route--was impossible to find at the time.

"I was staying in a nice, clean apartment in a tough district of Vienna. My host would drop me off there in the evening and I'd go up to my room. It wasn't a part of the city that I would go out at night in.

"On the inside of the door was a twisting-type lock and, boy, it was three times as wide and three times as long as a normal latch. So I twisted it and double-locked the door. I got up the next morning and I planned to go sight-seeing in downtown Vienna. I had the day off, so no one was coming that day for me.

"Well, I tried to open the door and it wouldn't open. I was sure I was gonna be there all day. I didn't know how I was gonna get out. I thought about breaking a window and jumping, but I was three stories up. And these were high stories. The first floor was a Chinese restaurant. So I was worried."

Especially since Klausing had no telephone with which to summon assistance. In addition, there were only two other apartments on the third floor, so rescue by a neighbor was unlikely.

"There was a narrow window to the side of the door that had bars on it, so I opened it up. There was no way you could get out that way.

"Finally a little old Austrian lady came by. She knew I was in trouble. I'm dangling the keys and telling her to try the keys in the door. She tried them but couldn't get them to work.

"I asked her if she spoke English and she said '*Nein.*' I finally said the word telephone [*Telephon* in German], which she understood. So I wrote the number of my host on a sheet of paper, gave it to her and she said, '*Ja.*' She goes and calls him and comes back and says, 'Coming, coming,' something to that effect."

His rescuers came, all right--armed with a sledgehammer. They shattered the lock and released the captive Klausing from his "prison" in Vienna.

Zone Coverage

American football is still fairly new to Europeans, who grow up following another kind of football--the game known as soccer in the United States. Even so, players on the Continent sometimes show more good sense than Americans.

"I'm out in pre-game practice one time and it's pouring down rain. In the States we would stay out there and keep warming up once we started, but the players in Europe ran off the field.

"They stayed in the locker room until about one minute before game time. And when they came out they had beach umbrellas. They'd sit on the bench, open up the beach umbrella and seven or eight kids would huddle under it. They just might be smarter than we are."

Call to Arms

Finland was the birthplace of perhaps the premier distance runner of all time, 12-time Olympic medalist Paavo Nurmi, but in recent years the nation has specialized in producing javelin champions.

Arto Harkonen and Tapio Korjus won Olympic titles at Los Angeles and Seoul, respectively, Heli Rantanen captured the women's gold medal at the Atlanta Games, Seppo Raty and Kimmo Kinnunen won top honors at the World Track & Field Championships in 1983 and 1987, respectively, and Tiina Lillak claimed the world women's title in 1983.

Turns out those good arms can be put to use on the football field, too, as Klausing discovered during one of his overseas sojourns.

"All the kids in Europe throw the ball differently than they do here. We teach players to rotate the thumb down as they throw a football, but kids in Europe like to sail a football. They turn the thumb up. They get a spiral, but they have no control of the football.

"Well, when I was in Berlin I ran into a quarterback from Finland--his first name was Pietro--who played for the Helsinki Roosters. He had one of the most beautiful throwing motions, the strongest arm, the quickest release of any young quarterback I've seen.

"I asked Pietro one day how he developed that throwing motion.

He told me it was exactly like the one used in the javelin throw. It seems he was a world-class javelin thrower.

A Masterpiece 'Vanishes'

Klausing and his wife have visited many popular tourist spots during their travels through Europe. Joann Klausing is invariably armed with a camera and has focused on numerous sights through her viewfinder.

But her flair for photography resulted in a rather unsettling experience in Italy.

"The main cathedral in Milan [the Duomo] is the second largest in the world. It's old--built to last a lifetime. We're walking in that cathedral when we bump into Mario Russo, a coach from Wisconsin who was there coaching the Milan team.

"After we exchanged greetings, he asked what we were doing. I said, 'Aw, we're just doing some sight-seeing.' He said, 'Can I take you and show you some things?' "

Russo graciously acted as the Klausings' tour guide, escorting them around Milan, a city of 1.5 million. One of their stops was at the Monastery of Santa Maria delle Grazie, where Leonardo da Vinci painted his famous fresco, the *Last Supper*, between 1495 and 1497.

Klausing hints that something supernatural occurred there.

"The remarkable thing, my wife's a great picture taker. Everybody who knows her says that she's the best camerawoman that they've ever run into. She watches how she takes photos and watches the background and everything.

"She said, 'Aw, I've just got to get a picture of the *Last Supper*.' And she took a picture. Then we see a sign: Please do not take photographs.

"We get home and we get our photos back. I think her camera had 36 shots on a roll. Well, 35 pictures came out perfectly. One is a blank--it's the picture of the *Last Supper*. Now what caused that picture to be blank?"

A 'Role' in Desert Storm

Klausing's most interesting foreign experience involves a country he's never even visited. One he's not likely to visit, either.

"I buy about 1,500 T-shirts each year that I give out to kids that come to my summer camps. I've been running these camps since 1954, so a lot of T-shirts are out there someplace with my name on them."

One even turned up in Iraq. On an Iraqi soldier.

"A high school coach from around the Greensburg area--he had been to my camp--told me this story. He was with a National Guard outfit that got called up during Desert Storm. They're going through the desert and the Iraqi soldiers are coming out of their pillboxes with their hands in the air, surrendering. The Americans were coming through with flame throwers and I guess they got scared.]

"These soldiers weren't what you'd call front-line troops. So one guy comes out of the pillbox with a pair of Bermuda shorts on and a white T-shirt. And the white T-shirt had 'Chuck Klausing's Wing-T Football Camp' on it. This coach goes up to the guy and he says, 'Can you speak English?'

"He says, 'Yes, I'm an American. My parents are Iraqis from Baghdad. I was over here visiting my parents when the war broke out. I was at a grocery store and the military was enlisting troops. They were just grabbing anybody off the street and giving them a rifle and saying, 'Get on the truck, you're going to the front.' I was afraid to tell them I was an American. This is how I was dressed.'

"This coach asked him, 'Where did you get the T-shirt?' He says, 'I'm from Canton, Ohio, and my son went to a football camp over in western Pennsylvania. And I wear his T-shirts at times. This is my son's T-shirt.' "

CHAPTER 10
Finding Utopia

In 1986, Chuck Klausing bid adieu to coaching--or so he thought--following a disappointing 5-5-1 season as Mike Gottfried's assistant at Pitt. But retirement lasted about as long as a sumo wrestler's diet.

The man who had worked his magic at Braddock, IUP, West Virginia and Carnegie Mellon found a new place to coach: Utopia.

That's what he called Kiski School. Klausing, long the tireless recruiter, wound up at Kiski because headmaster John Pidgeon turned the tables and, in effect, recruited *him*. Klausing didn't need much convincing to pack his bags for Saltsburg.

"When I announced I was leaving Pitt, I had six job offers the next day," he recalls. "Three of them were in college and three were offers to be athletic director and head football coach at large Quad-A high schools. None appealed to me."

Then Pidgeon called. He extolled the virtues of Kiski--the tradition, the academic standards, the focus on developing well-rounded individuals, even the pastoral beauty of the 400-acre campus--and invited Klausing for a visit.

"We sat down and, boy, Kiski sounded like Utopia to me," says Klausing. "I think Kiski has a very idealistic philosophy of athletics that I've always believed in. Every kid plays three sports. I've always been for the all-around athlete. It just seemed like the perfect place."

So perfect, in fact, that Klausing delayed retirement for seven years to coach there.

The Project

Danny Freiburger's rags-to-riches saga is one of Klausing's fondest memories from his tenure as the Cougars' football coach and athletic director.

A gawky quarterback with an Ichabod Crane physique and absolutely no football experience when he arrived at Kiski, Freiburger capped his career with a perfect performance.

"I'm starting preseason practice one year and there's a young man 6-foot-5, 160 pounds, skinny as a rail. He wants to play quarterback. He looked fairly athletic, but I had two quarterbacks who had been around our program for two or three years, so I figured this boy was going to be a third-string quarterback.

"I asked him, 'How much football have you played?' He said, 'Coach, I've never played football before.' In high school he had mono as a sophomore, his junior year he had a liver disease similar to mono and his senior year the coach didn't want him to play football.

"So in practice he was hardly getting a snap, just watching what the other guys were doing. We play our first two games and I tried each of the other two quarterbacks, but neither of them were coming through. Danny could throw the ball pretty well, so we decided we were gonna try him.

"The first game he gets in, on the first play, he goes up behind the right guard rather than the center to take the snap. He calls the signals and the ball goes on the ground. So I send in another play and he gives it to the team. This time, fortunately, he goes up behind the center. But he never calls the signal and the team jumps offside.

"I call timeout and I go out on the field and I ask the kids, 'What's wrong, what's happening here?' One of the players says, 'Coach, you're sending in the plays, you better start sending in the starting count, too. This guy doesn't know enough to be able to give us a starting count.' "

Klausing tried to calm his quarterback as best he could. Freiburger eventually shook off his first-game jitters and began playing like a seasoned veteran.

"After that Danny looked pretty decent. He threw a touchdown pass in that game and became our starting quarterback. And in the last game of the season he completed 12 of 12 passes for four touchdowns."

Kiski clobbered Shady Side Academy, 28-0.

Klausing mailed a tape of Freiburger to University of Miami quarterbacks coach Gary Stevens, now the offensive coordinator of the Miami Dolphins. Stevens was duly impressed, but he had already recruited his quota of quarterbacks. So he forwarded the film to Southern Methodist coach Forrest Gregg, who liked what he saw and offered Freiburger a scholarship.

By the time he finished at SMU, Freiburger had passed for 3,769 yards--he's ranked fifth on the school's all-time list, just ahead of "Dandy" Don Meredith--and established an SMU record for consecutive passes thrown without an interception (125).

Perhaps most impressive, Freiburger led the Mustangs to a 5-6 record in 1992, their best since the NCAA levied the so-called death penalty against the school in 1987 for an assortment of misdeeds. He's now an analyst on SMU radio broadcasts.

Klausing still marvels at Freiburger's metamorphosis from unheralded prep schooler to record-breaking collegian.

"He had a great career at SMU, was signed by the Philadelphia Eagles and seemed to have the Eagles made until they got Bubby Brister as a free agent. I think they wanted to go with a more experienced backup quarterback. But it's still amazing to me. How many times does somebody coach a senior in prep school who's playing for the first time and then is good enough to start for a major-college team?"

Near Miss on Morris

Klausing nearly had an opportunity to coach a one-time member of the Pittsburgh Steelers, a Texas Tech product who played against Freiburger in college.

"Two years after Danny goes to SMU, Forrest Gregg's son calls me. He says, 'I've got a great big running back for you. He'll scare everybody.' His brother was a wide receiver with the Chicago Bears, an ex-SMU football player named Ron Morris. This kid was a great high school player in Texas who went by the name of 'Bam.'

"So we could have had Bam Morris in our backfield. His brother paid his admissions fee, but they [Kiski administrators] looked at the boy and didn't feel they could help him. If they don't think they can help raise a kid's SAT scores enough, they'll reject him."

Morris went on to play for Texas Tech, where he rushed for 3,545 yards and 37 touchdowns in three seasons. He gained a Southwest Conference-record 1,752 yards in 1993, eclipsing the standard set in 1977 by Heisman trophy recipient Earl Campbell of Texas, then signed with the Steelers.

Morris was the leading rusher in Super Bowl XXX, gaining 73 yards on 19 carries and scoring a touchdown in a losing cause. He now plays for the Baltimore Ravens.

All in the Family

The highlight of Klausing's stay at Kiski was quite possibly winning the Interstate Prep School League championship in his final season--with his daughter Patti's son leading the way.

Jeff Simmons, a senior who started the 1993 season as the Cougars' No. 2 quarterback, directed Kiski to a 33-8 win over Shady Side Academy, wrapping up a 7-1 season--and his grandfather's illustrious coaching career. Klausing was thrilled that Simmons played a prominent role in the Cougars' run to the conference title.

"Jeff wanted to be the quarterback, but he was always the No. 2 man. We had the quarterback from the year before back and he had a year's experience, so Jeff sat on the bench [he did start on defense, at safety]. This kid could throw and he could run better than Jeff could ever hope to.

"But at halftime of the first game he tells us he's having knee problems. The doctor couldn't find anything wrong, but the kid didn't seem like he wanted to play in the second half. So we played Jeff. And he played so well that we never wanted to change."

The result was a championship season--the last of many in Klausing's 46-year coaching career.

Crime and Punishment

One of Simmons' roommates during his time at Kiski later gained notoriety for something that happened half a world away, in the tiny Asian republic of Singapore.

Michael Fay, charged with spray-painting cars and other acts of vandalism, found himself at the heart of a controversy that focused scrutiny on Singapore and what some termed its draconian criminal justice system.

Fay was sentenced to six lashes with a rattan cane, blows that quite often leave permanent scars. While some in the international community applauded Singapore for its crackdown on crime, many others expressed outrage over what they considered a brutal form of punishment.

President Clinton and others appealed for leniency, which prompted officials in Singapore to reduce the number of lashes to four. The sentence was carried out May 5, 1994.

The portrayal of Fay as a vandal and a troublemaker doesn't jibe with the picture Klausing has of him.

"Michael Fay, when I first met him, was a freshman at Kiski. He was Jeff's roommate then. We met his parents--they were real nice and so was Michael. I drove a van to church every Sunday and he rode with us. He seemed like a good young boy.

"He went out for football and played on the freshman team. He came out as a sophomore, too, but then he left school. I think the reason he left, his parents were divorced and his mother married a man from Singapore. So she took him to Singapore, where he got into trouble.

"My wife and I felt that maybe he fell in with the wrong crowd there and was in the wrong place at the wrong time. We just could not imagine him getting involved in something like that. He seemed to be a model citizen at Kiski."

Kiski's Gridiron Greats

Klausing played and coached at a number of schools that boast of superior football traditions. Penn State, Pitt, Army and West Virginia come immediately to mind, but the list certainly wouldn't be complete without Kiski.

The program was once a colossus on the national scene, its name as familiar to followers of football as any of those listed above. Kiski was especially prominent during the period between the two world wars--the school's halcyon era--when Latin teacher Jimmy Marks turned out future collegiate headliners in assembly-line fashion.

According to a story that appeared long ago in *The Boston Herald,* "Marks is rated, particularly by the Pennsylvania college coaches, as a man who can deliver football men to college with a fine grounding in the gridiron game and its many offensive and defensive niceties."

Perhaps the most notable player Marks "delivered" was Harry Stuhldreher, a 1921 graduate who quarterbacked Notre Dame's national championship team of 1924. Stuhldreher and his three backfield mates--fullback Elmer Layden and halfbacks Jim Crowley and Don Miller--were christened "The Four Horsemen" by legendary sportswriter Grantland Rice following a 13-7 Fighting Irish victory over Army at New York's Polo Grounds on Oct. 18, 1924.

Rice's famous lead in the next day's *New York Herald-Tribune* reads as follows:

> "Outlined against a blue-grey October sky, The Four Horsemen rode again. In dramatic lore they are known as Famine, Pestilence, Destruction and Death. These are only aliases. Their real names are Stuhldreher, Miller, Crowley and Layden."

The irony is that Stuhldreher went to Notre Dame--not yet a national powerhouse--almost as a last resort. That's the story he told Klausing.

"I got to know Harry when he was superintendent of the Edgar Thompson steel mill in Braddock [where Klausing coached the Braddock High School team to a 53-0-1 record between 1954 and 1959].

"He told me a story that's been verified by a number of his teammates at Kiski. Jimmy Marks said to him, 'Harry, it's a shame you're so small, that some major college won't take you. But I have a friend who's coaching at a little Catholic school out in Indiana and I'm gonna send you to him.' "

Knute Rockne welcomed the undersized (5-7, 151 pounds) quarterback with open arms. During Stuhldreher's three seasons on the Notre Dame varsity, the Irish posted a 27-2-1 record, defeated a vaunted Stanford team in the 1925 Rose Bowl and won the first of their 12 national championships.

The Kiski Rose Bowl

Klausing is fond of pointing out that 12 Kiski School grads--Stuhldreher among them--are members of the College Football Hall of Fame.

Back in the '20s and '30s, Kiski products were sprinkled through the lineups of top-flight teams from coast to coast. There's no better example of the school's national prominence than the Stanford-Columbia Rose Bowl of 1934, which featured five of Marks' former players.

In fact, both teams' captains once wore Kiski colors. Cliff Montgomery, a 1930 grad who was later enshrined in the Hall of Fame, led the Lions to a 7-0 victory.

Klausing met Montgomery and many of Kiski's grid greats either during his travels around the country or at the school's centennial celebration in 1988.

"Cliff went to Kiski as a postgraduate to get his grades up. He didn't get a scholarship offer out of high school--no one wanted him. Lou Little was the coach at Columbia at the time and he was a friend of Jimmy Marks, so Cliff wound up going to Columbia.

"When they got invited to the Rose Bowl, he was their star. Cliff was the tailback in the single wing--he was the runner, he was the passer, he was the kicker. And he was their captain. The captain of the Stanford team, [Robert] "Bones" Hamilton, was from Kiski, too."

Three other Kiski graduates played that day in Pasadena: Joe Ferrara for Columbia and James "Monk" Moscrip and Alf Brandin for Stanford. Moscrip eventually joined Stuhldreher, Montgomery and Hamilton in the College Football Hall of Fame.

'Bones' and Bob Hope

Montgomery briefly suited up for the Brooklyn Dodgers during the fledgling days of the NFL, when the league played second fiddle to the college game and salaries were scarcely a fraction of what they are today. Hamilton could have joined his fellow Kiski grad in the pros, but he passed on the opportunity.

Good thing, too. At least judging by a story Klausing likes to tell.

"Back then there was a Stanford connection with Kiski: Pop Warner, who was the coach at Stanford [he had previously guided Pitt to national championships in 1915, 1916 and 1918], was a friend of Jimmy Marks. So Bones wound up going to Stanford.

"Well, he was picked to the All-America team. Bob Hope had the All-America team on his radio program and afterwards he asked the players, 'Do any of you play golf?'

"Bones had learned to play golf at Kiski and he got to be pretty good. So they play and Hope was just amazed how great a golfer Bones was. He says, 'Bones, I'm playing in a member-guest tournament next week. Would you be my partner?' Bones says yes, he plays with him and they win the tournament at Hope's country club.

"So Hope says, 'Bones, what are you going to do when you graduate?' He says, 'Well, I was drafted by the Chicago Cardinals and I can play for them for $500 a game.' This was at a time when other people were getting about $75 a game.

"Hope says to him, 'Bones, you could make more money working for me. I'm going to buy a Plymouth dealership. I want you to be the manager and I'll give you the option to buy the business.'

"Well, Bones started to sell cars. Pretty soon it became a Chrysler-Plymouth dealership and later it became Rolls Royce . . . in Beverly Hills. He owned the largest automobile dealership in the state of California. Bones married one of the Swanson girls of the Swanson frozen foods family. And eventually he bought a home in Palm Springs."

Small wonder Hamilton never regretted turning his back on the NFL.

The Vow Boys

No team had appeared in three consecutive Rose Bowls until Stanford accomplished the feat from 1934 through 1936. Hamilton played on all three of those teams.

"When Bones was a freshman at Stanford, the freshman team went undefeated. So he says to the other freshmen, 'Let's vow that we beat Southern Cal three straight years and that we play in the Rose Bowl three straight years.' They were called the Vow Boys, the Stanford team. And they did beat Southern Cal three straight years and they did play in the Rose Bowl three straight years."

Stanford won the third game against SMU after losing the first two to Columbia and Alabama. That Alabama team featured a future college and pro Hall of Fame end named Don Hutson.

Incidentally, the Crimson Tide's other end later gained some measure of fame, too: Paul Bryant, better known as Bear.

The 'Burger King

Alex Schoenbaum, a long-time member of Kiski's Board of Trustees and a benefactor of the school, played football at Kiski and later at Ohio State (1936-38).

But he's better known for launching a revolution of sorts in America. Like the one sparked by a skirmish at the bridge in Concord, Mass., this revolution also had a lasting impact on millions.

"While he was at Kiski he was real hustler. He would go buy a loaf of bread and get some lunch meat and make sandwiches and sell them to the students in the dormitory at night.

"Later he invented the double-decker hamburger and started a hamburger joint. He changed his name a little bit and called the place Shoney's."

Instead of collecting dimes from fellow students, Schoenbaum was soon counting five-figure profits. Shoney's eventually expanded into a national chain that today encompasses 862 outlets in 34 states.

Schoenbaum's days of peddling sandwiches for pocket change were history.

"He recently sold the Shoney's business for, I think, $400 million."

Visitors from the North

During the fall of 1995, a Canadian team from outside of Toronto, Brampton Centennial Secondary School, played a regular-season game at Kiski School. But that wasn't the first visit to Kiski by a team from north of the border.

When Klausing coached the Cougars, he worked out an exchange program with several Canadian schools, including Trinity College School of Port Hope, Ont., alma mater of newscaster Peter Jennings and former NHL coach Roger Neilson.

"Our classes started around Sept. 15, so practice wouldn't start until Sept. 1. We had no one to scrimmage in the preseason because the PIAA [Pennsylvania Interscholastic Athletic Association] schools had already started their season. So I started to make arrangements with Canadian prep schools.

"I'd say, 'We'll bring you down to our place for a week and we'll practice for an hour and then we'll scrimmage each other for an hour. All it's gonna cost you is gasoline for your bus because we'll take care of your room and board.

"Then we'll go up to your place for a week. We'll do the same at your school.' Oh, they loved it. We did this for four or five years."

And just how did the teams resolve one of the biggest rules differences between American and Canadian football--the extra player favored by Canadian teams?

"When our offense was on the field, they took one guy off and it was 11 against 11. And then when they had the ball, they had 12 and we'd put an extra guy on the field and it was 12 against 12."

One of the Cougars' trips to Canada was especially memorable because of the unique housing accommodations.

"It was our turn to go to Trinity College School, but they had a problem because their dormitory was being remodeled. So they set up beds in the hockey rink for our team.

"At first our kids were a little disappointed, because they didn't have private rooms, but they ended up having one of the best times of their lives. They found hockey sticks, rolled up a piece of tape to make a ball and played hockey in this rink."

The Cougars merited praise for their creativity--and their good sense. They played only among themselves. They knew better than to challenge the Trinity players--Canadians reared on hockey--to a game.

The Son of Joseph

Klausing coached against Joe Paterno's Penn State teams when he was at West Virginia and Pitt and experienced nothing but heartache: zero wins in seven meetings.

When he retired as a college coach following the 1986 season, Klausing figured his days of dealing with Paterno were over. He was wrong.

"I got a phone call from Joe when I was coaching at Kiski. He told me his youngest boy, Scotty, needed a year or two at a boarding school and that he wanted him to play for me at Kiski."

So tackle Scott Paterno wound up playing two seasons for a coach whose teams had been dominated by his father's (composite score: 261-74).

"Scotty wasn't the most gifted athlete, but he was without a doubt one of the brightest kids I've ever coached. Also, something must have rubbed off from his dad because he was the smartest player on rules of any player I've ever coached. When I'd ask my team a question, something pertaining to rules, Scotty had the answer."

Unfortunately, his attention sometimes wandered when Kiski played on Saturday afternoons.

"Halftime of a game he'd be running to a phone, putting in a call to the State College Police Department, getting an update of the Penn State score. He was very loyal to his dad and I admired him for it."

The Round-Robin Game

One of the most memorable games during Klausing's seven years at Kiski School actually featured three teams.

Due to a mix-up, Penn Charter School of Philadelphia was scheduled to play both Kiski and Peddi, a New Jersey prep school, on the same day. But Klausing found a novel solution to the predicament.

"We had a home-and-home contract with Penn Charter. They

were to come to Kiski, we'll say, on Sept. 15. We get their schedule before the season and they have another game scheduled on Sept. 15. I had the contract in writing, so I sent them a copy. Their athletic director, who was also the coach, admitted he had made a mistake and scheduled Peddi on the same date I thought we were scheduled. He said he'd have to cancel the Peddi game because our contract was first.

"I said, 'Well, it's a shame that Peddi won't have a game.' This was like three, four weeks before the season started. I said, 'I'll tell you what we can do. Let's play a round-robin game. We'll come to your place for the second year in a row, but now you'll have to return two games to Kiski. Let's say we play you for a half, we take a two- or three-minute break, Peddi can be warming up, they come out and play us for a half while your players rest and then you can play a half with Peddi. The fans will see three halves of a game and we'll play a full game, you'll play a full game and Peddi will play a full game.'

"So that's what we did. We decided to score it like a [triangular] track meet. The fans loved it, the players loved it . . . everybody went home happy."

Especially the Cougars. They won by one of the strangest scores in football history: 7-6-0.

The T-shirt Gamble

Tom Klausing really went out on a limb in 1993. Then again, given his father's track record, maybe his T-shirt gamble was as much a sure thing as tomorrow's sunrise.

In the week leading up to the game that would cap Chuck Klausing's coaching career, Tom had a batch of T-shirts printed to commemorate the occasion. Under the heading "Chuck Klausing's Victory Tour," he included his father's record at each of his nine coaching stops.

Listed beside Kiski School were the numbers 29-22-4. Tom knew full well that win No. 29 would come about only if the Cougars prevailed against Shady Side Academy in the season finale. One misstep and those T-shirts were candidates for the trash heap. Fortunately, the game was decided early in Kiski's favor. Klausing got his first look at the T-shirts when players, family members and even fans donned them during an emotional post-game celebration.

"I didn't know anything about it. That was all Tom's doing. Everybody liked it, I'll say that. I was just glad that the record was accurate."

So was Tom Klausing. Otherwise he'd have lost his shirt.

CHAPTER 11
The Sunday Heroes

Chuck Klausing grew up in Wilmerding, not far from the birthplace of professional football. No, not Canton, Ohio. Pittsburgh, site of the first game to feature a paid player.

Former Yale All-American William "Pudge" Heffelfinger, an imposing specimen acknowledged as the premier player of his time, secretly accepted $500 to line up for the Allegheny Athletic Association of Pittsburgh in a Nov. 12, 1892, game against the rival Pittsburgh Athletic Club. Heffelfinger denied ever taking money, but he is regarded today as the first footballer to play for pay.

Lawson Fiscus and John Brallier, who rank sixth and seventh, respectively, on the list of earliest pros, were both products of IUP (known as Indiana Normal School back then), where Klausing coached for six seasons.

And like them, he had an opportunity to draw a paycheck as a professional football employee. The Pittsburgh Steelers offered Klausing a scouting position during his tenure at West Virginia, but he turned it down. Any regrets?

"No, not really," he says. "The money was very tempting and it would have opened up a lot of doors, more so in the administrative end. But I didn't want to be an administrator--I wanted to be a coach and a teacher. I've always been glad I did what I did."

This chapter focuses on professional football, ranging from the modern era back to 1920, when representatives of several teams gathered at the Jordan and Hupmobile Auto Showroom in Canton and formed the National Football League.

The Weekend Warriors

Klausing served as an assistant coach under Bobby Bowden at West Virginia during the 1970s and went to two Peach Bowls.

He nearly went to four Super Bowls instead.

Klausing was browsing through the lineups at a Steelers-Redskins game in 1973 when inspiration struck. His idea--certainly a revolutionary concept at the time--has since been adopted by all 30 NFL teams.

"I have a close friend in Art Rooney Jr. [the Steelers' vice president]. He used to invite me to sit in his box at Steeler games. One Sunday when the Steelers were playing the Redskins--this was when George Allen was coaching them--I was looking at the Steeler roster. After each name they would have D-1 or D-4 or D-9, to tell what round they were drafted in. There might have been one free agent and maybe another who came over in a trade.

"Then I looked at the Redskins' roster. There were a few players drafted, but, boy, you looked at the list and it was free agent, free agent, free agent, trade, trade, trade. The wheels started turning in my head. I said to Artie, 'How much money do you spend evaluating pro personnel?' They spent a lot of money evaluating college prospects. He said, 'Not a damn cent.'

"Well, I started thinking. Sometimes you're only one or two players away from having a good team and you can't wait for the next draft. George Allen would pick up a guy to fill a need. So I said, 'Maybe you ought to be evaluating pro talent the way you do college talent. You could have a scout in every pro city who could read the papers, watch tapes of that team, go to a game every Sunday and then write a report.'

"Artie calls me about two days later. He says he's talked to Dan [Rooney, the Steelers' president], who thought it was a good idea. He offered me a budget of $100,000, which was to include my salary. We were gonna call these scouts 'Weekend Warriors.' The next day I went up to meet with him and Dan and [head coach] Chuck Noll. I think the Steelers were the first team to have a pro scouting service. Now everybody in the NFL is big on pro scouting.

"Anyway, I went back to Bobby and told him about this offer.

Well, West Virginia matched my Steeler salary, so I decided to stay. I went up to Pittsburgh the next day and turned down the job with the Steelers.

"I passed up four Super Bowls."

See Jim Run

Bob Higgins, Klausing's coach at Penn State, figures in a tale about the early days of the NFL, when the legendary Jim Thorpe ran wild for the Cleveland Indians. Higgins was playing in 1921 for the Canton Bulldogs--Thorpe's old team--when he had a memorable encounter with the Sac and Fox Indian great.

"He tackled Thorpe and Thorpe gets up and says to him, 'All these people came to see Jim run. Why don't you let Jim run?' And Higgins said, 'You just try to come around my end again.' Next play Thorpe comes around end and barrels into him, knocks him over--knocks him out--and runs for a touchdown.

"Coming back after the touchdown, they line up for the kickoff and Higgins is still laying on the field. So Thorpe bends over, pats Higgins and says, 'Nice go, Hig. You let Jim run.' "

The Pride of Marquette

One of Thorpe's teammates with the Canton Bulldogs, Bob Shiring, hailed from Klausing's hometown of Wilmerding. Shiring, a center who tipped the scales in excess of 300 pounds, was good friends with Klausing's father, Chuck.

"My dad told the story about getting on the train and going down to Canton on a Saturday and meeting Jim Thorpe. He said the players would come in from all over the place. They would have two or three plays on a sheet of paper and they'd walk through them in a barroom. That's how they prepared for their big professional football games back then.

"My dad said they introduced the teams before the game. They would say, 'Jim Thorpe, Carlisle Indians,' and Jim Thorpe would run out on the field. And then they'd say, 'Tommy Davies, University of Pittsburgh,' and he would run out. They'd introduce the team and say what college you were from.

"They'd say, 'Bob Shiring, Marquette,' and he would run out on the field. They're going home on the train after the game and my dad says to his friend, Bob, 'Bob, it's not truthful saying that you went to Marquette--you never went to college.'

"Bob Shiring says to my dad, 'Chuck, where do you and I hang out at a couple nights a week?' My dad says, 'the Marquette Club.' Bob says, 'Well, that's where I got the name Marquette. So I'm not telling an untruth when I say I'm from Marquette.' "

Cash Crunch

Pro football has changed radically since the days of Thorpe, Higgins and Shiring. Nowhere has that change been more striking than the area of player salaries.

That point is illustrated by a story Klausing heard about former Geneva College standout Larry Bruno, better known today as Joe Namath's high school coach in Beaver Falls. Bruno once turned down a pro contract for a more remunerative offer: teaching high school students.

"Larry comes out of college--this was like 1946--and he tries out for the Pittsburgh Steelers. And he's making the team. On Aug. 17 he gets hired as the football coach at Monaca High School for, I guess, $2,400--$2,000 teaching, $400 coaching--and he leaves the Steelers.

"Well, the coach [Jock Sutherland] and Mr. Rooney go to see Larry. And Mr. Rooney says to him, 'Larry, you're gonna be our regular running back. Why are you leaving to take a high school coaching job?' And Larry says, 'Well, I always wanted to be a high school coach. That was my No. 1 goal in life. Plus, they're paying me more.' "

A Day with Lombardi

Klausing and Frank Cignetti--former and present IUP football coaches, respectively--worked together as assistant coaches at West Virginia for six seasons.

Every summer they would visit professional training camps, hoping to soak up knowledge they could utilize back at WVU. That's how Klausing came to spend a day with legendary coach Vince Lombardi, who led the Green Bay Packers to five NFL championships.

"We decided we wanted to see Lombardi, who was coaching the Washington Redskins then. They trained at Dickinson College in Carlisle. We get there at the start of morning practice and they had guards posted all around the field. Any coaches and fans had to stay in the bleachers. We couldn't see or hear what was going on.

"Frank got real disgusted. He said, 'The Eagles are practicing in Hershey. Let's go there.' I told him, 'No, I think I'll hang around here.' So Frank took the car and went to Hershey. The same thing happened in the afternoon practice. You couldn't get close enough to see or hear anything.

"After practice I ran into one of the Redskins' personnel people, Timmy Timerario, who used to coach at Penn with John Bateman [Klausing's boss at Rutgers]. I said, 'Tomorrow is a holy day of obligation and I want to go to mass. Can you tell me where the Catholic church is in town?' He tells me that at 7 o'clock the next morning they're having a private mass in Room 201, which is just two doors away from where I'm staying.

"I get up the next morning and go down to 201 at five minutes to 7. The priest is there and he asks me if I want to serve as the altar boy. So I say, 'Sure.' At one minute to 7, Vince Lombardi and a couple of his assistant coaches walk in.

"After the mass, I'm walking over to the dining hall, and Vince is walking ahead of me. He turned and waited until I caught up. He says, 'Hi, I'm Vince Lombardi.' I told him I was a college coach, that I was there to observe his practices. He told me how happy he was to have me there.

"Then he said, 'Do you want to have breakfast with me?' So we ended up having breakfast together. Then he asked me if I wanted to go to the quarterbacks meeting. Next thing I know I'm in the quarterbacks meeting with Sonny Jurgensen.

"We go outside later for practice and it's raining. I didn't have any rain gear, so Vince gets the equipment man to get me rain gear. He's riding a golf cart around the practice field and he says, 'Why don't you sit here with me?'

"I really had a great time that morning. In the afternoon it was the same thing. So Frank comes back from Hershey, looks out on the field and sees me there, riding around with Lombardi."

And was utterly flabbergasted.

"We're driving home later and he says, 'How in the world did you ever pull that off?' All I said was, 'Frank, did you go to mass this morning?' "

Scrambled Signals

Knowing the other team's signals does not always ensure success in the pros. *Thinking* you know the signals can bring even more disastrous consequences.

That was a lesson learned the hard way by a certain NFL coach, whom Klausing prefers not to identify.

"When I was at Carnegie Mellon, a friend of mine gets a head job in the NFL. He had heard that I had the ability to steal signals and decipher them. Most all the pro teams were using signals at that time. Since they have the radio system now, they don't have to do that.

"He sent me to a game that his upcoming opponent was playing. We took tapes of this particular team sending in their signals and I deciphered them. He played this team early in the season and beat them by a fantastic score, something like 50-7.

"Later in the year, with the same talent, he played the same team. Only by then they had changed their signals. So he didn't have the edge and he lost--by about the same score he'd won by earlier. That taught me what a difference knowing the signals can make."

Noll's First Practice

Following a 2-11-1 season in 1968, the Steelers fired Bill Austin and hired a new head coach, a long-time Browns assistant who was cut from a different cloth than his brethren.

Chuck Noll, imperturbable and undemonstrative, offered a stark contrast to most coaches, who would scream like Marine drill instructors and rage at even the most trivial of transgressions. Noll's calm demeanor made quite an impression on Klausing, a spectator at the Steelers' Latrobe training camp in 1969.

"I went to watch his first practice along with another football guy. It was the most unusual practice that we had ever observed. Almost every coach we'd ever seen was very vocal, especially the head coach.

"We go to the Steeler practice and you never heard Chuck Noll raise his voice. He would go up close to a player and you could see that he was discussing things with him. It was more of a businesslike discussion. We're riding back in the car and this guy says to me, 'Chuck, he will never win a game. There's no enthusiasm. He's not coaching.'

"I visited the Steelers camp and watched Noll many times after that and what I realized was he wasn't the kind of guy who would yell if you missed a tackle or you missed a block. The player knew that he missed the tackle or missed the block. Noll would go up to him and explain *why* he missed the tackle or missed the block.

"Once in a while he would get upset and be very vocal. And I think I realized something because of that. You know, if a guy's yelling all the time, it doesn't have much effect. But here was a guy who hardly ever yelled. So when he did yell, he really got your attention."

And the Steelers responded. Contrary to what Klausing's companion predicted, Chuck Noll did win some games in Pittsburgh--not to mention four Super Bowl trophies.

Diamonds in the Rough

Klausing and Dave Smith, the wide receiver who played for him at IUP and later started for the Steelers, joined forces in 1990 to stage the inaugural King All-America Classic, a matchup of major- and small-college all-stars.

Three subsequent games were played, with Smith organizing and promoting the event and Klausing assembling the talent and coaching the small-college squad. Their mission was to showcase players who, for a variety of reasons, were overlooked or underpublicized during their careers. Mission accomplished.

"We had 80 players in the first game. Of the 80 players that were in the Senior Bowl game that year, 62 got drafted. The East-West game, which had been in existence for 40-some years, had 52 players of their 80 drafted. The Hula Bowl had 49 players drafted and the Blue-Gray game had 44.

"Our game, playing for the first time, had 53 players drafted [24 others signed as free agents]. Here's the reason ours was so good: I only selected people that pro scouts had recommended."

By consulting the experts, Klausing discovered some hidden treasure: Bryan Cox of Western Illinois, now a linebacker with the Chicago Bears; Central State's Erik Williams (offensive tackle, Dallas Cowboys); Jacksonville State's Eric Davis (cornerback, Carolina Panthers); North Dakota State's Phil Hansen (defensive end, Buffalo Bills); Fred Barnett of Arkansas State (wide receiver, Miami Dolphins); Maine's Justin Strzelczyk (offensive tackle, Pittsburgh Steelers); and Eric Swann, who didn't even play college ball but now starts for the Arizona Cardinals at defensive tackle. The list goes on.

"We selected the kind of players who would not get invited to one of those other games--the Blue-Gray, East-West or Senior Bowl. A lot of those kids are in the NFL today. I visit two or three training camps every year and three or four players from every team will come up and remind me that I coached them in that all-star game."

High on Hugh

Klausing unwittingly unearthed another gem in 1994 as he was watching film of NAIA powerhouse Central State (Ohio) University, an upcoming IUP opponent.

"I'm looking at the tapes and they have a defensive end by the name of Hugh Douglas who is just beating up everybody he plays against. I look in the program and it says he's a junior, but one of the IUP coaches told me that he was a transfer who had actually played a year somewhere else and that this was his last year.

"So I called Tom Modrak, who had played for me--he's now the head of college scouting for the Steelers--and told him about this great defensive end at Central State. He looked at his records and said, 'Chuck, there's no report on anyone good enough to play pro football from Central State.' I said, 'Boy, you better look again.'

"I told him about Hugh Douglas, gave him his number, and he must have gone out and checked himself. He calls me back and says,

'Chuck, you're absolutely right. He's a real player and he *is* eligible for the draft. We'll be interested in drafting him.'

"Well, later that year I was talking with Rey Dempsey, who had played for me at Pitcairn. He was happy because he had been selected to coach the defense at the Hula Bowl, the college all-star game. I said, 'Boy, you ought to get a guy from Central State by the name of Hugh Douglas to play in the game.' So he requested him."

Smart move. Douglas, working against predominantly Division I players, harassed the West quarterbacks all game long and finished with four sacks.

"Hugh just dominated. I think that my recommending him to Tom Modrak and especially my recommending him to Rey Dempsey helped him to be a first-round draft choice."

The New York Jets selected Douglas with the 16th pick overall. Without the opportunity to display his skills in Honolulu, it's unlikely he would have been drafted that high.

Douglas paid immediate dividends with the Jets: He was a unanimous selection as the NFL's Defensive Rookie of the Year in 1995.

Finding Gold in South Dakota

These days, few players, no matter how tiny the school or how unheralded the program, escape the scrutiny of pro scouts--or talent hunters like Klausing. But not all that long ago, prospects could be easily overlooked.

Especially if they played in the backwaters of college football, far removed from the media spotlight. In Yankton, S.D., for example. That's where former All-Pro defensive end Lyle Alzado was discovered--quite by accident.

Klausing heard the story from Alzado himself, a coach at one of the camps he operated.

"We'd get the kids together and we'd tell stories at night. When he was a young football player out of New York, he went to the University of New Mexico to play. He got in trouble there--I don't know what he had done--but they wrote on his transcript, 'Don't accept him to any college in the country.' "

Alzado, his dreams of a major-college career dashed, was granted a second chance by little Yankton College, an NAIA school that played teams like Sioux Falls, Lea, Midland Lutheran, Dana and Westmar. The Greyhounds were so far removed from the Notre Dames, Penn States, USCs--even the New Mexicos--of the world that they didn't even take game films.

"He goes to Yankton and he's playing great football--he's dominating every football game he's in. He wanted to play pro football, but no scouts are coming to see him. Then one day there was a pro scout traveling through South Dakota and his car broke down."

That breakdown was Alzado's big break.

"The scout goes to a service station and they tell him its gonna take six to eight hours for the car to be repaired. He said, 'Well, I need to do some work. Is there a college near here?' There was a college nearby that they drove him to. And this college had films of their game against Yankton.

"Yankton did not even take films at that time. That's why Alzado was being passed over. This scout sees this player from Yankton just dominating everybody he plays against. And that's how he got drafted to play in the NFL."

Alzado played for the Broncos, Browns and Raiders, appeared in Super Bowls XII and XVIII and was named the AFC Defensive Player of the Year in 1978. He also took on three-time heavyweight champion Muhammad Ali in a memorable exhibition boxing match in 1979.

Speechless

Quarterback Terry Bradshaw, drafted first by the Steelers out of Louisiana Tech in 1970, arrived in Pittsburgh with a reputation as something of a backwoods country bumpkin. He did nothing to dispel that notion during one of his first public appearances in western Pennsylvania--a banquet where Klausing was to speak.

"Each year the Big 10 Conference of the WPIAL would put on a sports banquet at the Twin Coaches, about 30 miles south of Pittsburgh. It was a big affair where their all-star teams were honored. There would be a thousand people in the audience.

"A man by the name of Johnny Bunardzya, who was the sports

editor of the Charleroi newspaper and sort of the head guy of this affair, would invite about 20 college coaches to speak. Well, I was one of the 20 coaches. We'd each get up and tell jokes for about one minute.

"Bob Prince was the master of ceremonies. The main speaker was to be the young first-round draft choice of the Pittsburgh Steelers, Terry Bradshaw. Everyone was expecting an entertaining 15-minute speech from Terry. When the time comes he gets up and just about about opens his mouth and nothing comes out. He finally says, 'I have nothing prepared to say and that's it. If you want my autograph, I'll be in the back of the room.'

"Everybody was embarrassed. So Bunardzya and Prince came to me--I was doing a lot of speaking at the time--and asked me to save the night, to give my usual 10 or 15 minutes of humorous stories, which I did. Bunardzya thanked me to no end. I was told that Terry Bradshaw got a thousand dollars."

For a 10-second "speech." Bradshaw, now a Fox-TV NFL analyst, *has* improved considerably since bombing at the Twin Coaches.

"I read a *Sports Illustrated* article recently about the highest-paid [sports-related] speakers in the country and it said that [Miami Heat coach] Pat Riley is No. 1 and [University of Kentucky basketball coach] Rick Pitino is No. 2. Terry Bradshaw is No. 3."

The School of Hard Knox

Chuck Knox bummed a ride and a place to stay from Chuck Klausing in the '60s. He landed an NFL head coaching position as a result.

"Chuck was a high school coach in Ellwood City. I'm recruiting for Army, so I go into Ellwood City. He asked me if I was going to the national coaches convention and I told him I was.

"He had no money, so he rode with me to Cincinnati and slept on the floor in my hotel room. I helped him get an interview for a job at Wake Forest. He gets the job at Wake Forest, coaches there a year or two, and gets an assistant coaching job at Kentucky, working for Blanton Collier.

"Collier was a friend of Weeb Ewbank, who became the head coach of the New York Titans [later renamed the Jets], so Knox gets on with the Titans. Eventually he gets an assistant's position with the Detroit Lions. Then, while he's with the Lions, he gets an interview for the head coaching job of the Los Angeles Rams.

"This next part was written up in *Sports Illustrated*. Carroll Rosenbloom, the owner of the Rams, said the turning point of the interview--what impressed him most about Knox--was him telling the story of how he used to go to football clinics and sleep on the floor to get a greater knowledge of football.

"So I sort of feel I helped launch a career."

The $100 Super Bowl Trip

Fans of the Pittsburgh Steelers shelled out thousands of dollars apiece for Super Bowl XXX packages that covered transportation, lodging, meals and game tickets.

Klausing chuckles at the thought. He and his son, Tom, went to the Steelers' first Super Bowl on $100. Total.

Klausing was working as an assistant at West Virginia when the Steelers defeated Oakland 24-13 in the AFC championship game to land a berth in Super Bowl IX. Tom, then a junior at WVU, talked his father into making the trip to New Orleans. And what a trip it was. The Klausings not only survived on $100--they attended exclusive parties, met Billy Eckstine and Jackie Mason, listened to Cab Calloway, rubbed elbows with Frank Sinatra and chauffeured the Steeler coaches in their run-down Chevy, affectionately dubbed "Old White."

"Both my son and I were big Steeler fans. We went to every home game. When the Steelers got into the Super Bowl, Tom comes begging me to make the trip. I didn't have the money to make that kind of trip--I had three kids in college--but he kept begging me. He said he had saved some money to go to Florida over spring break--he had $100 and we could use that $100 to make the trip."

Turns out that's *all* they needed.

The journey commenced six days before the game, when the Klausings fired up Old White. Literally.

"We had two cars. Actually, the one was my recruiting car and we called it Old White. The speedometer had gone around three times--it had over 300,000 miles on it. We had difficulty starting it in the winter, so I used to have to take the air filter off and I'd throttle it with a window scraper. When I had the throttle open, I'd get in the car and start it. A flame would shoot up in the air and the car would always start."

Old White carried the Klausings to New Orleans, where they were to stay with Steeler assistant coach Paul Uram, Chuck's former Slippery Rock teammate and roommate. But when they arrived Wednesday, Uram greeted them with a long face.

"I had called him and he said his wife was not making the trip, that we could stay in his room. But when we get to New Orleans, Uram sees me and says, 'Chuck, I have bad news. My wife decided to make the trip.' "

Fortunately, defensive coach Bud Carson overheard the conversation and suggested a solution. Since punter Bobby Walden didn't expect his wife to arrive until Saturday night, perhaps he would be willing to share his room for three days. The Klausings breathed a sigh of relief when Walden consented.

Once the lodging problem was solved, Chuck and Tom could focus their attention on having fun in New Orleans. They made the most of the opportunity, attending several Steeler practice sessions, meeting comedian Jackie Mason and "crashing" some parties.

"We were walking by the Royal Sonesta Hotel, which is, I think, the most plush hotel in New Orleans. I said to Tommy, 'Let's go in.' I thought maybe I'd see my friend, Art Rooney Jr., who had gotten us our tickets for the game. We walked into the lobby and there's an old friend, Sam Rutigliano, who I knew back when he was a high school coach in Brooklyn, N.Y.

"I asked Sam what he was doing. He said he was an assistant coach for the New Orleans Saints, but his duty that night was to be the doorman for the owners' party. He said, 'Boy, Chuck, Frank Sinatra just went in there.' It was a very private party of about 200 people. He said, 'Do you want to go in?' I said, 'Well, if it's OK.' "

Klausing entered and headed for the buffet table. He was loading his plate when long-time Steeler owner Art Rooney sidled up to him.

"His words were, 'Chuck, what are *you* doing here?' I said, 'Oh, Mr. Rooney, if I shouldn't be here, I'm sorry, I'll leave.' He says, 'No, I want you here. But I'd like to now how you got in.' So I explained that the doorman was my friend."

The Klausings found themselves at another party the following night, no small thanks to Old White.

"The Steeler coaches were gonna go to [NFL commissioner] Pete Rozelle's party Friday at the convention center, which was a good distance from the hotel. None of them had a car. I'm the only guy who has a car. So they rode in Old White with their wives--there was Tommy and I, Bad Rad [Dan Radakovich] and his wife, Paul Uram and his wife and Bud and Linda Carson. Eight of us went in a six-passenger car. We get to the convention center, but Tommy and I had no tickets. The coaches said, 'Look, you've done us a favor, we'll get you in.' "

And so the Klausings crashed another party.

"We go in and they have about 10 bars and 10 buffet lines and two bands. One of the bands was Cab Calloway. And one of the entertainers was Billy Eckstine. I went up and introduced myself. He was born in Braddock, where I coached at one time [1954-59]. He thought that was great, that someone from his hometown was there."

The Klausings attended a more sedate function the next day--a mass for the Steeler players and coaches and their families.

"Mr. Rooney brought in a priest from Ireland--a Father Dugan--who talked with an Irish brogue. He gave a beautiful homily. Then we had prayers, where you usually pray for the sick and deceased members of the parish. And he said [here Klausing mimics the priest's accent], 'Please pray for the poor soul who's going to have to play opposite Mean Joe Greene.' "

Klausing had a prayer of his own--to find a place to stay that night. That prayer was answered, in part because the Super Bowl was played at Tulane Stadium, with Tulane University acting as official host.

"I went and asked the Tulane coaches if they had any room. One of them said, 'Well, we have two players from New Orleans who usually go home on the weekends.' So they got the keys for this one room. It belonged to a guy by the name of Steve Foley, who was the Tulane quarterback. He later played 11 years for the Denver Broncos as a defensive back."

The Klausings caught another break the next day. While most fans spend money at the big game, they *earned* some.

"We'd pretty much gone through our budget. I was fortunate Bud Carson gave me four 50-yard line tickets to sell at the game. He said, 'You can keep whatever you get for them.' We sold the tickets at $10 each for $40, so we had enough money to go home."

All in all, it was quite a trip. Quite an inexpensive one.

"Our housing was free and a lot of our meals were taken care of. We had to pay for gasoline, for snacks and for parking. But we got by with a budget of $100."

Inconceivable though that seems. For a hundred dollars wouldn't have purchased even the cheapest ticket to Super Bowl XXX.

CHAPTER 12
That's Incredible

Back in the '80s, former NFL quarterback Fran Tarkenton, singer John Davidson and actress Cathy Lee Crosby--ex-wife of another NFL quarterback, Joe Theismann--co-hosted *That's Incredible*, a television program that related all sorts of unusual tales. Viewers provided material by sending letters

The program's producers could've saved a mint on mailroom expenses by simply contacting Chuck Klausing, who most certainly would've reduced--or perhaps even eliminated--the need for viewer contributions. Trot out Klausing and he could've filled a season's worth of episodes with an assortment of offbeat tales from his years in coaching.

When Klausing jogs his memory nowadays, after more than a half century in football, all sorts of incredible--some might even say outrageous--stories come spilling out. The ones in this chapter could just as easily find a home in one of Robert Ripley's believe-it-or-not books.

Ringers in the Rose Bowl

Earle "Greasy" Neale bettered his chances in the 1922 Rose Bowl by acquiring better players--on the way to California.

Neale played right field for the Cincinnati Reds in the 1919 World Series, coached the Philadelphia Eagles to NFL championships in 1948 and 1949 and co-coached the storied Steagles, the team formed when war-time manpower shortages forced a merger between the Steelers and Eagles in 1943.

But to Klausing, Neale's name evokes images of ringers in the Rose Bowl.

Neale coached Washington & Jefferson's unbeaten football team in 1921, back when the Presidents were a major-college power. They were invited to the Rose Bowl, a great honor since it was the *only* bowl game in those days. But the team that played the unbeaten California Bears in Pasadena on Jan. 1, 1922, apparently bore little resemblance to the one that departed Pennsylvania with a 10-0 record.

At least according to a former W&J player who crossed paths with Klausing long ago.

"My critic teacher in practice teaching at Wilkinsburg High School was a guy by the name of John Browning, who played on the W&J team that went to the Rose Bowl in 1922. Browning told the story that they'd gone through the season undefeated, beaten West Virginia, beaten Pitt, and got invited to the Rose Bowl.

"You know, in the '20s and '30s, there were maybe 30 players on a team and maybe only 20 of them or 15 of them were scholarship players. So Neale posts the travel squad. All 30 expected to be going, but there were only 15 names on the list.

"The walk-ons came in to see Greasy and said, 'Coach, aren't we all going to the Rose Bowl?' He says, 'Naw, you're not good enough to play in the Rose Bowl.' These were kids that hardly ever got into a game anyway.

"Well, according to Browning, the team got on a train out of Pittsburgh and the train went through Canton, Ohio. He said there were four or five of the biggest guys you ever saw with football shoes over their shoulders and shoulder pads under their arms and they got on the train.

"The train stops again in Chicago and they pick up four or five more guys. It stops in St. Louis and there were a couple more. These were all guys who had played on Sundays with Greasy Neale. Greasy played for the Canton Bulldogs.

"Browning said by the time they got to California, they had one heckuva team. They played against California, which had one of the greatest offensive teams in the nation. But Browning said, 'We could've played all day and they never would've scored on us.' "

The Presidents, bolstered by their reinforcements, battled the Bears to a 0-0 draw.

Ironically, Neale later served as head coach at West Virginia (1931-33), where Klausing spent six seasons as an assistant. He was elected to the College Football Hall of Fame in 1967 and the Pro Football Hall of Fame two years later.

Railroad Record Breaker

According to the record book, the longest punt in NCAA history, regardless of division, carried 99 yards. Klausing begs to differ. He heard of a punt that traveled 18 *miles.*

"Arnold Koepka from Trafford was kicking for Waynesburg College back in the '30s. He was in his own end zone and he shanked the punt. The ball bounced into a railroad car and the train ended up in Brownsville."

Eighteen miles away. The tracks back then--as now--run right behind the visitors' bench at College Field.

The official record of 99 yards was set in 1950 by Nevada's Pat Brady, who later punted for the Steelers (1952-54).

Brute-al Treatment

Klausing has encountered some colorful individuals during his half-century in football. "But if I wrote a book about the most unforgettable characters I've ever met, 'Brute' Kramer might be No. 1."

Who else could treat a college president with undisguised contempt and wind up getting hired by the man? Kramer was working as the scholastic sports editor of the *Pittsburgh Post-Gazette* when Klausing, then an assistant coach at Army, paid him a visit.

"I had come in to Pittsburgh to recruit the weekend of the Dapper Dan banquet. So I go to see Brute and he says, 'Chuck, as soon as I finish writing my story for tomorrow's paper, we'll go to the Dapper Dan banquet. There's a real nice cocktail party beforehand I'll take you to.'

"Al Abrams, the sports editor of the *Post-Gazette,* comes in just then and he says, 'Brute, the president of Parsons College [in Iowa] is coming to the Dapper Dan banquet. I want you to go out to the airport and pick him up because he's gonna give out a scholarship to a local athlete.'

"Brute says, 'Aw, Al, I'm not gonna be able to do that. I've already promised Chuck I'm gonna take him to a party beforehand.' And Al says, 'Brute, you work for me. You've got the assignment to pick this guy up.'

"So he's mad. We go out and pick this guy up and Brute treats him rude--throws his bag in the trunk, hardly talks to him. We're riding in from the airport and he doesn't even say a word to anybody. We get to the Hilton Hotel in Pittsburgh--it's like 5:45--and Brute says to the president, 'Look, there's a cocktail party at 6. If you're at the door at 5:59, I'll take you in. If you're not, you're on your own.'

"The poor guy had to run up and change shirts and put a tie on and so forth. He's one of these respectful, Ivy League-type college presidents. He's waiting at the door, so we take him to the party.

"Well, Brute knows everybody there. We walk in, he sees Johnny Weissmuller and he goes, 'Johnny Weissmuller, Windber, Pa. Johnny, how are you?' Weissmuller says, 'Oh, Brute, I'm fine. How are you?' Brute says, 'I want you to meet my good friend, Chuck Klausing. And this jerk here is a college mpresident.'

"Rocky Marciano was there that night and Paul Brown--every big name in sports was there, and Brute knew them all. He'd introduce me and he'd introduce the president the same as he did the first time: 'This jerk is a college president.'

"So during the banquet Brute comes up to me and says, 'Chuck, there's a real good party after this affair. Let's go there afterwards.' Just then Al Abrams comes up to Brute. He says, 'Brute, the president has to get a midnight plane. I want you to take him to the airport.'

"And again Brute's mad. So we're driving out to the airport after the banquet and the president hasn't said a word. All of a sudden he goes, 'Mr. Kramer.' I think to myself, Uh-oh, here it comes."

But instead of upbraiding Kramer, the president showered him with compliments. Both Klausing and Kramer were dumbfounded.

"He says to Brute, 'I want you to know I've never been so impressed by a man in my life. You know everybody. I'm looking for a public relations director at my college and I think you would be the right man for the job.'

"So Brute says, 'You don't have enough money in Iowa to pay me.' The president says, 'Well, I don't know how much you're making'--I'm guessing Brute's making about $5,000 a year at the time--'but I'm willing to give you a three-year contract: $15,000 the first year, $16,000 the second year, $17,000 the third year. Unlimited budget.'

"Brute pulls that car right off the highway. He says, 'Chuck, you heard him. We're gonna draw up a contract right now.' He pulls an envelope from his pocket and starts to write, 'This is a valid contract between Parsons College and Charles Kramer for $15,000, $16,000, $17,000.' The president signed it and Brute went to work for him."

Kramer later played an indirect role in the greatest offensive explosion by an individual in IUP basketball history. He contacted Klausing--then the school's football coach and athletic director--and scheduled a game between the Indians and Parsons at tiny Waller Gym during the 1964-65 season.

It wasn't much of a game, really. Mel Hankinson highlighted a 126-87 IUP vistory with a school- and conference-record 59-point performance.

Hankinson, incidentally, is now an assistant basketball coach at West Virginia, where Klausing once served as a football assistant.

Horning in on the Action

By the time Klausing arrived at Carnegie Mellon in 1976, the fabled football rivalry between the Tartans and Pitt had long since ceased, a relic from the seemingly ancient past.

But at one time, the Panthers and Carnegie Tech, as the school was known, were both major powers who battled not only for bragging rights within the city, but for national acclaim.

What was arguably the most memorable game of the series took place in 1938. Tech marched into Pitt Stadium a heavy underdog, the defending national champion Panthers having vanquished all six of their opponents to extend their unbeaten streak to 22 games (three ties). But the Tartans were not intimidated by Jock Sutherland's team or even All-America halfback Marshall Goldberg, the centerpiece of

Pitt's heralded "Dream Backfield."

Tech's 20-10 victory over the Panthers was later hailed as a classic. Classic, too, is the story of Jack Purcell's "instrumental" role in the Tartans' success. And he didn't even play.

"Right before the first half ended Tech was on a drive and they threw a pass into the end zone. Merlyn Condit caught the pass for a touchdown. John Chickerneo had been covering him man for man.

"The Kiltie Band from Carnegie Tech was near the end zone, massing for their halftime show. Some of them were standing right on the end line. Chickerneo told me that Jack Purcell, the trombone player, stuck his trombone out and tripped him and that's why he wasn't able to cover Condit."

That touchdown turned the tide irrevocably in the Tartans' favor. Jubilant Tech students celebrated the upset by yanking down one set of goal posts and toting them to their campus, nearly a mile away.

Identity Crisis

Pitt waged three epic battles against Fordham University and its famed "Seven Blocks of Granite" defense--Vince Lombardi was one of the immovable Blocks--in 1935, 1936 and 1937. All three games were scoreless ties. The Panthers broke through at last in the opening seconds of the 1938 clash at Pitt Stadium, no small thanks to Marshall Goldberg. Or was it Harold Stebbins? To a young broadcaster named Mel Allen, who would achieve lasting fame as the voice of the New York Yankees, the difference was indistinguishable.

Klausing heard Allen tell the tale of Stebbins' dramatic touchdown on the banquet circuit.

"On the opening kickoff, he says, 'Fordham kicks off to Pitt and Goldberg takes the ball on the 10. He's up to the 20, he's to the 30.' The guy who was his spotter was saying, 'It's not Goldberg, it's Stebbins who has the ball.' "

Allen paid him no heed.

"He says, 'Goldberg crosses the 50, he's to the 40, Goldberg's to the 30.' The spotter nudges him--'It's not Goldberg, it's Stebbins.' 'And Goldberg is to the 20, he's to the 15.' 'It's not Goldberg, it's Stebbins.' Finally Allen says, 'And Goldberg laterals to Stebbins, who goes over for a touchdown.' "

The spotter likely grimaced, which is what Fordham coach Jim Crowley--one of Notre Dame's famed Four Horsemen--did most of the afternoon. The Panthers ran roughshod over his team, 24-13.

Grin and Bear It

Allen figures in another tale involving long-time Alabama football coach Bear Bryant, whose candor caused a television sponsor to cringe back in the '50s. And had viewers--Klausing included--howling with laughter.

"There used to be professional fights every Friday night on television. One of the sponsors was White Owl cigars. Rocky Marciano was just starting out then--I think he had 19 straight knockouts--and he was on this one night.

"They had prepared as if Marciano was gonna win again with another knockout. Right after the fight he was gonna be interviewed by Mel Allen. What happens, Marciano has a bad fight--he wins, but it wasn't a knockout. He leaves the ring and he's walking down the aisle and Mel's introducing him. 'Here comes Rocky Marciano, the great young heavyweight. Rocky, will you come over here and say a few words to your public?'

"But Rocky doesn't want to talk. He just keeps going. Mel Allen has to be quick afoot. He had sitting right next to him his college classmate from Alabama, Bear Bryant, who was coaching Kentucky at the time. He asks Bear if he wants to be interviewed. Bear wants to help his friend, so they talk for two or three minutes about football and so forth.

"Well, Mel would always end his show the same way. So he says, 'Bear, thank you for the interview. And for your smoking pleasure, here's a box of White Owl cigars.' Bear Bryant looks at the box and he says to Mel, on the air, 'Mel, you know I hate cigars.' "

The Scam Man

Some Penn State fans suffered through two losses at homecoming in 1955. Navy made off with a 34-14 victory and a scam artist made off with their money.

"My wife and I went to the game and afterwards we went to a fraternity party. I had a cousin who belonged to this fraternity. The bar was going and music was playing--college kids having a good time. In came an old-timer who worked his way around the room, telling everybody he was back visiting, that he had graduated 20 years before and this was his fraternity.

"After about 15 minutes he stands up on the bar and he goes, 'Give me your attention, please.' He says, 'I feel ashamed. All us old-timers here and we're drinking these kids' liquor. I'm gonna pass a hat around. Everybody throw in what you can.' And he threw $20 in the hat.

"He went around the room and he had a hat full of bills. I think I threw $5 in. Well, 15 minutes later we don't see the guy. Finally, some of the fraternity kids go looking for him, but they never find him.

"Later they get a phone call from a fraternity down the street, telling them, 'Look out, there's a guy on campus who's a con artist. He was just here, passed a hat and took all our money.' "

The Long Haul

Klausing saw something as a spectator in 1948 that he'll never forget: a kickoff in excess of 100 yards that owed its success more to deception than execution. Vince Sundry, a doctor now living in Tarpon Springs, Fla., scored easily on the play.

"I went to a game between St. Vincent and Geneva at St. Vincent College. On the opening kickoff, Geneva kicks the ball into the end zone and Vince Sundry catches it. He must have semi-planned this--had the referee in on it.

"Usually if a kid didn't want to return a kickoff, he would kneel down. So Vince gets the ball in the end zone and he takes a deep-knee bend, but he's telling the referee, 'Don't blow the whistle, I'm gonna run with this ball.'

"The Geneva kids see him almost kneeling down and then

pretending he's gonna hand the ball to the referee, so they start to walk toward the bench. And Sundry just takes off down the field, more than a hundred yards for a touchdown. I thought it showed savvy and ability."

Sundry recalls the distance as "101, 103 yards at the most." Impressive as that was, it could not equal the significance of his 47-yard punt return in the 1950 Tangerine Bowl at Orlando, Fla., which set up a touchdown and helped St. Vincent defeat Emory & Henry, 7-6.

Sundry, incidentally, was coached by a fellow Blairsville product who is enshrined in the Indiana County Sports Hall of Fame along with Klausing: Al DeLuca. His uncle.

Water Break

DeLuca played at Duquesne University under Elmer Layden, renowned as one of Notre Dame's Four Horsemen. Layden imported some Irish traditions when he landed the Duquesne job in 1927, which initially put Benny Rosenberg on the spot.

Rosenberg was a Jew on a predominantly Catholic team.

"Al told the story that one of the traditions Layden brought from Notre Dame was that right before the game, they would pass a bottle of holy water around and the guys would bless themselves, hope they wouldn't get hurt and ask, if it was God's will, that they might win the game.

"So Al gets the holy water and he blesses himself. Sitting right next to him is Benny Rosenberg. He tries to hand the holy water to Rosenberg and Rosenberg won't take it. He's afraid to even touch it. Well, the next player over is Armand Niccolai--he was later a great placekicker for the Steelers [1934-42]. So Niccolai takes the holy water and blesses himself and then passes it on to the next player.

"Well, in that game Niccolai kicked two field goals and four extra points and DeLuca runs for three touchdowns. And neither of them gets even a scratch. Rosenberg, who is a guard, gets a black eye, his shoulders are all bruised up, his knee's bummed up, his ankle is sprained--he's just beat up.

"The next week they're sitting in the locker room and Layden brings out the Notre Dame tradition again. DeLuca blesses himself and then starts to pass the bottle. He doesn't want to offend Rosenberg in any way, so he tries to pass the holy water around Rosenberg and over to Niccolai."

Only Rosenberg intercepted the pass. This time he would take no chances. For the first time in his life, the Jewish lad doused himself with holy water.

Cold Cuts

Baseball broadcasters often speak of a line drive as a frozen rope. In one memorable game, the adjective was especially fitting.

Klausing's long-time friend, Brute Kramer, went to extremes to earn some cold cash after arranging a game with manager Cumberland Posey's vaunted Homestead Grays, one of greatest teams in Negro League history. In their heyday, the Grays featured future Hall of Famers such as Josh Gibson, Cool Papa Bell, Oscar Charleston, Buck Leonard, Martin Dihugo and Judy Johnson.

"Brute was always a manager. He was the manager of his high school football team in Braddock. He somehow made friends with Paul Birch, the great professional basketball player out of Pittsburgh. Brute became the general manager of the Fort Wayne Pistons, which are now the Detroit Pistons, because Birch was the coach.

"One of Brute's first experiences was as manager of the Braddock Merchants semi-pro baseball team. He booked a game with the Homestead Grays for the Fourth of July. He and Cum Posey were arguing over who should get the heavy percentage of the gate--should it be 60-40 or what?

"Finally, Brute says to Cum, 'What are you afraid of? Let's play winner-take-all.' Cum says, 'Brute, you have to be the dumbest guy in the world, trying to play winner-take-all against us.' And they signed a contract.

"Well, Brute goes to a sporting goods store, buys a dozen baseballs, takes them to a butcher shop and freezes them. He went and hired the best semi-pro pitcher he could find to pitch for him that day. And he had his own umpires.

"The Grays were sitting on the first-base side, so the umpire had the frozen balls in his right pocket and the good balls in his left pocket. When the Grays come to bat, out goes the right-pocket ball. This pitcher Brute hired is putting the ball in there pretty good. When the Grays did make contact, the ball would just dribble to the shortstop, so they knew something was up."

Braddock was clinging to a 1-0 lead heading into the last inning.

"What the Grays started to do was foul off the frozen balls. Finally all 12 balls were lost. Now the umpire had only the balls from his left pocket. One of the Grays players hits a solid one into the left-center field gap, turns around and yells at his teammates, 'The good ones are in there now.' And they went on to win the game."

Something to Kick About

Roger Staubach won the Heisman trophy in 1963 and led Navy to a No. 2 ranking nationally. But the Midshipmen owed their success in one early-season game to kicker Fred Marlin. He used his head--not his foot--to help Navy beat Virginia Military Institute.

The Midshipmen went ahead to stay when Marlin scored what might well rank as the oddest touchdown in college history.

"When I was at West Point, I'm scouting Navy vs. VMI. Navy tries a field goal, but it's just too far. The ball goes on a line drive to the VMI safety man, who's standing in the end zone. He just bats the ball to the ground, because he feels the play is over."

So did everyone else except Marlin, who, according to a newspaper account, "raced straight up the middle and dived on the ball for a touchdown." Marlin then added the extra point.

"Ten of Navy's 11 players were walking off the field, but the kicker knew the rules. He knew that it was a live ball."

Marlin's pivotal play enabled the Midshipmen to survive an upset scare from unheralded VMI. They won, 21-12.

Mr. Opperman's Prospects

Henry Opperman, a businessman in the western Pennsylvania town of Connellsville, was a fan of Notre Dame football. So much so that he actually recruited players for head coach Frank Leahy--even though he wasn't a coach himself.

"At that time, recruiting was different because no one had films to evaluate prospects. You had to take the word of someone. Mr. Opperman was a friend of Frank Leahy and he told him about two prospects, Johnny Lujack and John Schroyer.

"So Leahy recruited the two best backs out of the state of Pennsylvania. I'm gonna say this was the fall of 1942. A lot of people thought Schroyer was the better of the two. Well, Mr. Opperman gets a phone call one Sunday from Leahy. He says, 'Those two bums you sent me are on the afternoon train out of Chicago--you can pick them up.' He doesn't even question Leahy about why.

"The two of them got off the train and Mr. Opperman asks, 'What did you do?' Leahy had a rule you had to go to mass on Sunday and they had missed mass. Mr. Opperman says, 'Let's call him up and apologize.' They do, so Leahy says, 'Put them back on the train, we'll take 'em back.'

"About two weeks later Mr. Opperman gets another phone call from Leahy. 'That bum Schroyer missed mass again. Pick him up at the train station.' When he arrives, Mr. Opperman goes, 'John, why did you miss mass?' And John says, 'Two reasons: one, I'm not Catholic, and two, there was a really good softball game going on.'

"Well, World War II is on so Schroyer joins the Army, goes to France, steps on a land mine and loses both legs. When he comes back home, Mr. Opperman meets Schroyer at the airport and he says, 'John, if you had only gone to mass, you'd have been the All-American at Notre Dame, not Lujack.' "

Lujack, a quarterback, won the Heisman trophy in 1947, earned All-America honors in 1946 and 1947 and led the Irish to national championships and unbeaten seasons both years.

He signed with the Bears out of college and in 1949 set an NFL record by passing for 468 yards in a victory over the Chicago Cardinals. Lujack played only four seasons with the Bears because of shoulder and knee injuries before returning to Notre Dame--as Leahy's quarterbacks coach.

The Tavern Tandem

College recruiting usually involves finding players to fill future needs. But in one instance, Klausing was called on to recruit a player or two to meet an immediate need.

West Virginia placekicker Frank Nester took a blow to the thigh during a win over Tulane in 1972 and was sidelined for the following week's game against Penn State at Mountaineer Field. Klausing, the kicking coach, suddenly found himself in a quandary.

"Big program like ours and we did not have a backup placekicker. Bobby Bowden says to me, 'Chuck, what are we gonna do?' I said, 'This is a big university. Let's advertise in the school newspaper that we're gonna have a tryout and we're gonna pick one or two placekickers to kick against Penn State.'

"We couldn't believe it--we had almost a hundred kids show up for this tryout. We finally narrowed it down to two guys. One guy could kick off pretty good--his name was Sheets. He was about 6-foot-6, skinny kid, looked more like a basketball player. The other kid's name was Stillwell and he looked like pear. He was about 5-foot-10, 240 pounds, big pot belly. He could kick extra points. He was accurate. So we felt safe.

"We received the kickoff against Penn State and I still remember, Kerry Marbury returns it 100 yards for a touchdown [the longest in school history]. Here comes Stillwell into the game. He kicks the extra point--I think it hit the crossbar and just rolled over--so we're ahead 7-0.

"Out trots Sheets to kick off. He shanks it to the right and the ball goes up into the bleachers. At that time you got penalized five yards, so he's back at the 35. I'm up in the press box and the guy in charge of the coverages gets on the phones and he says, 'Chuck, can he kick off?' I said, 'Don't worry, he can kick off.'

"He kicks the second one out of bounds, so now we're back to the 30. This coach is moaning like anything. He says to me again, 'Chuck, can he kick off?' I said, 'He's coming right by you on the sidelines, put him on the phone, let me talk to him.' So he gets on the phone and I tell him, 'Sheets, relax and kick the ball straight.' Well, there was wind to his back and he kicks the ball straight and it sails right through the goal posts.

"We hadn't beaten Penn State in a long time [not since 1955] and we're playing them nip and tuck. Late in the game we get down inside the 5-yard line and we can't score. It's fourth and goal on the 4. Bobby gets on the phone and says, 'Chuck, can Stillwell kick a field goal?' I said, 'I think he can.'

"So he kicks it--a 21-yard field goal--and we go ahead with four minutes to play. Again Sheets gives us a great kickoff. But Penn State goes on a drive the length of the field and they score and beat us.

"Now I have a daughter, Marylou, who was a student at West Virginia at the time. After the game she says to me, 'Dad, why did you use Sheets and Stillwell as placekickers?' I said, 'Well, they were the best we had because Nester was out with an injury.'

"She says, 'But, Dad, they're not students at West Virginia--they both work as bouncers at a local bar.'"

The 'Cured' Ham

Fritzie Zivic of Pittsburgh reigned as the welterweight boxing champion of the world in 1940 and 1941. But before he reached the big-time, Zivic struggled to make ends meet.

That's why, like many Americans in the '30s, he headed to California to seek his fortune. During the subsequent cross-country trip, Zivic discovered a novel method for "curing" hams.

Klausing heard this uproarious tale during his tenure as IUP's head football coach. Zivic was then working as a steeplejack at the nearby Homer City Generating Plant.

"Fritzie tells the story that at that time, for an eight-round fight in Pittsburgh, he'd get from $200 to $250. For a 10-round main event, it was about $350. Well, he hears that out in California it was $500 or a thousand dollars for a fight.

"So he and his manager, Bunny Buntag, decided they were gonna drive to California. What's a drive to California in those days? Six days? So Fritzie's mother baked a ham and baked a couple loaves of bread and fixed them a picnic basket. They were gonna stop and eat on their own during the trip.

"They drive to Wheeling, W.Va., and stop at a service station. The manager says to Fritzie, 'I didn't eat anything today. I'm hungry.

Why don't you get that ham out and make me a ham sandwich? I'm going in to pay the gasoline bill.'

"Fritzie gets the ham out--it's an old car, with a running board--and he's cutting a piece of ham on the running board when the ham slips into the mud and grease. So the manager comes out and sees this ham just covered with mud and grease. He tells Fritzie, 'Oh, just wash it off in the ladies room, because I've been in the men's room and it's not very clean.'

"So Fritzie takes it into the ladies room and he sees there's no wash basin. All it is is a john. So he takes the ham and he dips it in there and cleans it off the best he can. He comes out and the manager cuts a piece of ham and some bread and says, 'How about yourself, Fritzie, do you want a sandwich?' He says, 'Naw, I'm not hungry.'

"They drive for half a day and they're getting hungry again. The manager says to Fritzie, 'Cut a piece of ham, let's make a sandwich.' So he cuts a piece of ham and makes a sandwich for the manager. And Bunny goes, 'Fritzie, aren't you gonna have something?' He says, 'Naw, I have to make weight.'

"So they drive for another half a day and the manager gets the ham out. He goes, 'Fritzie, you've got to have something to eat.' And Fritzie says, 'Bunny, I've got a confession to make. You remember in Wheeling when that ham fell in the mud and I took it into the ladies room to wash it off? There was no place to wash it off. I just dumped it in the john.'

"Bunny looks at him and he says, 'Fritzie, you're full of blank.' And Fritzie says, 'No, Bunny--*you're* full of blank.' "

Appendix
Chuck Klausing--By The Numbers
Braddock's National-Record Unbeaten Streak
Game by Game

1953
1. W Rankin*..........................15-7

1954
2. W Wilkinsburg....................7-6
3. W Homestead.....................14-0
4. W McKees Rocks...............20-7
5. W Elizabeth.......................39-6
6. W Brentwood....................27-0
7. W Swissvale......................25-0
8. W New Brighton..............33-6
9. W North Braddock..........13-12
10. T Midland.........................7-7

1955
11. W Springdale...................25-0
12. W Homestead..................8-6
13. W McKees Rocks............25-0
14. W Elizabeth....................30-7
15. W Brentwood..................32-0
16. W Swissvale....................13-6
17. W New Brighton............19-0
18. W North Braddock.........20-0
19. W Derry Township.......26-13

1956
20. W Springdale..................26-0
21. W Homestead...............32-20
22. W McKees Rocks.............20-6
23. W Elizabeth....................26-0
24. W Derry Area................12-7
25. W Swissvale...................39-0
26. W New Brighton............26-0
27. W North Braddock.........26-0
28. W Carmichaels..............38-0

1957
29. W Homestead...............25-13
30. W McKees Rocks............32-7
31. W Elizabeth....................53-7
32. W Swissvale...................33-0
33. W New Brighton............41-7
34. W Canonsburg................35-0
35. W North Braddock.........25-6
36. W Derry Area................27-6
37. W Glassport....................14-0

1958
38. W Homestead................31-7
39. W Schenley....................38-7
40. W Midland......................9-7
41. W Derry Area................27-0
42. W Swissvale...................32-6
43. W New Brighton...........27-13
44. W Canonsburg................46-0
45. W North Braddock.........9-6
46. W Waynesburg...............21-0

1959
47. W Homestead..................47-0
48. W Hopewell..................27-13
49. W Midland.....................25-7
50. W Derry Area................32-7
51. W Swissvale...................34-7
52. W Monaca......................28-8
53. W Canon-McMillan#...45-27
54. W North Braddock.......15-12
55. W Waynesburg...............25-7

1960
56. W Kittanning @.............25-6

*last game coached by Henry Furrie

#surpassed existing national record

@first game coached by Bob Teitt

Chuck Klausing Through the Years

Year(s)	School	Record
1948-53	Pitcairn High School	30-22-2
1954-59	Braddock High School	53-0-1
1960	Rutgers University (assistant)	8-1-0*
1961-63	Army (assistant)	19-11-0
1964-69	Indiana University of Pennsylvania	47-10-0
1970-75	West Virginia University (assistant)	42-26-0
1976-85	Carnegie Mellon University	77-15-2
1986	University of Pittsburgh (assistant)	5-5-1
1987-93	Kiski School	29-22-4
TOTALS		310-112-10
	Totals as head coach	236-69-9
	Totals as assistant coach	74-43-1
	Totals as college coach	198-68-3
	Totals as high/prep school coach	112-44-7

*also coached Rutgers freshman team to 5-1 record

Chuck Klausing Year by Year

Pitcairn		Army		Carnegie Mellon	
1948	3-6-0	1961	6-4-0	1976	6-1-1
1949	1-7-1	1962	6-4-0	1977	8-1-0
1950	6-3-0	1963	7-3-0	1978	9-2-0
1951	8-1-0			1979	10-1-0
1952	5-3-1	IUP		1980	8-1-0
1953	7-2-0	1964	8-2-0	1981	7-1-1
		1965	7-3-0	1982	6-3-0
Braddock		1966	7-2-0	1983	9-1-0
1954	8-0-1	1967	8-1-0	1984	6-3-0
1955	9-0-0	1968	9-1-0	1985	8-1-0
1956	9-0-0	1969	8-1-0		
1957	9-0-0			Pitt	
1958	9-0-0	West Virginia		1986	5-5-1
1959	9-0-0	1970	8-3-0		
		1971	7-4-0	Kiski School	
Rutgers		1972	8-4-0	1987	5-1-1
1960	8-1-0	1973	6-5-0	1988	2-6-0
		1974	4-7-0	1989	4-3-1
		1975	9-3-0	1990	5-3-0
				1991	2-4-2
				1992	4-4-0
				1993	7-1-0

Career Totals

10 unbeaten regular seasons: Braddock 1954-59; IUP 1968 (lost 31-24 to Delaware in Boardwalk Bowl); Carnegie Mellon 1979 (lost 15-6 to Ithaca in NCAA Division III semifinals), 1983 (lost 16-14 to Salisbury State in Division III quarterfinals), 1985 (lost 35-22 to Salisbury State in Division III quarterfinals)

   39 winning seasons
   24 consecutive winning seasons (1950-1973)
   41 seasons at .500 or better

All-Time College Coaching Leaders

The list below includes all NCAA coaches with a winning percentage of at least .800 (through the 1995 season), regardless of division, with a minimum of 10 seasons. Bowl and playoff games are included.

Coach (Alma Mater) (Colleges Coached, Tenure)	Years	Won	Lost	Tied	Pct.
Knute Rockne (Notre Dame) (Notre Dame 1918-30)	13	105	12	5	.881
Frank Leahy (Notre Dame) (Boston College 1939-40; Notre Dame 1941-43, 1946-53)	13	107	13	9	.864
Bob Reade (Cornell College) (Augustana, Ill. 1979-94)	16	146	23	1	.862
Doyt Perry (Bowling Green) (Bowling Green 1955-64)	10	77	11	1	.855
Larry Kehres (Mount Union) (Mount Union 1986-)	10	96	16	3	.848
George Woodruff (Yale) (Penn 1892-1901; Illinois 1903; Carlisle 1905)	12	142	25	2	.846

Jake Gaither (Knoxville) (Florida A&M 1945-69)	25	203	36	4	.844
Dave Maurer (Denison) (Wittenberg 1969-83)	15	129	23	3	.842
Mike Kelly (Manchester) (Dayton 1981-)	15	145	27	1	.841
Paul Hoereman (Heidelberg) (Heidelberg 1946-59)	14	102	18	4	.839
Barry Switzer (Arkansas) (Oklahoma 1973-88)	16	157	29	4	.837
Don Coryell (Washington) (Whittier 1957-59; San Diego State 1961-72)	15	127	24	3	.834
Percy Haughton (Harvard) (Cornell 1899-1900; Harvard 1908-16; Columbia 1923-24)	13	96	17	6	.832
Bob Neyland (Army) (Tennessee 1926-34, 1936-40, 1946-52)	21	173	31	12	.829
Chuck Klausing **(Slippery Rock)** **(IUP 1964-69; Carnegie Mellon 1976-85)**	16	124	25	2	.828
Fielding Yost (Lafayette) (Ohio Wesleyan 1897; Nebraska 1898; Kansas 1899; Stanford 1900; Michigan 1901-23, 1925-26)	29	196	36	12	.828
Tom Osborne (Hastings) (Nebraska 1973-)	23	231	47	3	.827
Al Bagnoli (Central Connecticut State) (Union, N.Y. 1982-91; Penn 1992-)	14	114	25	0	.826

Bud Wilkinson (Minnesota) (Oklahoma 1947-63)	17	145	29	4	.826
Vernon McCain (Langston) (Maryland-Eastern Shore 1948-63)	16	102	21	5	.816
Jock Sutherland (Pitt) (Lafayette 1919-23; Pitt 1924-38)	20	144	28	14	.812
Ron Schipper (Hope) (Central Iowa 1961-)	35	280	64	3	.811
Bob Devaney (Alma) (Wyoming 1957-61; Nebraska 1962-72)	16	136	30	7	.806
Biggie Munn (Minnesota) (Albright 1935-36; Syracuse 1946; Michigan State 1947-53)	10	71	16	3	.805
John Luckhardt (Purdue) (Washington & Jefferson 1982-)	14	118	28	2	.804
Sid Gillman (Ohio State) (Miami, Ohio 1944-47; Cincinnati 1949-54)	10	81	19	2	.804

NOTE: Updated information, taking into account the 1996 season, was not yet available from the NCAA as this book went to press.

Chuck Klausing--A Man of Letters

People Write about Chuck Klausing

Coach Klausing has had a profound impact on many people. Following is a sampling of comments made through the years in letters, on television, at Hall of Fame award banquets. The words included come from nationally known coaches, from other football coaches, from school administrators, from sportswriters and from former players and students.

Letters of Recommendation

I have known this young man and his work for quite some time. In every instance, it has been of the best, and I feel sure that he is fast approaching the top of his profession. Without question, Chuck Klausing would represent your institution and your people exceptionally well. He is understanding, completely cooperative and would fit in to the complete team.

Harry A. Stuhldreher,
Former quarterback, Four Horsemen of Notre Dame

This [note] is written only out of total loyalty to Chuck Klausing. Frankly, it would be my selfish wish that you do not hire him, because I cannot replace him on our staff. However, friendship for Chuck and honesty to both you and him compels me to tell you that I feel you would be most lucky if you were able to secure his services.
Paul F. Dietzel,
Former head football coach, Army

Chuck was an immensely successful high school coach in the tough Western Pennsylvania A league, and from there went to Rutgers and then to Army as an assistant. He was named head coach at IUP and had nothing but winning seasons, going to the Boardwalk Bowl in 1968. When he went there, IUP was a state college, but when it gained university status, it become ineligible for state championship competition and had to turn to a cross-country independent schedule. As a result, Chuck accepted the opportunity to go to WVU as assistant head coach and administrative assistant to Bobby Bowden. Quite frankly, I was greatly surprised when he did not receive the head job at Pitt in 1969, as he would have been my top selection had I been AD at that particular time. *Frank Carver, former athletic director, University of Pittsburgh*

Anyone from western Pennsylvania with any football background knows that Chuck Klausing is monumental in the tradition of WPIAL and college football. I remember being one of the victims of Chuck's long winning streak in high school as a member of the Derry football team. I thought he was old then! He continued to coach with distinction for decades and I hold him in high esteem. I think very highly of you, Chuck.
Lou Tepper, former head football coach, University of Illinois

I am very sorry that I missed you after your presentation...I heard many fine things about your talk....many people told me that all the seats were taken and many people had to sit on the floor. We had a great clinic.
Don Lessner, Duffy Daugherty Coach of the Year Clinic

There is no way I can express to you how much you have meant to me in my career. I fell in love with you the first time I met you. I knew you were something special and you are. Thanks for being a friend.
Bobby Bowden, Head Football Coach, Florida State University

I have known Chuck Klausing for most of my life. When I needed a speaker for a high school banquet that would relate to the audience, I would call Chuck. Not only would he be down-to-earth, but his message about attitude and winning would be easily accepted. He is a living example of how to become successful in athletics and life.
Darrell Hess, Chairman of the Board, Pennsylvania Sports Hall of Fame

Thank you for speaking at the Pee-Wee Football banquet. The message was truly inspirational. I look forward to chatting with you about the Pee-Wee program.
Dr. Earl Hewitt

Coach Klausing is an outstanding coach, speaker, clinician, and leader. He cares about others--coaches, players, youth, etc. This humanistic concern has positively touched the lives of so many, many individuals. I have been part of his audience a number of times and look forward to similar future occasions. He has helped me become a better teacher, coach, and person. At our Senior Awards Night banquet, he held the attention of all in attendance, young and old alike. He is truly a remarkable person and I admire and respect him very much.
Jerry Page, Head Football Coach, Laurel Valley High School, New Florence, Pa.

Letters to the Editor

Never Lost a Game first took shape in the form of a series in *The Indiana Gazette*, titled "The Klausing File." The 12-part series generated an overwhelming response from readers. Following is a selection of letters sent to the newspaper.

I have read a couple of Bob Fulton's articles about Chuck Klausing, titled "The Klausing File." I am sure many others in addition to his former players would enjoy Coach Klausing's interesting and humorous recollections.
Rev. Bruce R. Leonatti, Irwin, Pa.

I very much enjoyed "The Klausing File." The thought that came to my mind was that this guy should write a book....He could give a humorous side of the sport and the people involved. *Don Poluszek, WVU Football Staff*

Chuck's distinguished career as a player and coach is well documented, but many of the human interest stories and acquaintances he has made would make an interesting book. *Carmine and Angie Cortazzo, Darragh, Pa.*

If anyone would have a handle on the high school and college football scene, it certainly would be Chuck--I'm sure he would fill more than one book with his knowledge of the game and his experience. I'll look forward to more from "The Klausing File." *Bill Camperlino, Camillus, N.Y.*

I have known Charles Klausing in a professional capacity for the past several years. He has proven to be a most interesting and pleasant man...In fact, you may wish to consider compiling these articles in book form at some time.
Edward T. Szabo, M.D., Latrobe, Pa.

I strongly urge your paper to insist that Mr. Fulton and Coach Klausing record in book form the experiences of this amazing gentleman and "America's Coach." *Dale L. Hamer, NFL Official, Murrysville, Pa.*

I have had occasion to read some of Chuck Klausing's reports in your paper. They are very enjoyable, and I feel all sports fellows would love to read more of the same. *A.T. Marucci, Oakland, Md.*

I enjoy the stories in "The Klausing File" very much. If Chuck would write a book, I, for one, would buy it.
John Devlin, Defensive Coordinator, Bloomsburg University

I wish to express my thanks to you for the articles you printed about Chuck Klausing. I enjoyed the interesting stories about his coaching career and his account of the people, coaches and players that were a part of his coaching experience. *Ralph Glott, Indiana, Pa.*

I am sure that a book authorized by Coach Klausing would appeal to football lovers on all levels. Chuck is a true raconteur of football stories of many meaningful and frequently humorous situations. A book of such anecdotes would not miss in the football hotbed of western Pennsylvania. There is no question that your publishing collaboration with Chuck would make another winning combination. *Thomas P. Jessup, Saltsburg, Pa.*

Just a note to let you know how much I enjoyed "The Klausing File." Keep up the good work.
Pete Antimarino, former football coach, Gateway High School

Let's face it, college football news either centers around the glamour being achieved by the major colleges and their players or the troubles they encounter (NCAA probation, criminal activity, etc.). "The Klausing File" brings college football, and athletics in general, down to earth. The moments of this man's coaching career deserve to be preserved and shared.
Bob Basehore, former IUP player, Columbus, Ohio

I have just read some of the Chuck Klausing stories. They are very good and I know there are other real good stories to come. Thanks and keep it up.
Art Rooney Jr., Pittsburgh Steelers

Klausing's career, thank God, is unusual and unique. The book could be a treasure. *Steve Klipa, captain at Pitcairn High School,*
the first team Klausing coached, in 1948

He has won the esteem and respect of all of us who have had the privilege of being associated with him. It would be very nice to see the life of this outstanding individual put into book form. Think about it.
Louis V. Kasperick, Derry, Pa.

He's a real superstar/hall of fame person and it's great that he is back in town with us after all these years. Young men and women and families need to know who lives in our area and what great careers they have.
Jack Frank, Indiana, Pa.

I really enjoy "The Klausing File." I hope something is done to preserve, in book form or whatever, the true real stories of Chuck Klausing.
Bob Davis, Davis Supermarkets

This is such a great man with such a long and wonderful career in coaching. I had the opportunity to play for Coach in 1988. He was my first football coach and without a doubt the *best* I ever worked with. After one year at Kiski, I received a full scholarship at SMU. There is no question in my mind that if I had never met Coach "K," I would not have had the fantastic experience of playing quarterback at the collegiate level.
Danny Freiburger, McVean Trading and Investments

I got some of the clippings on "The Klausing File" and sure did enjoy them and would like to see more of them. Hope that you can continue the series. I believe that somebody could make a nice book out of it.
Bobby Bowden, Head Football Coach, Florida State University

Being a former football player of his, I was already aware of the wealth of knowledge Coach Klausing has regarding football. I look forward to reading many more articles and suggest that these articles be put into book form so that many others can enjoy and learn from his experiences.
Brian Curran, University of Pittsburgh

I have really enjoyed reading "The Klausing File." It has been interesting and humorous reading. I would love to see it put in book form.
Thomas D. Florence, WVU, '76,
Florence Realty, South Charleston, Ohio

Some old friends of mine have sent me several articles written by Chuck Klausing. Just want you to know that I really enjoyed them and hope they continue. Chuck ought to write a book.
Bill McDonald, Edinboro University